CW01333294

THE BRITISH AMBASSADOR'S
RESIDENCE IN PARIS

EXECUTIVE EDITOR
Suzanne Tise-Isoré

EDITORIAL COORDINATION
Sarah Rozelle

ART DIRECTION
Styles and Design

PROJECT EDITOR BRITISH EMBASSY
Susan Nemazee Westmacott

COORDINATOR BRITISH EMBASSY
Donna Brabon

COPYEDITING
Lindsay Porter

PREFACE TRANSLATED FROM
THE FRENCH BY
Deke Dusinberre

PROOFREADING
Helen Woodhall

PRODUCTION
Élodie Conjat-Cuvelier

COLOUR SEPARATION
Bussière, Paris, France

Printed by
Toppan, China

Simultaneously published in French as
*La Résidence de l'ambassadeur
de Grande-Bretagne*
© Flammarion SA, Paris, 2011

English-language edition
© Flammarion SA, Paris, 2011

Text © Tim Knox

House plans: Christopher Hawkesworth Woodward

Genealogical chart: Wheeler M. Thackston

All rights reserved. No part of this publication
may be reproduced in any form or by any means,
electronic, photocopy, information retrieval
system, or otherwise, without written
permission from Flammarion.

Flammarion SA
87, quai Panhard et Levassor
75647 Paris cedex 13
France
editions.flammarion.com

Dépôt légal: 10/2011
11 12 13 3 2 1
ISBN: 978-2-08-020078-5
Printed in China by Toppan

Fimalac

Page 4: Detail of the ironwork on the Staircase. Created by blacksmith Antoine Hallé in 1724–5, the sun in splendour motif may allude to Louis XIV, the 'Sun King', under whom the Béthune-Charost family had flourished.

THE BRITISH AMBASSADOR'S
RESIDENCE IN PARIS

TIM KNOX
PHOTOGRAPHY BY FRANCIS HAMMOND

Flammarion

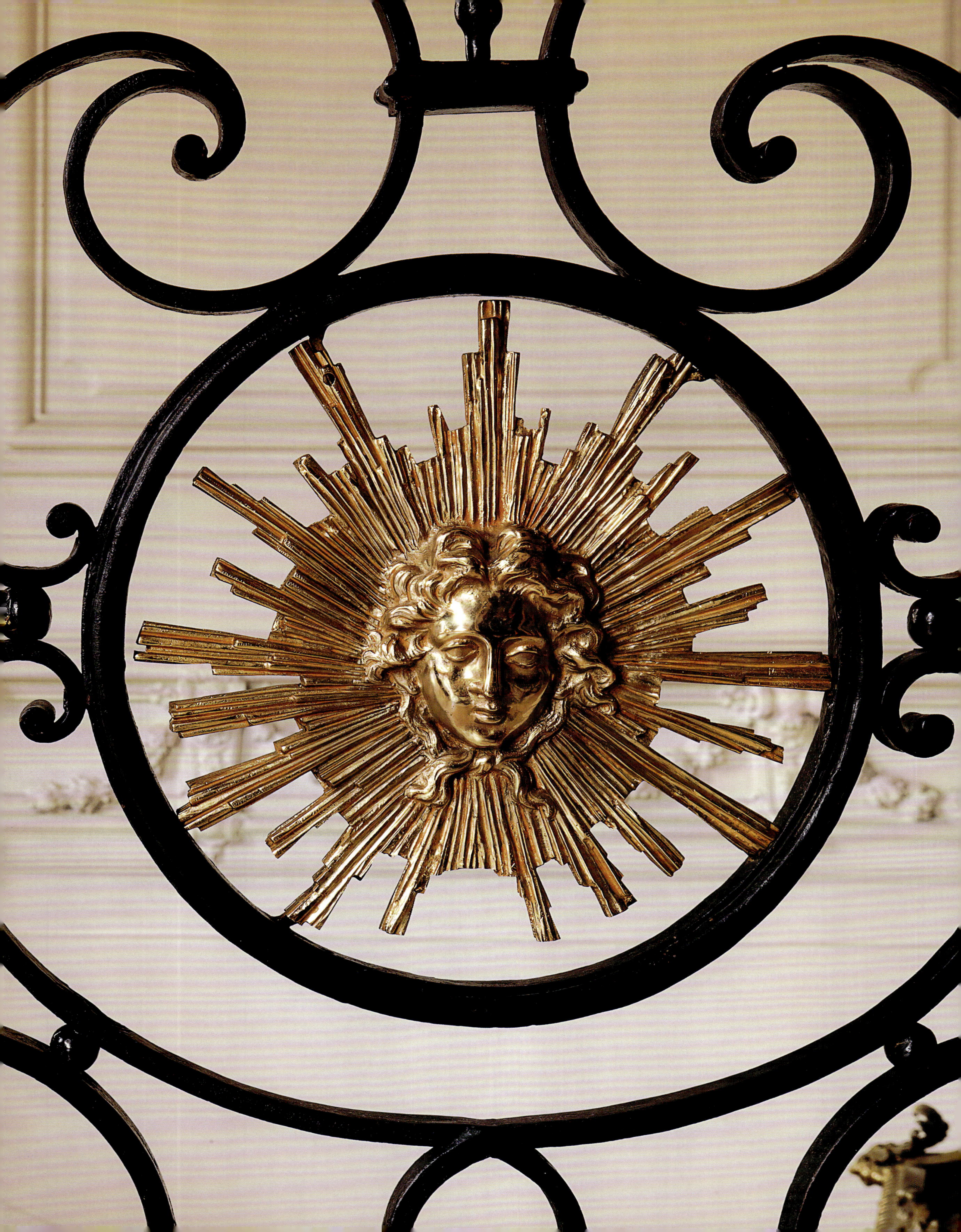

	9	FOREWORD HRH THE PRINCE OF WALES
	10	PREFACE MARC LADREIT DE LACHARRIÈRE
	13	INTRODUCTION SIR PETER WESTMACOTT
	16	EVENTS AT THE RESIDENCE
	20	ACKNOWLEDGEMENTS
FROM ARISTOCRATIC TOWN HOUSE TO AMBASSADORIAL RESIDENCE	22	
THE HISTORY OF THE HOUSE AND ITS OCCUPANTS	28	
THE HOUSE ROOM BY ROOM	70	
	72	HOUSE PLANS 1814–2011
	74	ENTRANCE FRONT AND COURTYARD
	76	ENTRANCE HALL AND STAIRCASE
	80	SALON ROUGE
	90	SALON BLEU
	94	SALON PAULINE
	100	THRONE ROOM
	104	BALLROOM
	112	GALLERY
	116	STATE DINING ROOM
	122	ANTE-ROOM
	126	SALON JAUNE
	132	TAPESTRY DINING ROOM
	136	SALON VERT ET OR
	142	SALON VERT
	146	COOPER BEDROOM AND BATHROOM
	152	DUFF COOPER LIBRARY
	156	WELLINGTON ROOM
	158	GARDEN FRONT AND GARDEN
RESIDENTS OF THE HOUSE	164	
GENEALOGICAL CHART	166	
SELECTED BIBLIOGRAPHY	168	
INDEX	170	
PHOTOGRAPHIC CREDITS	174	

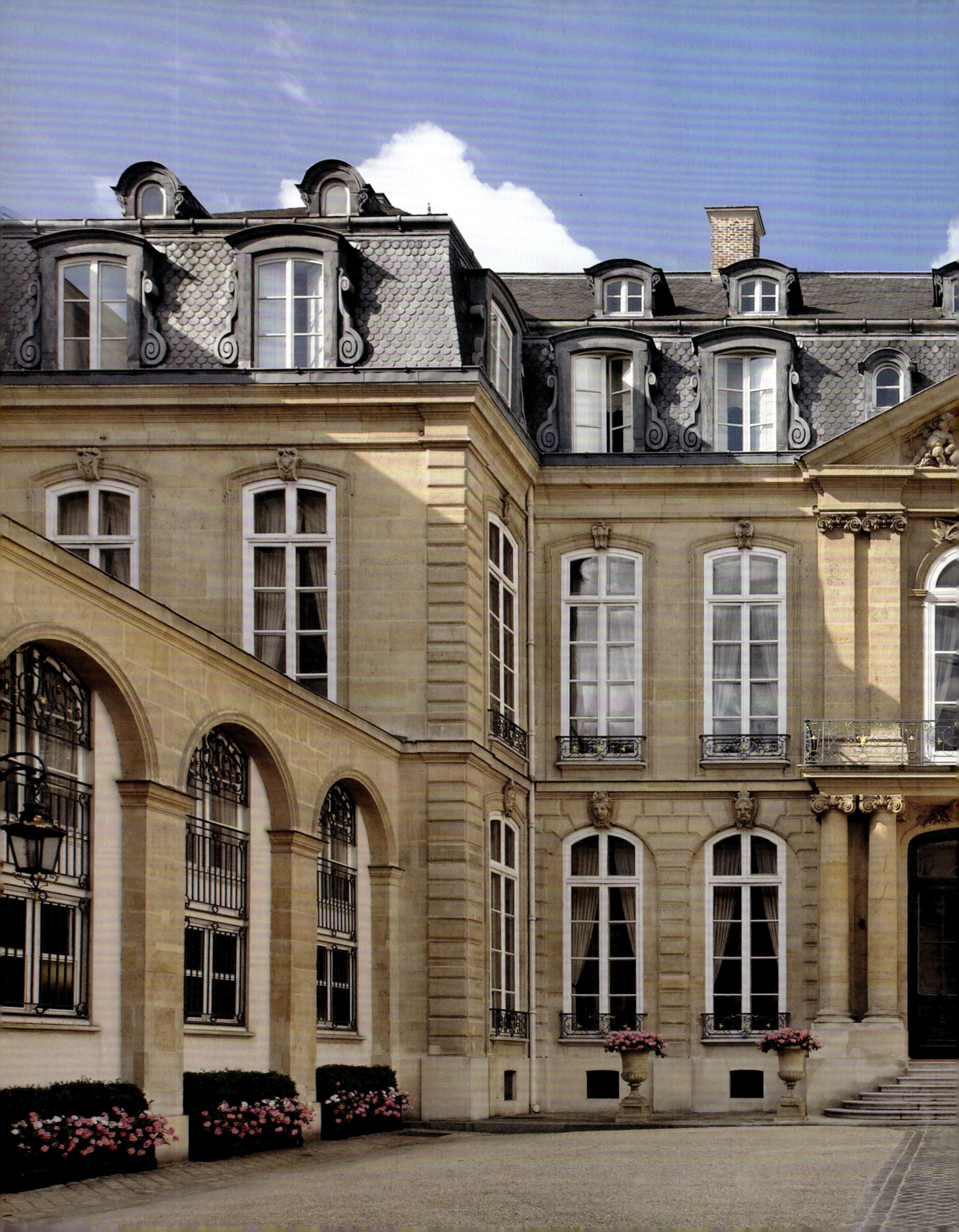

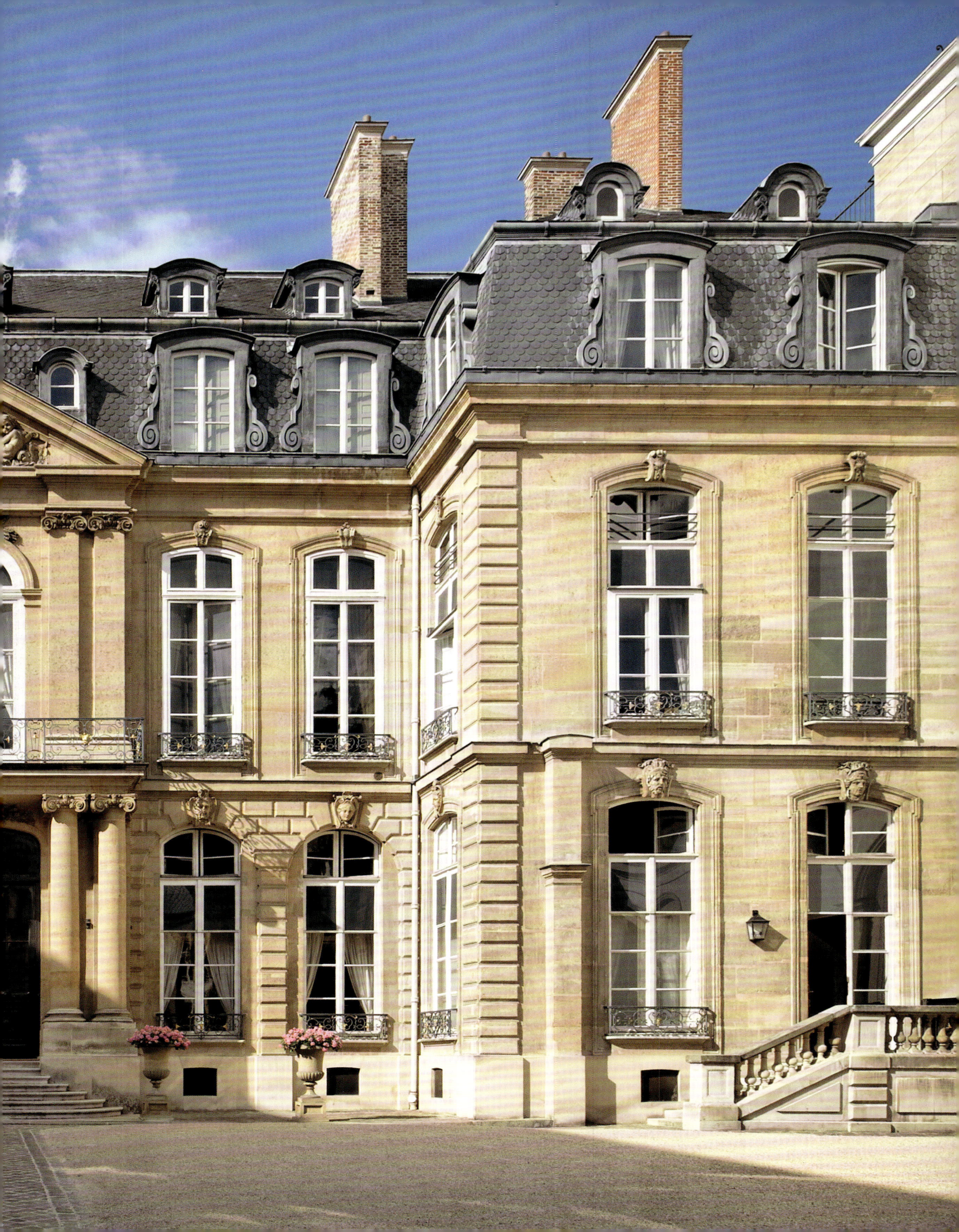

HONI SOIT QUI MAL Y PENSE

DIEU ET MON DROIT

CLARENCE HOUSE

For some 200 years, the Hôtel de Charost has been the beating heart of British diplomacy in Paris. When The Duke of Wellington was appointed British Ambassador to France in 1814 he urgently needed a home and had the excellent good sense – and taste – to acquire the house of Napoleon Bonaparte's sister, Pauline Borghese. He also had the wisdom to purchase the contents. To the great credit of successive British Governments, every effort has been made to keep the collection intact and preserve the character of the original building. As a result this marvellous eighteenth century building continues to house a unique collection of French Empire furniture, clocks, candelabra and chandeliers.

Today, the building remains the Ambassador's Residence and is in constant use as a means of bringing together the people of the two countries. Every walk of life crosses the threshold, ranging from politics, business, the arts and finance to the often otherwise unsung heroes and heroines of the voluntary sector. Activities range from promoting the excellence of British goods and services to the search for practical solutions to climate change and the protection of the World's increasingly fragile ecosystems. The house provides a literally inspirational setting for these vital discussions and, I rather suspect, has a subtle convening power all of its own…

This book serves not only as a guide to a magnificent house and its treasures, but also as a touchstone of the cultural heritage which the United Kingdom and France have developed together over the last two centuries – and that is of enduring importance in an increasingly uncertain world.

HRH The Prince of Wales

PREFACE

Fimalac is delighted to be associated with the unveiling of an artistic and historic gem, namely the Paris Residence that has served as the home of British ambassadors to France for nearly two hundred years.

The publication of this book testifies to an extraordinarily rich relationship between Britain and France — the Residence known as the hôtel de Charost, located in the heart of Paris at 39 rue du Faubourg-Saint-Honoré, embodies and symbolises the harmonious relations between the two countries. It is notably famous for having been home to the 1st Duke of Wellington, who bought it from the no less illustrious Pauline Bonaparte Borghese, and ever since it has borne the singular imprint of great British diplomats — and their wives — who have each left his or her mark on its history.

An inside view of this glamorous, typically eighteenth-century residence with its equally precious furnishings is now possible outside the one day a year that restricted heritage sites are opened to the French public. On that day, visitors crowd the Residence to appreciate its Empire furniture, English garden, and all the other wonders found in the hôtel de Charost.

As a friend of Great Britain and a lover of art, I was highly aware of the human and artistic appeal of such an undertaking, led with talent and energy by His Excellency Sir Peter Westmacott and his wife, Ms. Susan Nemazee Westmacott. This volume now provides access to these wonderful treasures to all, specialist scholars and general public alike, here and abroad.

Marc Ladreit de Lacharrière
Member of the Institut de France
CEO of Fimalac

Pages 6-7: The front façade of the Residence facing the courtyard off the rue du Faubourg-Saint-Honoré.
Page 8: The Royal Arms of George III in gilded plaster decorating the north end of the State Dining Room.
Facing page: The Ante-Room with a bronze statuette of Edward VII on horseback by William Goscombe John (1860–1952), dated c. 1905.

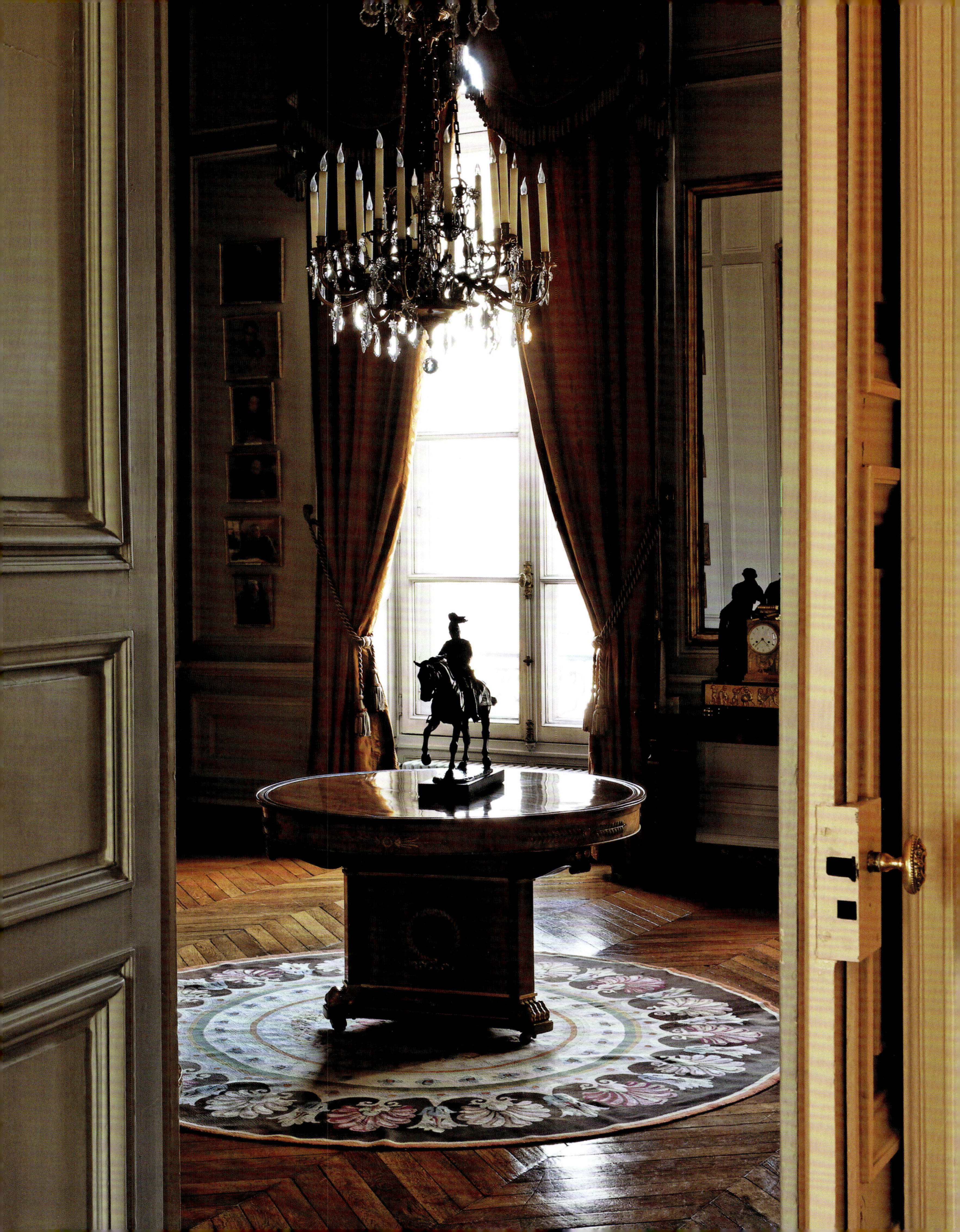

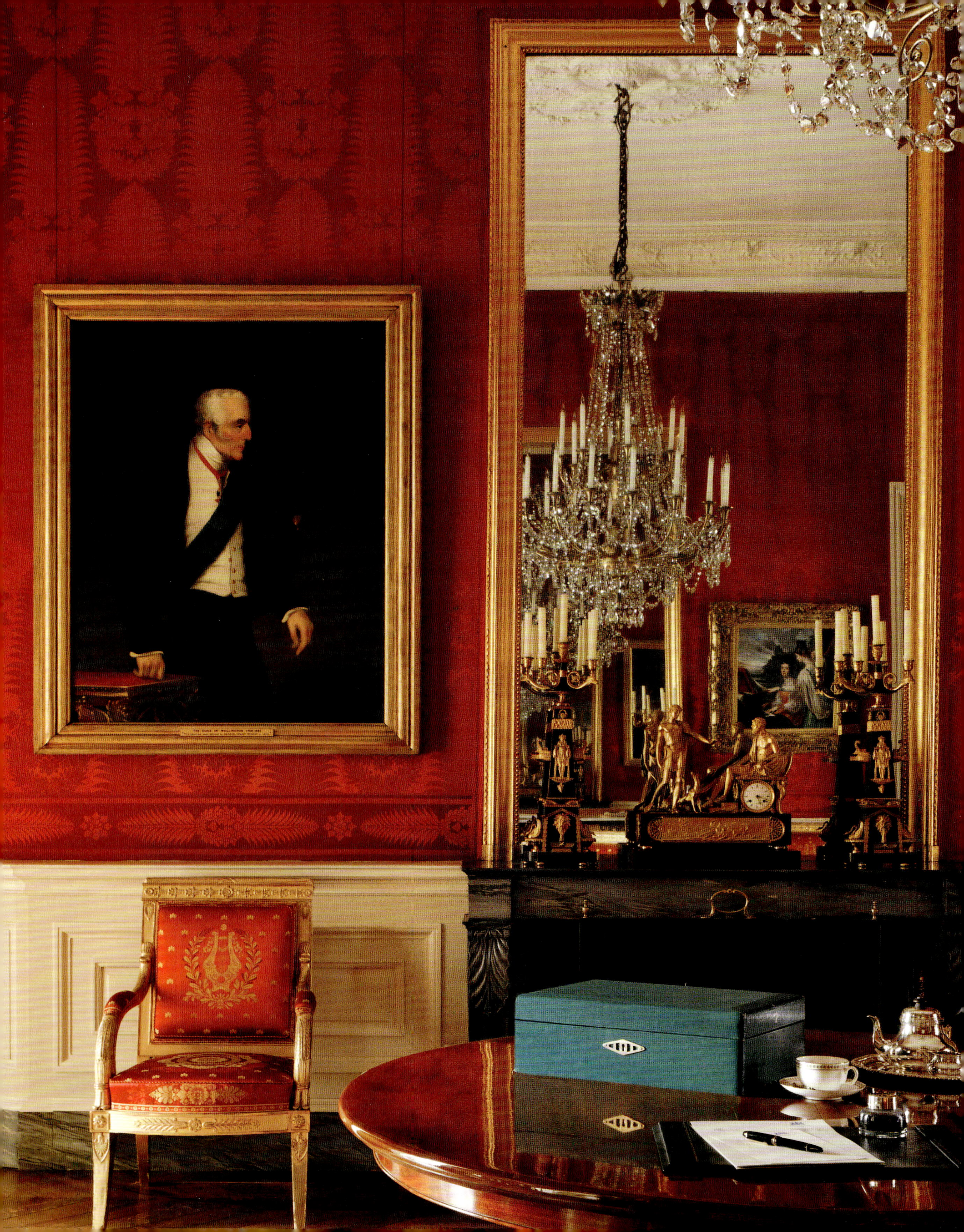

INTRODUCTION

It is an enormous privilege to serve in Paris as British ambassador and to be entrusted with what is probably the most beautiful, and certainly the most historically important, British ambassador's Residence in the world.

As The Prince of Wales points out in his foreword, when the Duke of Wellington acquired the house in 1814, he bought the contents too, much of which can still be seen in the Residence today. Pictures loaned by the British Government Art Collection, many associated with the house and its previous occupants, add to the spirit of the place. It is a shared inheritance: French in origin and nature but carefully maintained for two hundred years by appreciative British governments and successive ambassadors.

In the early nineteenth century, an Embassy was both home and the place where the ambassador and his staff worked. As the role of diplomatic missions expanded, separate premises came to be acquired for the offices while ambassadorial residences became the focus of entertainment and representational activity. Since 1947, it has been our great good fortune in Paris to have the two buildings next door to each other.

If we were looking for a new home for the British ambassador to France in the twenty-first century, we would not select as grand an historic monument as the hôtel de Charost. But it is part of our history, a unique asset in the heart of the city, and the envy of countries less magnificently represented. With ownership of such a building comes the responsibility both to take good care of it and to ensure that it earns its keep, so that it makes a real, living contribution to closer links between Britain and France. Hardly a day now passes when the Residence is not used for an official function of some kind.

The creation of the European Union has changed the way governments work together, and moved much of the negotiation to Brussels. But the need for the leading member states of Europe to talk to one another, to understand each other, and to deal with bilateral business has never been greater. Every British prime minister since Winston Churchill, whose parents were married here in 1874, has stayed in the house, as have many members of the Royal Family. Today, we regularly put up ministers, members of parliament, senior officials and members of the armed forces. We receive some 15,000 visitors a year.

The house itself is part of the history of relations between France and the United Kingdom. This book explains its role from the times of Napoleon and Wellington, through the Paris Commune and two world wars up to the present day. The Duke of Wellington may have been obliged to return to soldiering and is now probably best known for defeating Napoleon at Waterloo on 18 June 1815. But at the Congress of Vienna that year, and as 'the arbiter of Europe' over the next three years while commander of the allied armies occupying France, he successfully fought for better terms for France than Austria and Prussia wanted; was a strong advocate of allowing France to be a major player in the new European balance of power; and in 1818 settled the tangled issue of war reparations in France's favour.

Today, the house the Duke bought remains a focal point of the relationship that has been known since 1904 as the Entente Cordiale (although the expression was already in use fifty years earlier). It has often

Facing page: The Salon Rouge, with its crimson damask hangings and portraits of former ambassadors. The portrait of the Duke of Wellington by Alfred Guillaume Gabriel de Grimaud, comte d'Orsay (1801–1852), painted in 1845, is visible to the left of the mirror. *Page 15:* Books from the Library — the memoirs of successive ambassadors. Books given by Sir Alfred Duff Cooper still form the nucleus of the working library of the Residence.

been witness to major events. Its role in the Commune of 1871 is well described in this book. During the two world wars, when the ambassador was evacuated to the provinces, the house was left in the care of a skeleton staff who denied entry even to Hermann Goering. In the late 1940s, the salons of Sir Duff and Lady Diana Cooper helped put Parisian social life back on the map after the occupation. In the 1960s, the house was witness to the sometimes stormy relationship between President de Gaulle and Sir Christopher Soames — ambassador and son-in-law of the president's old friend and rival, Winston Churchill — as the two governments debated whether the United Kingdom should be allowed to join the European Community. Over two decades later, in November 1990, it was on the steps of the Residence that Margaret Thatcher was filmed reacting to the results of the first round of the Conservative Party leadership contest which led to her resignation as prime minister two days later.

In good times and bad, the Residence has remained a focal point of diplomacy and friendship between the peoples of Great Britain and France. In 1997, it had to respond instantly to terrible news that Princess Diana had been fatally injured in a car crash near the Pont d'Alma. In 2004, when the British and French governments were in disagreement over the war in Iraq, The Queen paid a highly successful state visit marking the hundredth anniversary of the Entente Cordiale.

Tony Blair and Jacques Chirac were respectively prime minister and president of the Republic for ten years between 1997 and 2007. Towards the end, war in Iraq and EU budgetary issues sometimes came between them. In 2008, when both had retired, they met again in the Residence. At the end of a long reminiscence, Jacques Chirac remarked: "It wasn't always so, Tony, but I have greatly enjoyed our time together this evening." Later that year, when the world's economies were hit by a financial tsunami, Blair's successor, Gordon Brown, visited Paris four times in the month of October alone. On 6 May 2010, five TV crews and hundreds of guests came to the house to witness the early results of an historic UK general election. Just nine days after becoming prime minister of a new coalition government, David Cameron came to stay for his first visit abroad in his new role.

The house makes its contribution in an increasing variety of ways. Events organised in the Residence vary from political and business breakfasts, lunches, dinners and receptions — for anything from a handful of people to thousands — to conferences, seminars, trade fairs, workshops, cultural events, product launches and even fashion shows. In September each year, we take part in France's country-wide Patrimony Days to welcome some 3,000 members of the public who do not normally see the house and its garden. There is great demand, too, for the tours we arrange for school children and organisations interested in the history and architecture of the house. Sponsored events, organised at no cost to the taxpayer, offer British and Franco-British business the opportunity to take advantage of the unique surroundings, the history of the building and its cachet to entertain their contacts and promote their products and services.

Not least for the manner in which this remarkable building has adapted to the changing needs of modern diplomacy, I am very proud that we have been able to produce this magnificent new book, with text by Tim Knox, photographs by Francis Hammond and the support of the Government Art Collection. I should add that the project would never have seen the light of day without the determination and hard work of my wife, Susan Nemazee Westmacott, and Donna Brabon at the Residence, or without the endless patience of our editor, Suzanne Tise-Isoré, and the very generous sponsorship of Fimalac and its president, Marc Ladreit de Lacharrière. I am immensely grateful to them all.

Sir Peter Westmacott
British Ambassador to France

COUNTESS
1810-1845
EDITED BY
THE HON.
BRITISH
EMBASSY
PARIS
AND
LITERARY
LETTERS
OF
THE EARL OF
LYTTON
VOL. I.
Edited by
ARTEMIS
COOPER
COLLINS
DUFF
COOPER
THE
DIARY
OF
LORD
BERTIE
1914-1918
STOUGHTON

Above: The Residence receives up to 15,000 visitors a year. Many are likely to sign the Visitors Book, which provides a written record of who has been to the house, when they came, and on what occasion. *Facing page:* A selection of invitation cards giving an impression of the range of events organised at the Residence.

Invitation 1
E II R

On the occasion of the State Visit to the Republic of France of
Her Majesty Queen Elizabeth II
and His Royal Highness The Prince Philip, Duke of Edinburgh
the British Ambassador
is commanded by The Queen to invite

....

to a Din...

Ambassador's Residence

Pour Mémoire

Invitation 2
Ambassade de Grande-Bretagne

DESIGNED IN BRITAIN

Invitation 3
To celebrate the Fiftieth Anniversary of the signing of the Treaty of Rome
The British Ambassador, Sir Peter Westmacott

invites ....

to attend the Rome50 Lecture by

The Rt Hon Lord Patten of Barnes
(Former European Union Commissioner)
"Europe: Wave of the future or blast from the past?"

Tuesday 3rd April 2007 at 18h45 precisely
followed by drinks

British Ambassador's Residence
39 rue du Faubourg Saint-Honoré
75008 Paris

RSVP

This invitation and proof of identity will be requested on arrival

Invitation 4
A l'occasion d'Expofil
l'Ambassadeur de Grande-Bretagne et Lady Mallaby
et The British Wool Textile Export Corporation

prient

de leur faire l'honneur d'assister à une réception
qui aura lieu

... l'Ambassadeur

Invitation 5
SEEDA — South East England Development Agency
Working for England's World Class Region

UK Trade & Investment

The British Ambassador and Lady Holmes
and
The South East England Development Agency
request the pleasure of the company of

....

...pment Agency's
...30pm

Invitation 6
L'Ambassadeur de Grande-Bretagne, Sir Michael Jay

a le plaisir d'inviter

....

à participer au séminaire

"... sir son implantation au Royaume-Uni"

organisé par

Invest • UK

et

... de Commerce Française de Grande-Bretagne

Invitation 7
The British Ambassador, Sir Peter Westmacott,
requests the pleasure of the company of

....

at the new Spring / Summer 2010 Collection Presentation
&
Retrospective
of the last British Haute Couture House in existence

SAINT-HILL & VON BASEDOW

on Tuesday 26th January 2010
Exhibition 12h - 18h
Champagne Reception 17 - 18h
British Ambassador's Residence
39 rue du Faubourg Saint-Honore - 75008

RSVP
Bismarck Phillips Communications & Media
parisrsvp@bpcm.com • +33142966666

Invitation 8
In the presence of H.R.H. The Princess Anne
Mrs Mark Phillips

Fashion Show

In aid of the Hertford British Hospital, Paris

Her Britannic Majesty's Ambassador and Lady Hibbert
request the pleasure of the company of

....

at a Fashion Show on Wednesday 4 June at 15.45h.

The British Embassy
39 rue du Faubourg St Honoré
Paris 8ème

Please bring this card with you.   Refreshments

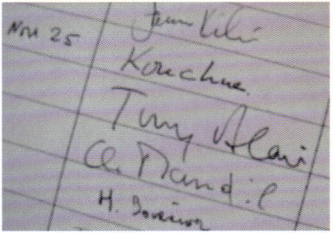

The Residence hosts a variety of events to promote the best of Britain across a wide range of sectors and activities from receptions for business people and government officials to art and fashion exhibitions and concerts. *Above:* A collage of photographs of events held at the Residence, signatures in the Visitors Book, and distinguished visitors, including The Queen, The Prince of Wales, successive British prime ministers, and senior French political figures.

Ambassade de Grande-Bretagne

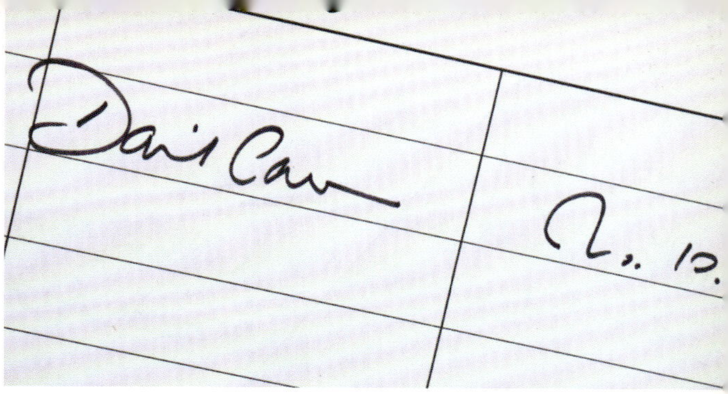

Elizabeth R
Philip

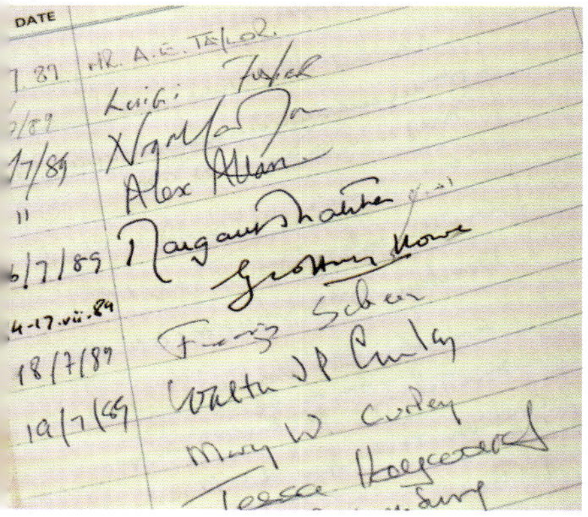
DATE

Adour turbofan
Adour turbofan

ENTENTE CORDIALE

ACKNOWLEDGEMENTS

This book could never have been written without Joseph Friedman's magisterial four-volume unpublished typescript: *British Embassy, Paris: History of a House 1725–1985* (1985), and the additional two-volume *A Catalogue of the Bonaparte-Borghese Collection of Furniture and Bronzes, British Embassy, Paris* (1985). I am also indebted to my friend the late John Cornforth, for his excellent guide book, with Mary Beal (formerly of the Government Art Collection), *British Embassy, Paris. The House and its Works of Art* (1992). The scholarly study of the Empire furniture and works of art by Jean Nérée Ronfort and Jean-Dominique Augarde, *À l'ombre de Pauline: La résidence de l'Ambassadeur de Grande-Bretagne à Paris* (Paris, 2001) was also helpful. John Julius Norwich, Viscount Norwich, told me some delightful stories about his parents' time at the Embassy. Joseph Friedman and Jonathan Harris's comments on my draft text were also invaluable. Lord and Lady Balniel very kindly allowed me to illustrate an interesting early watercolour in their collection showing the Residence, and arranged for its photography. Niall Hobhouse tipped me off about the Fontaine drawing for a canopy over the front door of the Palais Borghese, and my thanks to Bertrand Gautier of Galerie Talabardon et Gautier, Paris, for permission to reproduce it in this book. Christopher Hawksworth Woodward who uncomplainingly and expertly did the plans.

For the hospitality of the Residence, my thanks to the ambassador, Sir Peter Westmacott, and Lady Westmacott, who made me very welcome. Their enthusiasm, and success in finding a sponsor and publisher, has finally enabled the long-held ambition of the Embassy to update the 1992 book on the Residence to be realised.

Thanks, too, to Penny Johnson, Julia Toffolo and Philippa Martin of the Government Art Collection, who generously provided information on the works of art in the house and suggested I write the book; to Barbara Bryant for information about the artist Sir George Hayter. Also to Jan Carter from the FCO Interior Design Team, with whom I have got to know the Residence over the years. I would also like to thank Suzanne Tise-Isoré from Flammarion, who worked so efficiently and quickly to make this book come about, and Francis Hammond, who took the beautiful new photographs.

Thanks are also due to the staff of the Residence, notably the Residence manager, Eileen Flude; Donna Brabon and Miranda Westwood, who carried out helpful additional research; the indefatigable Residence butler, Ben Newick, and his staff; and particularly the chef, James Viaene, who sustained me while writing this book.

To Todd Longstaffe-Gowan for his forbearance.

Facing page: A silver crown finial from a tureen made by Robert Hennell in 1824. The Embassy silver, much of it acquired for the use of early nineteenth-century ambassadors, is still regularly in use today.

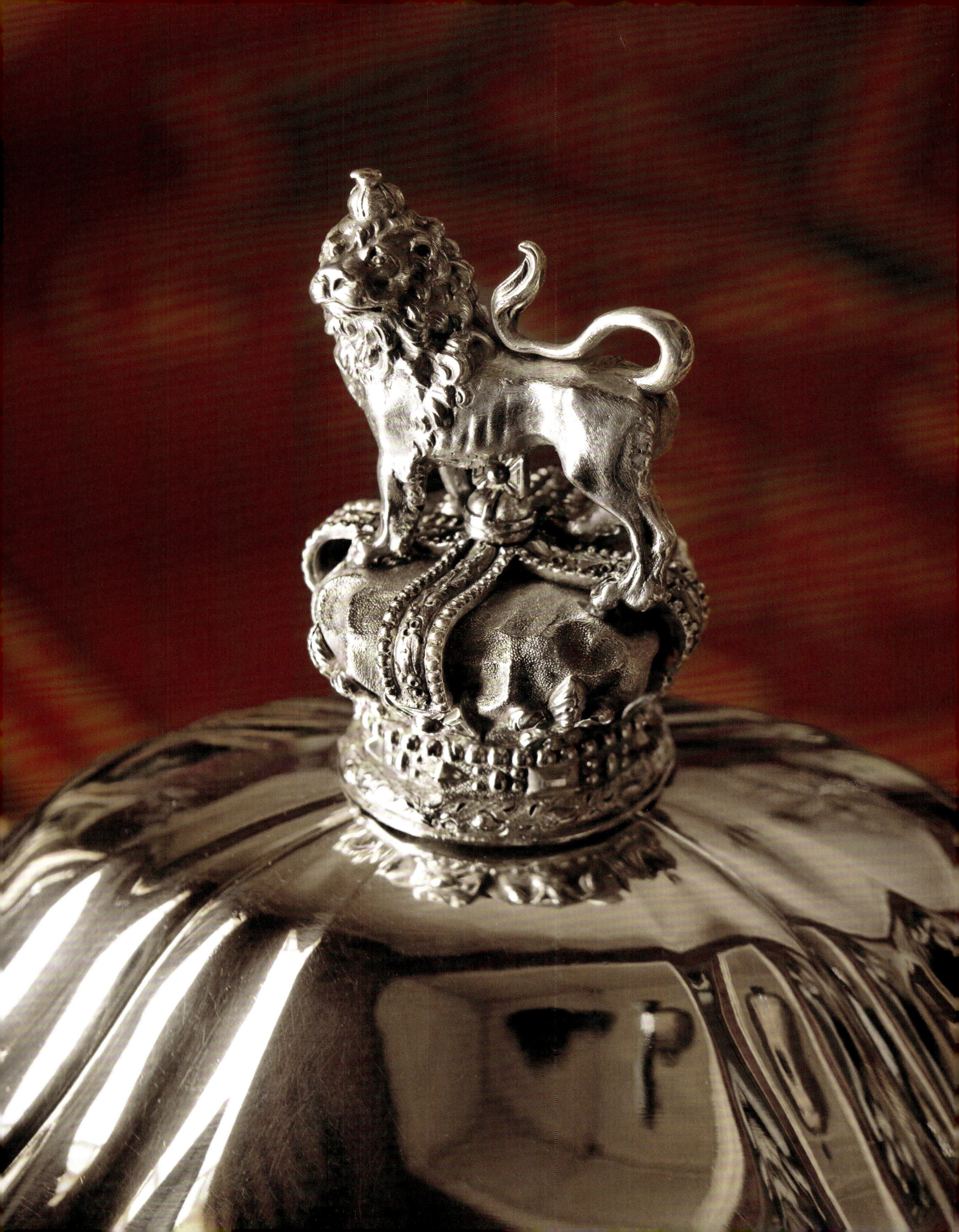

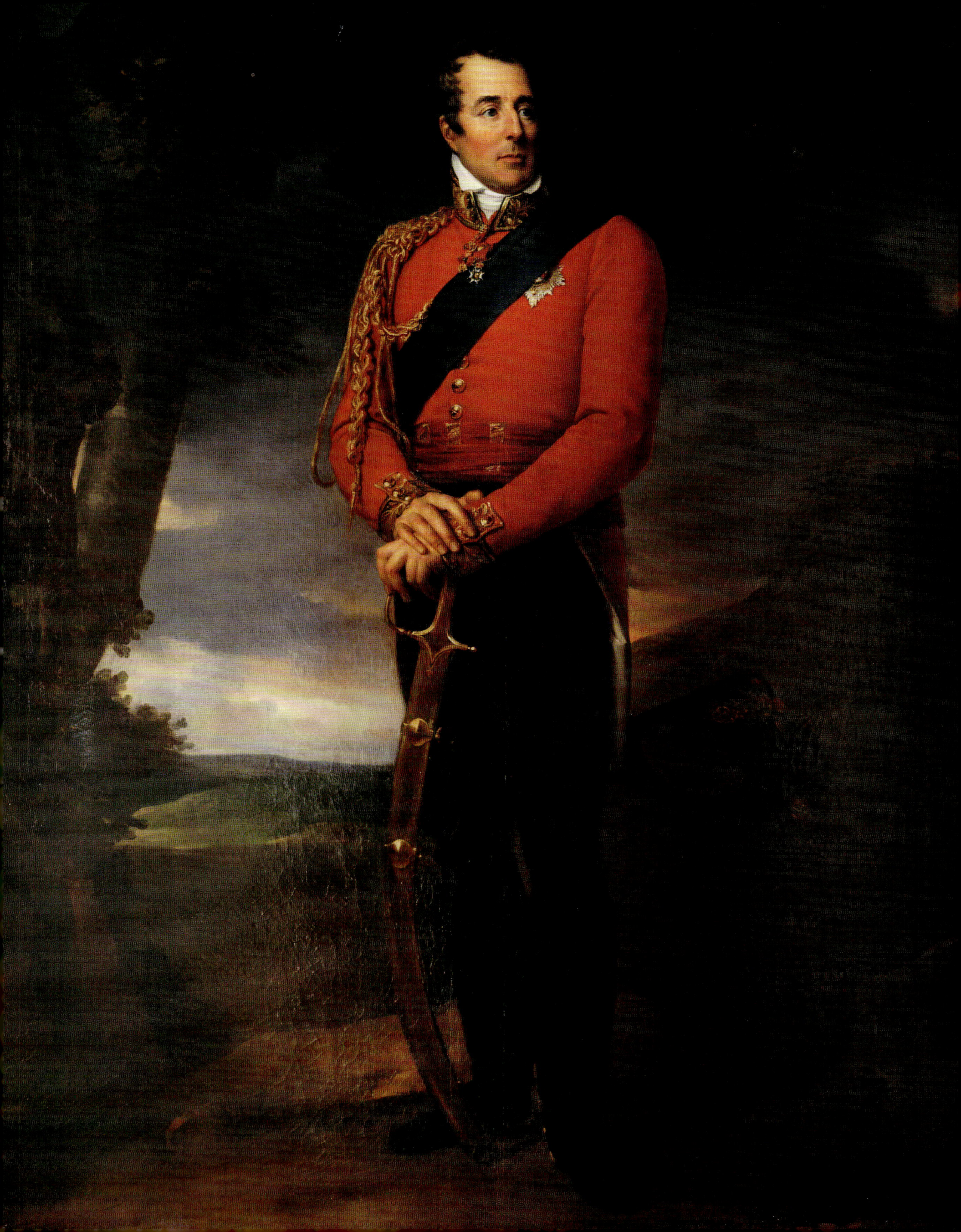

FROM ARISTOCRATIC TOWN HOUSE TO AMBASSADORIAL RESIDENCE

It was one of Britain's greatest military heroes, the 1st Duke of Wellington, who established the British in this grand old house in the rue du Faubourg-Saint-Honoré in the heart of Paris. In May 1814, Wellington arrived in Paris to join the Allied Sovereigns who had invaded France following the defeat of Napoleon at the Battle of Leipzig in October 1813. The former town house of the ducs de Charost, then known as the Palais Borghese, stood unoccupied with all its magnificent furnishings, having been hurriedly vacated by its owner, Napoleon's sister, Pauline Borghese. Although for a while it had been commandeered as the temporary residence of the emperor of Austria, it was now for sale, and Wellington was looking for a place to live following his recent appointment as British ambassador to the restored king of France, Louis XVIII. The Palais Borghese, opulently decorated in the height of fashionable Empire taste by Napoleon's extravagant sister, impressed him as an ideal place to establish his new embassy, and he ordered his aide-de-camp, Sir Charles Stuart, to inquire about its purchase. The negotiations were conducted between Pauline's comptroller, Jean-Paul Louis Michelot, and Quentin Craufurd, a wealthy expatriate Scot. By late August 1814, a deal had been struck, and the duke persuaded the British Government to pay 861,500 francs (approximately £40,000) for the house, furniture and stables.

Up until this time, during the eighteenth century, ambassadors leased their houses in the host country. Known as mission houses, these generally combined both living quarters and the Chancery, the offices for embassy business. Two earlier embassy premises had been custom-built in what was then Constantinople, (begun in 1801), and in Tehran (1811), but the Duke of Wellington's was the first embassy to be purchased, and has remained the home of the British ambassador to France ever since.

The Duke of Wellington did not occupy his splendid new residence for long, as he left Paris in January 1815 to take over from Lord Castlereagh as British representative at the Congress of Vienna, the conference at which the four Allied Powers who had defeated Napoleon assembled to remake the continent of Europe. The house survived unscathed Napoleon's brief return to power in March 1815 — when he escaped from the island of Elba, during the period known as the Hundred Days — and was the scene of festivities to celebrate Wellington's great victory at the Battle of Waterloo in June 1815. Since then, still retaining many of its original Empire furnishings, it has been home to over thirty British ambassadors to France and their families, and welcomed a host of famous people through its hospitable doors, from Queen Victoria to Elizabeth II, from Winston Churchill to Margaret Thatcher, and from William Makepeace Thackeray to Marcel Proust.

Successively an aristocratic town house, military offices, an imperial palace, and an embassy and diplomatic residence, it still bears the scars and embellishments of all its uses and occupants. Today, its ducal and imperial grandeur softened by almost two centuries of English decoration and taste for informal living, it is also one of the most beautiful and interesting of all ambassadorial residences in Paris, as well as being by far the most impressive British diplomatic residence abroad. This book is both a guide to, and a celebration of, a very remarkable house.

Facing page: The 1st Duke of Wellington, by François Pascal Simon Gerard 'Baron Gerard', painted in 1814, shortly after the duke became ambassador to France. This portrait hangs in the Ante-Room.

THE INVENTORIES

The hôtel de Charost is unusual in that it is exceptionally well documented by inventories. Such inventories, lists of the fittings and contents of the house and its outbuildings, were typically compiled on the death of persons of property, to assist with winding up their legal affairs, although they were also drawn up to record the state of a house prior to its lease or sale. The inventories of the hôtel de Charost minutely record the furnishings of the house and the uses of the rooms on the death of family members. Thus, there are inventories following the death of the duchesse de Béthune in 1737 and the duc de Béthune in 1759, while the lease of the hôtel to the comte de La Marck in 1785 is commemorated by the document *État des Lieux* of 1787 which has been very useful as a record of the house prior to its alteration. Another inventory was taken in 1792, at the request of the creditors of La Marck, while Pauline Borghese had another done — right down to all the clocks, firedogs, and the colours of the upholstery — to assist the sale of her house to the Duke of Wellington in 1814. The vicissitudes of the house in the nineteenth century are fully recorded in the inventories taken on the appointment or recall of ambassadors, and even today inventories play an essential role in maintaining the Residence in proper order.

THE ROOM NAMES

Over the centuries, the house has adapted gracefully to its many incarnations and functions. Room names that reflected normal usage for an aristocratic family of the eighteenth century, such as the *'grande chambre'* of the duchesse de Béthune, gave way to the *'chambre de parade'* in the household of an imperial princess. The same room later became known as the Victoria Room until redecoration in the 1980s led to its present name, the Salon Pauline.

Thus, Lady Granville's 'Glazed Galleries' of the nineteenth century are today simply known as the 'Gallery'. The 3rd duc de Charost's *cabinet* became Pauline Borghese's library before it was known as 'the Ambassadress's Bedroom' (*chambre à coucher de Milady*), becoming the 'Cooper Bedroom' at the end of the twentieth century, when all the bedrooms acquired names of illustrious ambassadors past — Stuart, Granville, Bertie and Monson among them. One bedroom, Wincham, is even named after the fictitious ambassador in Nancy Mitford's novel *Don't Tell Alfred* (1960).

Above: Title page of the inventory made for the sale of the hôtel de Charost in 1814. *Facing page:* Title page of the *État des Lieux* – an inventory made in 1787 for the 5th duc de Charost describing the condition of the hôtel de Charost prior to its lease to the comte de La Marck. Now conserved in the Archives de la Ville de Paris, it is one of a group of documents that help us reconstruct the history of the Residence.

État des Lieux
d'un Grand hôtel,
Rue du fauxbourg St honoré,
occupé par M. le Comte
De la Marck.

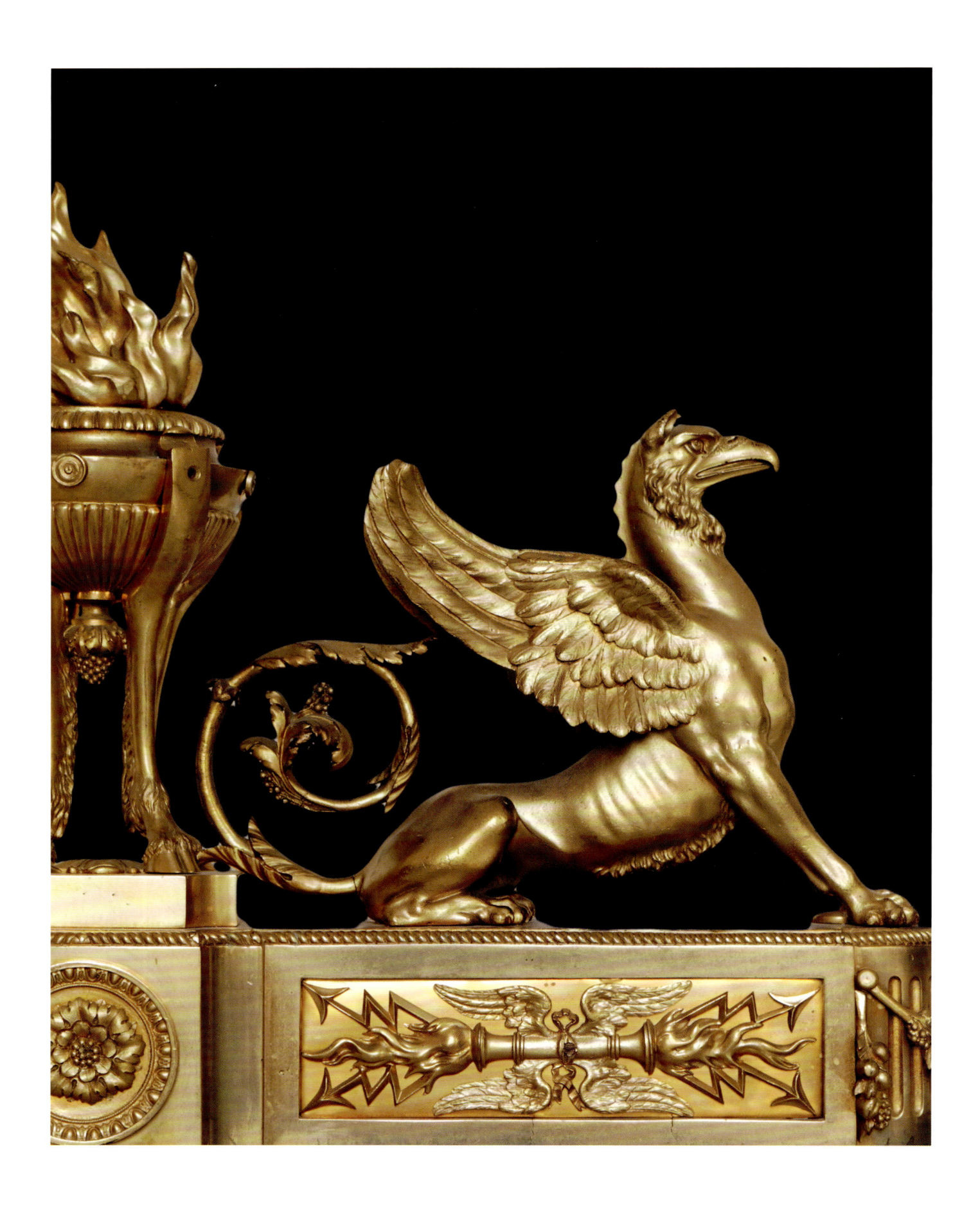

Above: One of a pair of bronze firedogs in the Salon Vert et Or. *Facing page:* Detail of the finely chiselled ormolu mounts from the psyche mirror in the Salon Pauline.

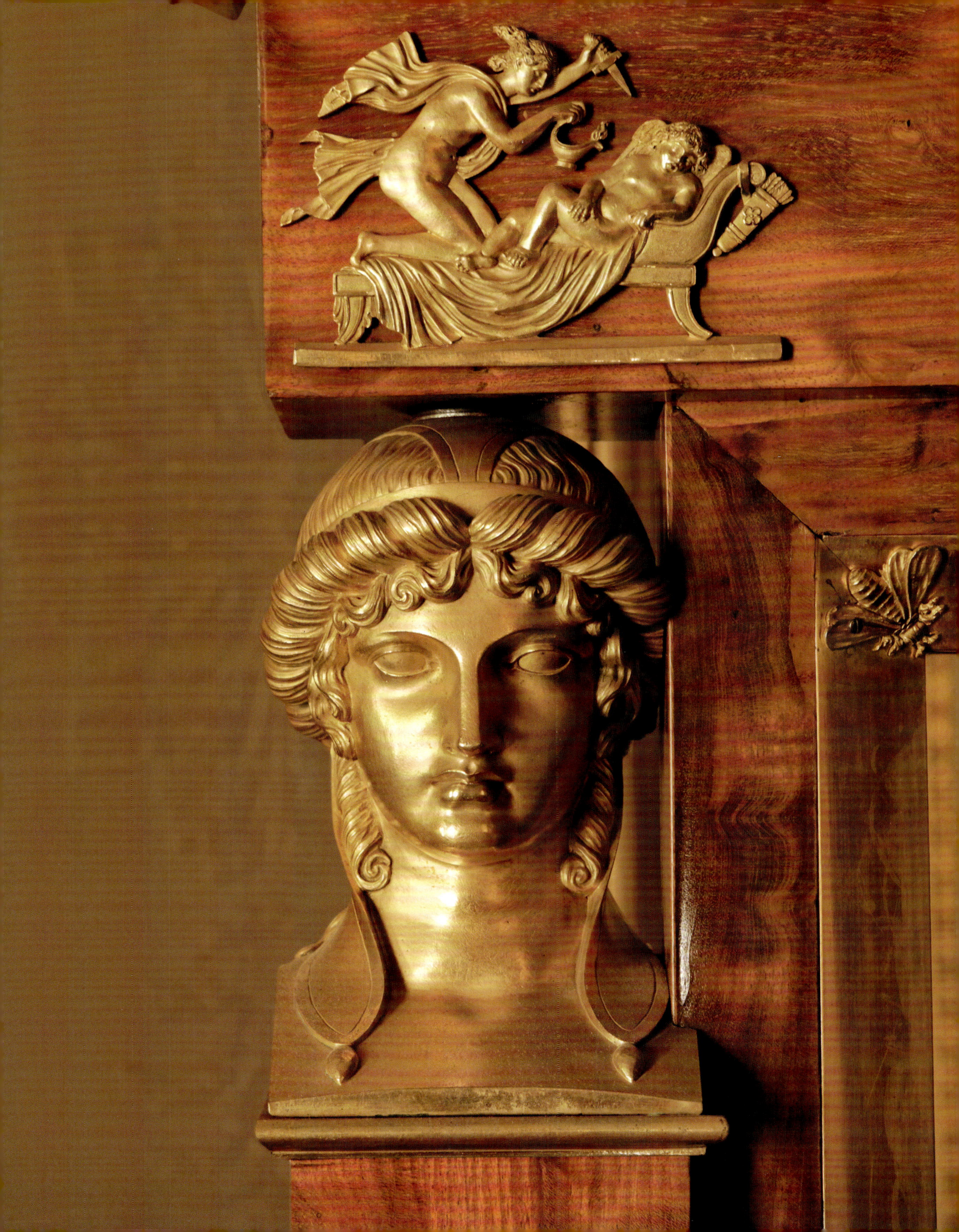

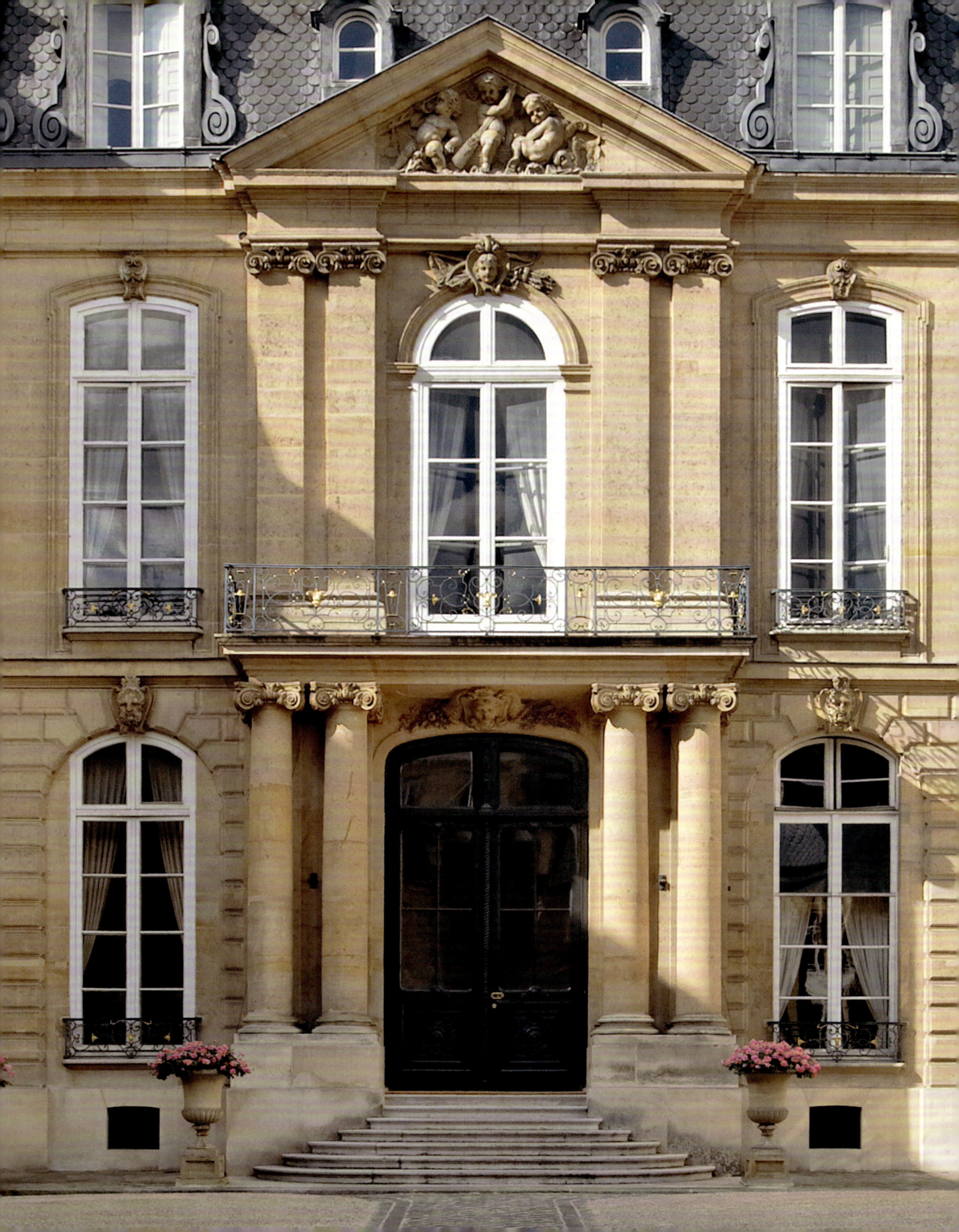

THE HISTORY OF THE HOUSE AND ITS OCCUPANTS

Facing page: The entrance front of the British Ambassador's Residence in Paris is still much as it was when it was built in 1725.

The Faubourg Saint-Honoré lies to the west of the Louvre, the old centre of Paris. Until the late seventeenth century it was still largely undeveloped, an area of scattered hamlets and farms along the road leading out of the city to Versailles. It was, one commentator noted in 1698, '*rien de singulier ni de remarquable*' ('neither special nor remarkable'). The site of what was to become the hôtel de Charost — the name of what is now the official residence of the British ambassador to Paris — was used at this time as market gardens.

As the death of Louis XIV approached, the aristocratic families who had followed the court to Versailles began to return to Paris. As a regency under the king's nephew, the duc d'Orléans, seemed likely, aristocratic life now centred around his establishment in the Palais-Royal and, after Louis's death in 1715, the Tuileries Palace, then the residence of the five-year-old Louis XV, the dead king's great-grandson. But rather than settle in the crowded and unsanitary centre of the capital, some of the more enterprising grand families began to acquire sites further out of town, along the rue du Faubourg-Saint-Honoré. The destination proved so popular that eventually the authorities attempted — unsuccessfully — to halt the expansion of Paris to the west. Among the new residences was the hôtel d'Évreux — now the Elysée Palace — which began construction in 1718. One of the noblemen taking part in this westward expansion was Paul François de Béthune-Charost, marquis d'Ancenis (1682–1759), who bought the site on the rue du Faubourg-Saint-Honoré, where he began building what

Above: A sundial still tells the hours on one of the curved walls of the gatehouse facing the Courtyard.
Facing page: Plan of the rue du Faubourg-Saint-Honoré of 1740 showing the property as it was in 1725. The hôtel de Charost can be found opposite the rue d'Aguesseau, flanked by a property owned by the president de Montigny and a large vacant site. The newly built hôtel d'Évreux — now the Elysée Palace – lies to the right.

30

Hôtel d'Evreux

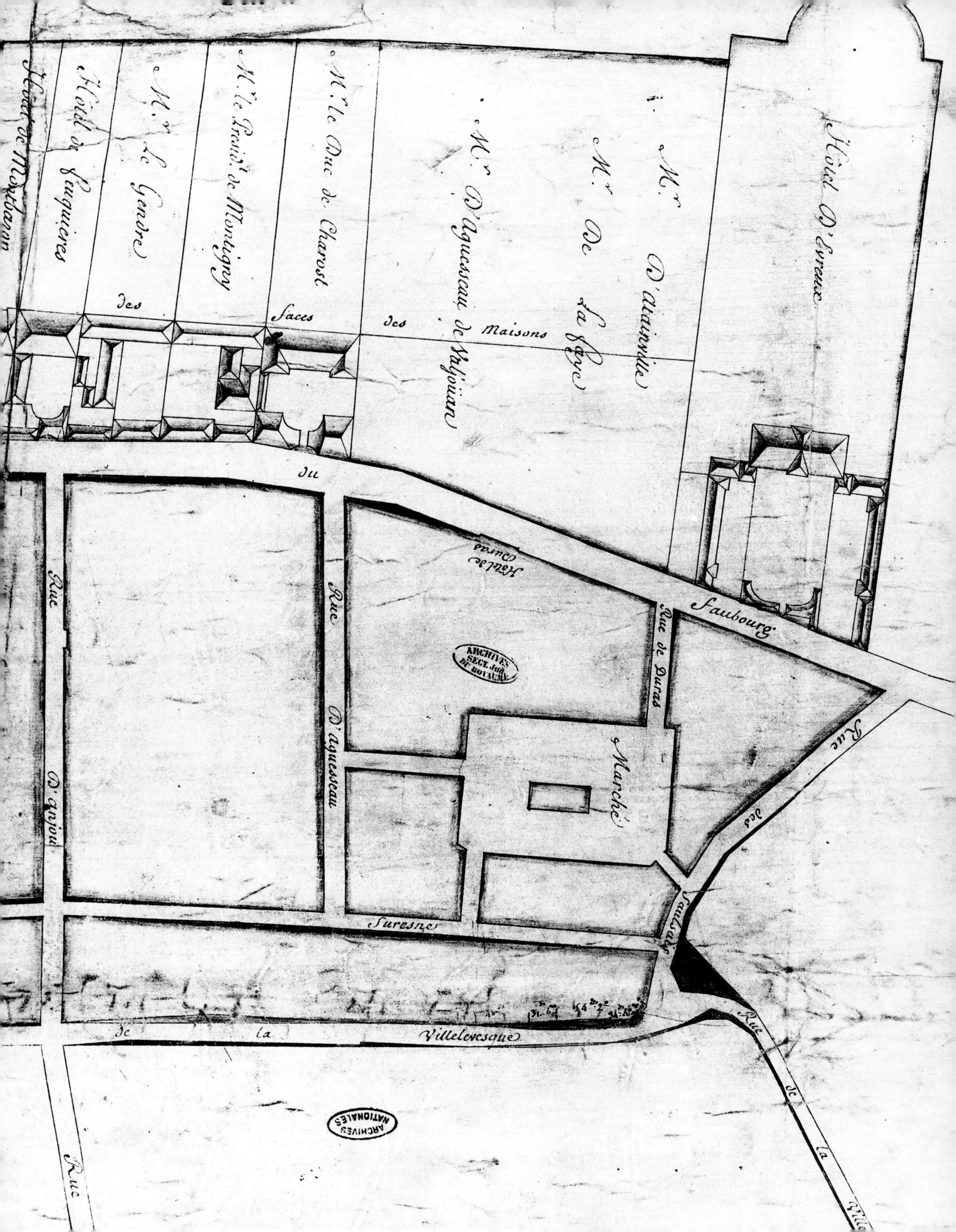

M. D'Étainville
M. De la Baye
M. Le Duc de Charost
M. Le Prest de Montigny
M. Le Gendre
M. De Fuguières
Hôtel de Montbazon

M.r D'aguesseau de Valjouan

faces des Maisons

Rue du Faubourg

Rue de Duras

Marché

Rue d'Aguesseau

Rue d'Anjou

Rue de Suresnes

Rue des Saussaies

Rue de la Villelevesque

Rue de la Ville

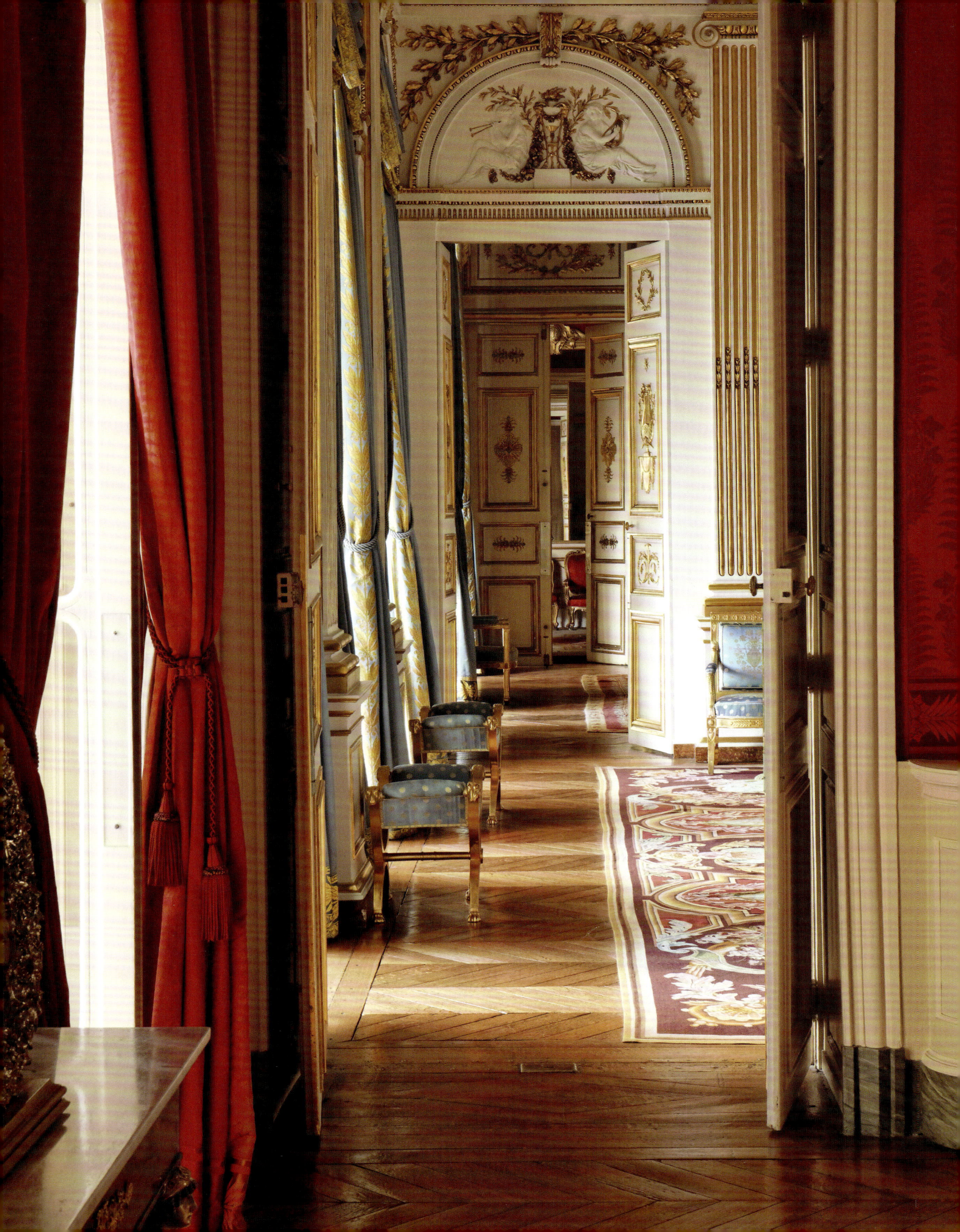

would become the hôtel de Charost. The Béthune family could trace its noble ancestry back to the tenth century, but the cadet branch of Béthune-Charost owed its rise to the favour of Louis XIII and Cardinal Richelieu, and later to Louis XIV. (Their frequent changes in title due to death, inheritance and unusually, early preferment, make any account of the Béthune-Charost family confusing. A simplified family tree showing the relationships of the principal occupants of the house is provided on page 167.)[1]

The marquis d'Ancenis, who was Captain of the King's Bodyguard, chose as his architect Antoine Mazin (1679–1740), a native of Marseilles described in contemporary documents as an '*ingénieur du roi*', and whose previous experience had been chiefly the design and construction of fortifications. Plans for the new house were supplied on 20 April 1722. These are now lost, but several agreements with the craftsmen employed survive, including those between Ancenis and the mason, Louis Paignault; with the master-carpenter, Jean-Baptiste Lardin; and with the blacksmith, Antoine Hallé. The internal fittings of the house were entrusted to the joiner, Robert Vitry. The contracts reveal the extent of the works and the considerable costs involved; the mason Paignault received 38,255 livres for his work in June 1723, with another 119,802 livres owing in 1725. Ancenis was compelled to sell estates to pay for the works, and Mazin was still owed money on his death in 1740.

The house was ready for occupation in December 1725. Like most *hôtels particuliers* — or great townhouses — it was not solely the residence of Ancenis and his immediate family. His father, the head of the extended family, Armand de Béthune, 3rd duc de Charost (1663–1747), occupied the most important apartment on the first floor overlooking the garden. Ancenis had rooms facing the courtyard, while his wife had a large suite of five rooms downstairs. Each suite comprised an ante-room, a reception room, a bedchamber and a cabinet or private closet. The second floor accommodated their six children, while a swarm of servants who attended the various households lodged in the entresols and over the stables and household offices in the courtyard. Nor was the hôtel de Charost the family's only residence; it was one of a series of houses and apartments they occupied as they followed the court to Versailles, Fontainebleau and Marly, in addition to their estates in the country.

Protected from the noise of the street, and taking advantage of the light and air of the garden, this type of Parisian town house contructed 'between courtyard and garden' was based on a model used for more than six centuries in France.

The occasional occupation of the new hôtel is partly due to the fact that, three years earlier, in August 1722, the duc de Charost had been appointed as governor of Louis XV. Although he held this position for only a few months — Louis XV came of age and was crowned at Reims in October that year — this meant that the family once again basked in royal favour and Charost was increasingly required to attend the king at Versailles, where the court had once more returned. Ancenis also profited from the new regime, with pensions and access to the royal circle, and, in 1724, over a game of cards, the king granted him the title of duc de Béthune, by which he was known ever since.

The completed hôtel de Charost, although spacious and well built, but not architecturally exciting, aroused little comment from contemporaries. One of the few who noticed it was Germain Brice,

Facing page: The gilded enfilade of state rooms on the ground floor of the Residence facing the garden: the Salon Rouge, Salon Bleu, Salon Pauline and, just visible, the Throne Room.
[1] Thanks are due to Pierre Arizzoli-Clémentel and Richard Flahaut for their invaluable assistance with the establishment of the genealogy of the Béthune-Charost family.

author of the famous guidebook, *Description de la ville de Paris*, who drily observed in 1752 that it was '*très vaste*'. An inventory of the hôtel de Charost drawn up in 1737, following the death of the duchesse de Béthune, gives us a good idea of its furnishing and decoration. The principal rooms were hung with tapestries, and the cornices and architectural woodwork — much more than survives today — were gilded, with overdoors and overmantels incorporating paintings. Much of the effect of the rooms depended on rich textiles and upholstery, but there were also inlaid cabinets, marble-topped console tables, oriental porcelain and ormolu-mounted clocks.

The fortunes of the family waxed and waned. By the late eighteenth century, the politically progressive heir to the house, Armand Joseph, 5th duc de Charost (1738–1800) — who had abolished feudal rights and privileges on his estates as early as 1769, and resided elsewhere in Paris — decided to rent out the hôtel de Charost. In 1785, he signed a lease with a distant relation, Auguste Marie Raymond d'Arenberg, comte de La Marck (1753–1833), who agreed to pay an annual rent on condition that Charost carried out various improvements. An inventory made in 1787, known as the *État des Lieux*, now conserved in the Archives de la Ville de Paris, describes the house prior to these works. These included replacing the old-fashioned windows with larger panes, creating an English-style garden, and the introduction of running water. Much of the gilding in the apartments was overpainted in white at this time.

The principal legacy of the comte de La Marck's time in the house is the Salon Bleu, a music room on the ground floor, which was remodelled with fashionable neoclassical panelling. However, the comte and his family were not to enjoy their house for long. With his regiment stationed in Strasbourg, he was often absent from Paris, and he was also becoming increasingly involved in the political turmoil of the French Revolution. La Marck particularly cultivated the comte de Mirabeau, the dynamic tribune of the National Convention, lending him large sums of money, possibly in an attempt to broker a deal between the Revolutionary party and the Royalists. In June 1788, Mirabeau was entertained at the hôtel de Charost, and after the events of 1789 — the storming of the Bastille and the bringing of the royal family from Versailles to the Tuileries — the comte de La Marck redoubled his efforts to act as go-between. In March 1790, he arranged for a secret meeting between Mirabeau and the Austrian ambassador the comte de Mercy-Argenteau at the hôtel de Charost, where they conspired to help Louis XVI and Marie-Antoinette flee Paris. But Mirabeau's sudden death in April 1791 and the royal family's failed attempt to escape to Varennes a few months later precipitated a crisis. The La Marcks retired to their estates in the country, from where — after again attempting to help Marie-Antoinette — the comte fled to Flanders.

In February 1792, the comte de La Marck sublet the hôtel de Charost to the Portuguese ambassador Dom Vicente de Sousa Coutinho (1726–1792), who died after only a few months' residence. By this time La Marck was an exile and heavily in debt, so his creditors demanded that seals were fixed to the hôtel (a common measure in cases of debt, preventing anything from being removed from the premises). A detailed inventory was taken of the ambassador's property, down to the hams, chocolates and coffee in the larder, and some of the Embassy servants were kept on to look after the house and feed the guard dog. Outside, the situation was desperate: the king was guillotined in the place de la Révolution (now the place de la Concorde, scarcely five hundred metres from the house) in January 1793,

Above: A sneering male mask — one of fourteen surviving stone masks over the doors and windows of the courtyard, minor masterpieces of Louis XV architectural sculpture. *Facing page*: A stone relief depicting a mastiff taking a large bite out of a wild boar makes for an appropriately sanguinary overdoor to the entrance to the Kitchen from the Courtyard.

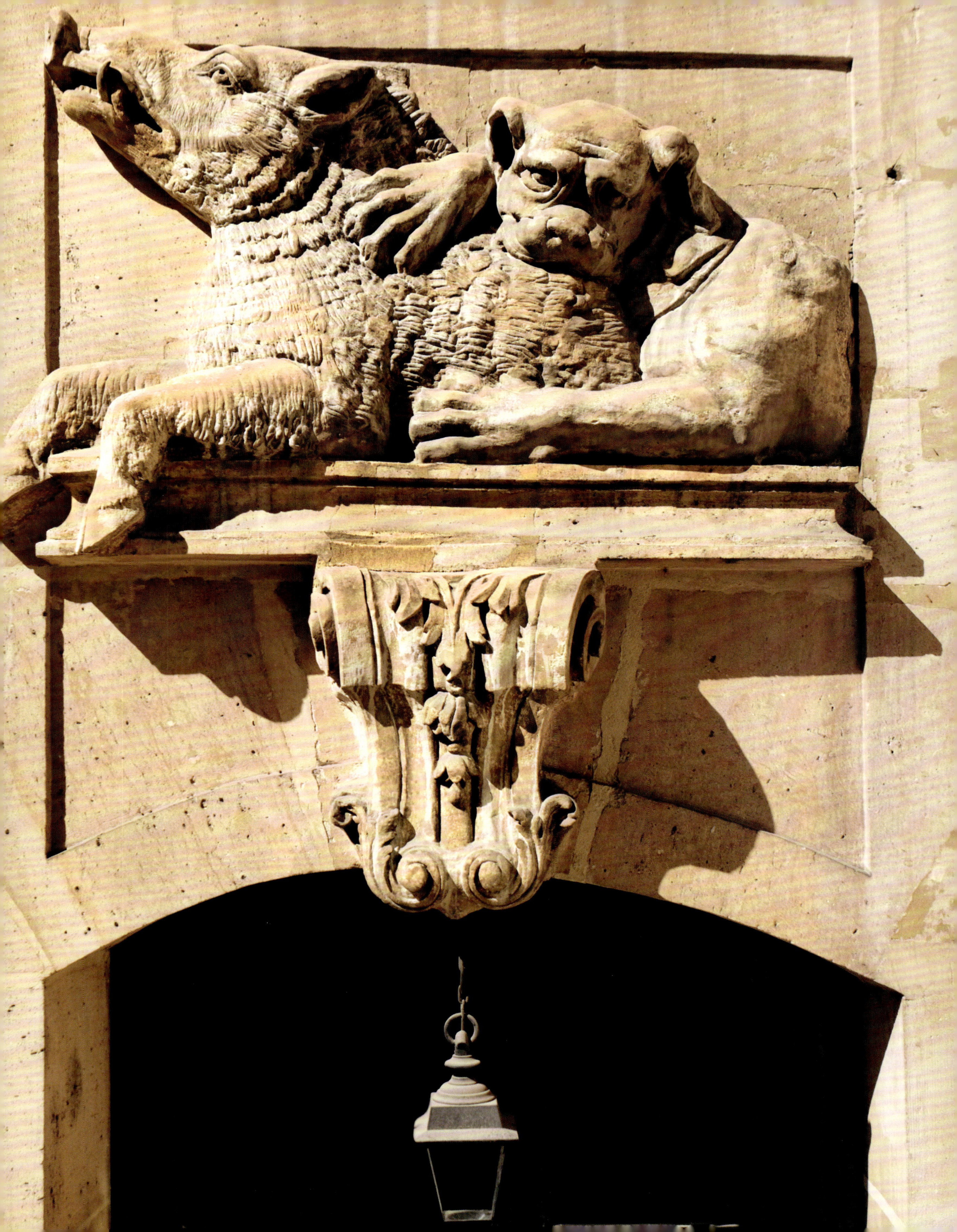

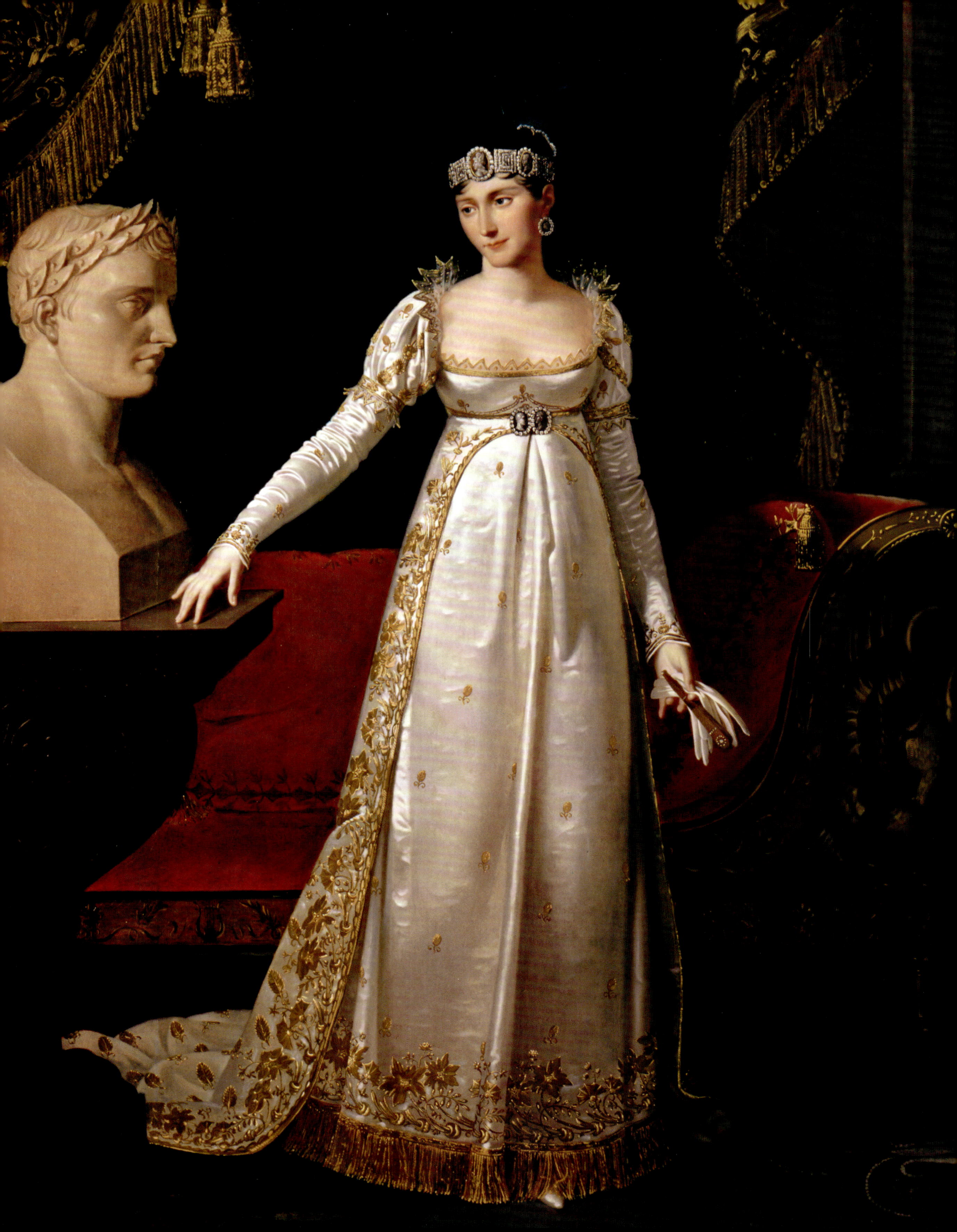

followed by the queen in October. On 28 April 1794, the duc de Charost's eldest son, the comte de Charost, went to the scaffold too. Like so many aristocrats, he had been arrested trying to escape to England. The duc de Charost was also arrested and confined in La Force prison, despite his staunch support for the principles of the Revolution. Luckily he was released soon afterwards, possibly due to representations from the grateful tenants on his estates. As La Marck himself had also fled France, he was subject to the confiscation of his property, so the contents of the hôtel de Charost were put up for auction in July 1795. Shortly afterwards, the duc de Charost managed to secure the return of his property, including the family hôtel, by this time largely stripped of its contents. He did not reoccupy the house, but in 1799 leased the building to the Régie Nationale des Hôpitaux Militaires (a body responsible for the administration of military hospitals) to be used as offices. Two years after his death in 1800 — from smallpox, caught, it is said, on one of his charitable visits to an institute for deaf-mutes — his widow, the duchesse de Charost, let the house to the British ambassador, the Earl Whitworth (1752–1825), who moved in with his wife, the dowager Duchess of Dorset. Their occupancy was short-lived, and they were forced to move the following year when diplomatic relations between England and France, then under the rule of the First Consul, Napoleon Bonaparte, were broken off.

On 1 February 1803, a twenty-two-year-old widow, Marie-Paulette Leclerc, and her infant son, Dermide, arrived in Paris and took up lodgings in her brother Joseph's palatial house, the hôtel Marbeuf in the rue du Faubourg-Saint-Honoré. She was none other than Napoleon Bonaparte's sister, known as Pauline (1780–1825), newly widowed following the death of her husband, General Victor Emmanuel Leclerc, from yellow fever contracted on an expedition to suppress a slave rebellion on the Caribbean island of Santo Domingo the previous year. Pauline returned to find her brother the ruler of France; he had been appointed First Consul for life in May 1802, giving the Bonaparte family unprecedented wealth, power and influence.

Despite her recent misfortunes, Pauline was young, beautiful and perhaps the most nakedly ambitious of all her siblings. It was therefore only natural that she should wish to capitalise on her position. By this time, almost all the Bonaparte family had acquired large and splendid residences in Paris, which they refurbished luxuriously with the help of their brother. Pauline wanted one too, and she set her sights on the hôtel de Charost.

Therefore, in the spring of 1803, she made a substantial offer for the house to its owner, the duchesse de Charost. The fact that she did not have the means to seal the bargain did not seem to trouble Pauline. The current occupants' lease still had several months to run, and in any case Pauline was absorbed with preparations for her second marriage to the Roman nobleman, Prince Camillo Borghese. The match had been arranged by Napoleon, who was keen to ally his upstart house with the grandest families in Europe, but Pauline was impatient and clandestinely married the prince in a secret ceremony in August. The marriage contract was signed at the hôtel de Charost — in which Pauline was somehow already installed. Her brother was furious: it was less than a year since the death of her first husband, and it was important to keep up appearances. By the terms of the marriage contract, Pauline's Paris residence was to be her property alone — the problem was she still didn't have the funds to pay for it.

Before Pauline departed for Rome with her new husband, she entrusted the refurbishment of the hôtel de Charost to an architect. It is often claimed that this was the most fashionable architect of the day, Pierre François Léonard Fontaine (1762–1853), who did, indeed, undertake work on another of Pauline's houses, the château de Montgobert.

Facing page: Princess Pauline Borghese by Robert Lefèvre, 1808. Since 1976 on loan to the British Ambassador's Residence from the Rayne Foundation through the Government Art Collection. *Following pages:* Pierre François Fontaine, *Project for the round tent requested by Her Imperial Highness (Princess Pauline Borghese)*, c. 1803.

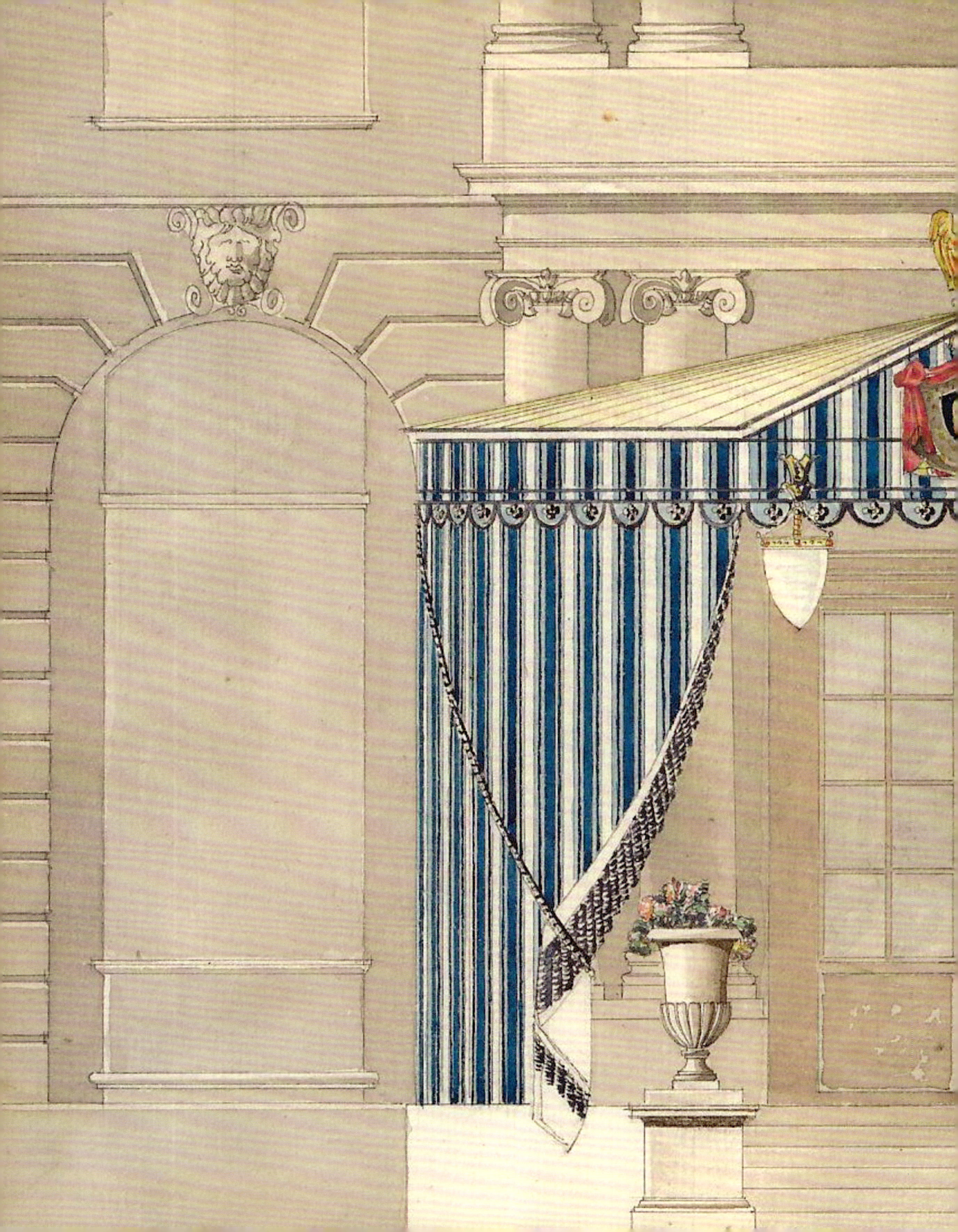

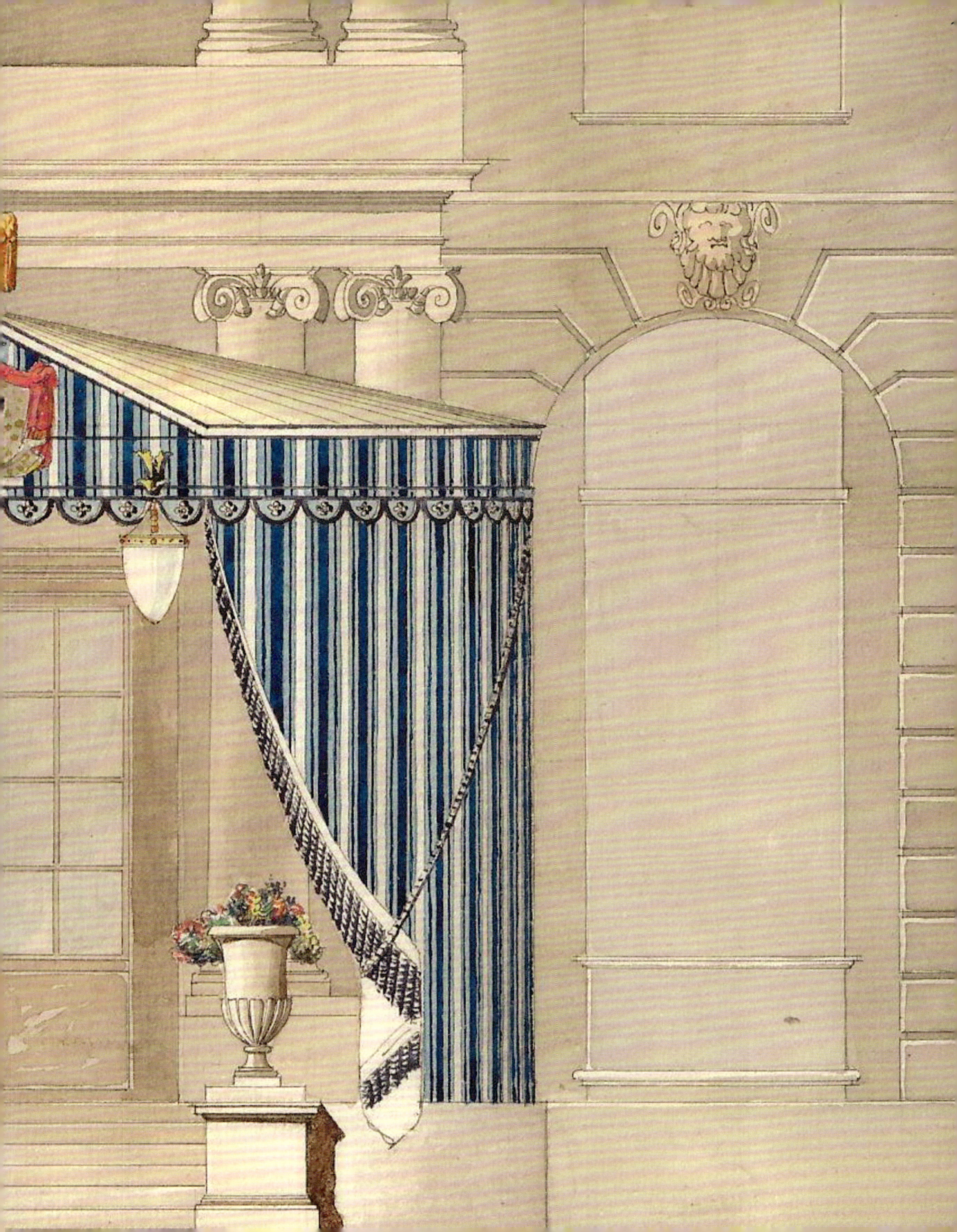

The recent discovery of Fontaine's design for a tented canopy bearing Pauline's coat of arms designed for the entrance façade of the hôtel de Charost corroborates this theory. It is not known if this was ever carried out, but it seems that Fontaine subsequently became engaged in an acrimonious dispute with his imperial client over unpaid bills. According to recent research, Pauline then employed the architect Pierre Nicholas Bénard (d. 1817), a student of Etienne Louis Boullée,[2] who also worked for Camillo Borghese's brother. But because of her precarious financial situation, much of the transformation of the old-fashioned Louis XV interior was carried out by decorators and upholsterers, with comparatively few architectural changes to Mazin's original structure.

> *'If she had lived in the time of Raphael, he would have painted her as one of those amours who lie so voluptuously on lions at the Farnesina.'*
>
> Chateaubriand on Pauline Borghese, *Mémoires d'Outre-Tombe*, 1841.

Despite the expense of new panelling, chimneypieces, textiles, furniture and bronzes, Pauline spent nothing like as much as Eugène de Beauharnais, Napoleon's stepson, did on the hôtel de Beauharnais across the river (now the German ambassador's residence), which resulted in some of the finest Empire interiors in Paris. However, despite the floor plan of the hôtel de Charost remaining largely unchanged, a very different spirit prevailed in its decoration. What survived of the old-fashioned carved woodwork was replaced by simpler panelling, lavishly gilded. This was combined with rich silks or velvets, all woven in France, demonstrating patriotic support for the French silk industry, with each room having a different colour or theme.

The furniture was specially designed to complement its architectural setting, so serried ranks of gilded chairs and sofas lined the walls of the state rooms, upholstered to match the wall-hangings, while the marble tops of the monumental console tables were laden with rich gilt-bronze candelabra and clocks. Everything was designed in the severe but magnificent Empire taste, the official style of Napoleon and his court, which was characterised by a massive simplicity combined with strong colours, embellished with forms and motifs derived from ancient Greece, Rome and Egypt. Despite the expense and magnificence of the furnishings, not everything was specially designed for the new house; many of the bronzes were obtained from specialist suppliers who dealt in such luxury items. Pauline was impatient for everything to be complete as soon as possible. Paying for the house and its refurbishment, however, remained problematic.

Although Pauline had borrowed large sums of money from Joseph, the eldest of her four brothers, her capricious behaviour angered Napoleon, who refused to help, hoping that by forcing Pauline to give up her house in Paris she would settle down in Rome — which she hated — and become a dutiful wife to Borghese, whose vapid good nature she rapidly came to despise. Pauline's comptroller, Michelot, was harried by agents of the duchesse de Charost and by other creditors. Joseph Bonaparte was asked to intercede and Napoleon eventually relented and settled the bill in April 1804. Following the tragic death that summer of six-year-old Dermide, Pauline's son by Leclerc, Napoleon allowed his sister to return to Paris in late 1804 — in time for his grandiose coronation as emperor in December. By this time works were largely complete on the house, which was rechristened the Palais Borghese to provide a fitting setting for the household of not just a Roman, but an imperial, princess.

The Palais Borghese was soon filled with Pauline's own court, which was deliberately modelled on

Facing page: The clock in the Salon Rouge by Moinet Aîné. The superb ormolu — or gilt-bronze — mounts by Thomire depict a statue of Minerva — the goddess of wisdom — on a litter borne by maidens.

[2] Jean Nérée Ronfort and Jean-Dominique Augarde, *À l'Ombre de Pauline: La résidence de l'Ambassadeur de Grand-Bretagne à Paris*, p. 13.

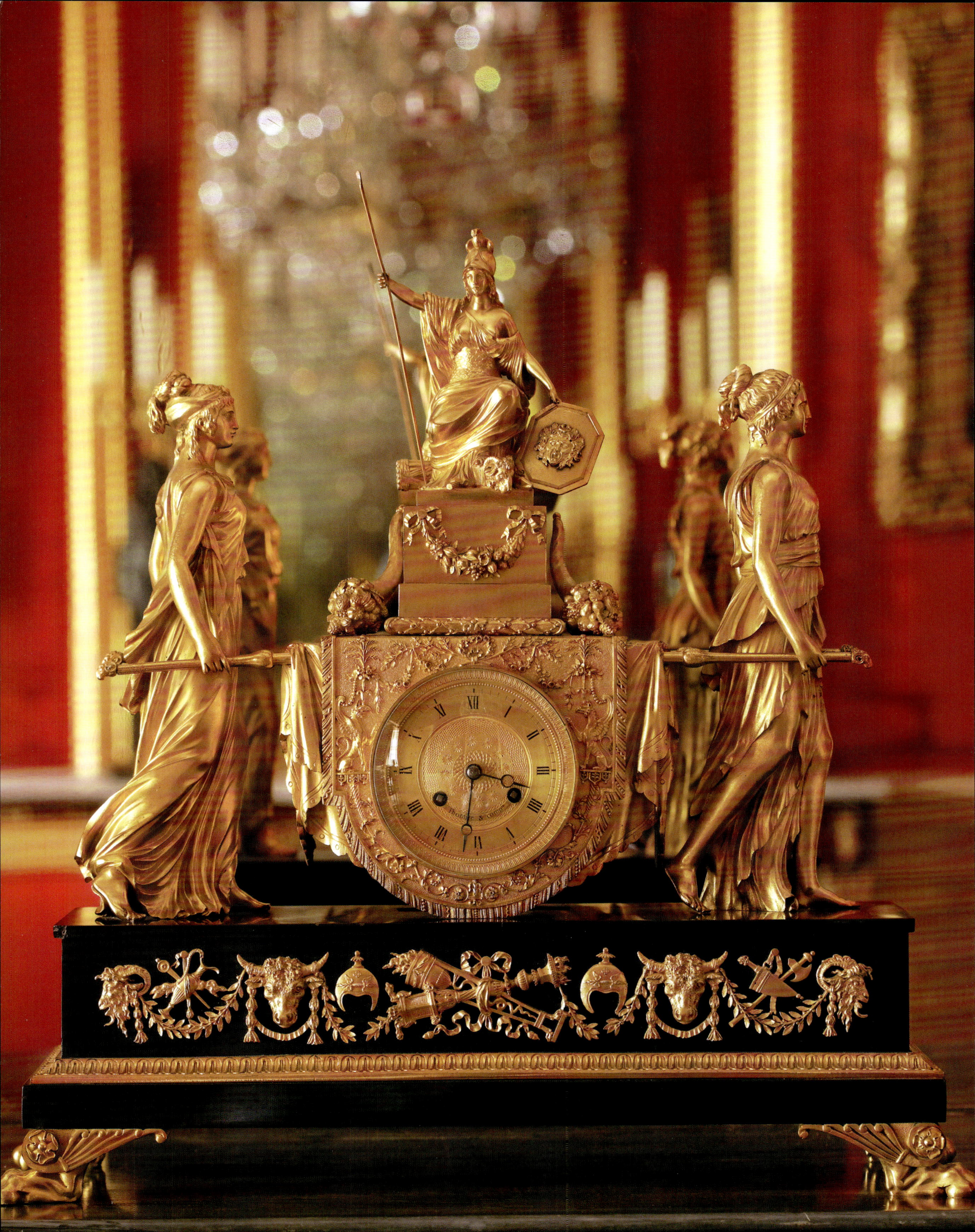

The rich collection of Empire furniture in the Residence has been conserved since Pauline's day. Among the most opulent styles in the history of the decorative arts, the Empire style drew its inspiration from Graeco-Roman antiquity — thereby linking Napoleon's reign with the great civilisations of the past through an ornate iconography of classical motifs, seen here in details of ormolu mounts from the rich collection of Empire furniture in the Residence.

Facing page (clockwise from top): Amorous deities from *La Liseuse* clock in the Salon Vert et Or; a Victory from a console table in the Salon Rouge; tortoises support the base of a pair of marine-themed candelabra in the Salon Vert et Or. *Above (clockwise from top left):* Detail from a console table in the Salon Rouge; the other candelabra base in the Salon Vert et Or; Cupid firing a dart, an ormolu furniture mount from a console table in the Salon Rouge.

43

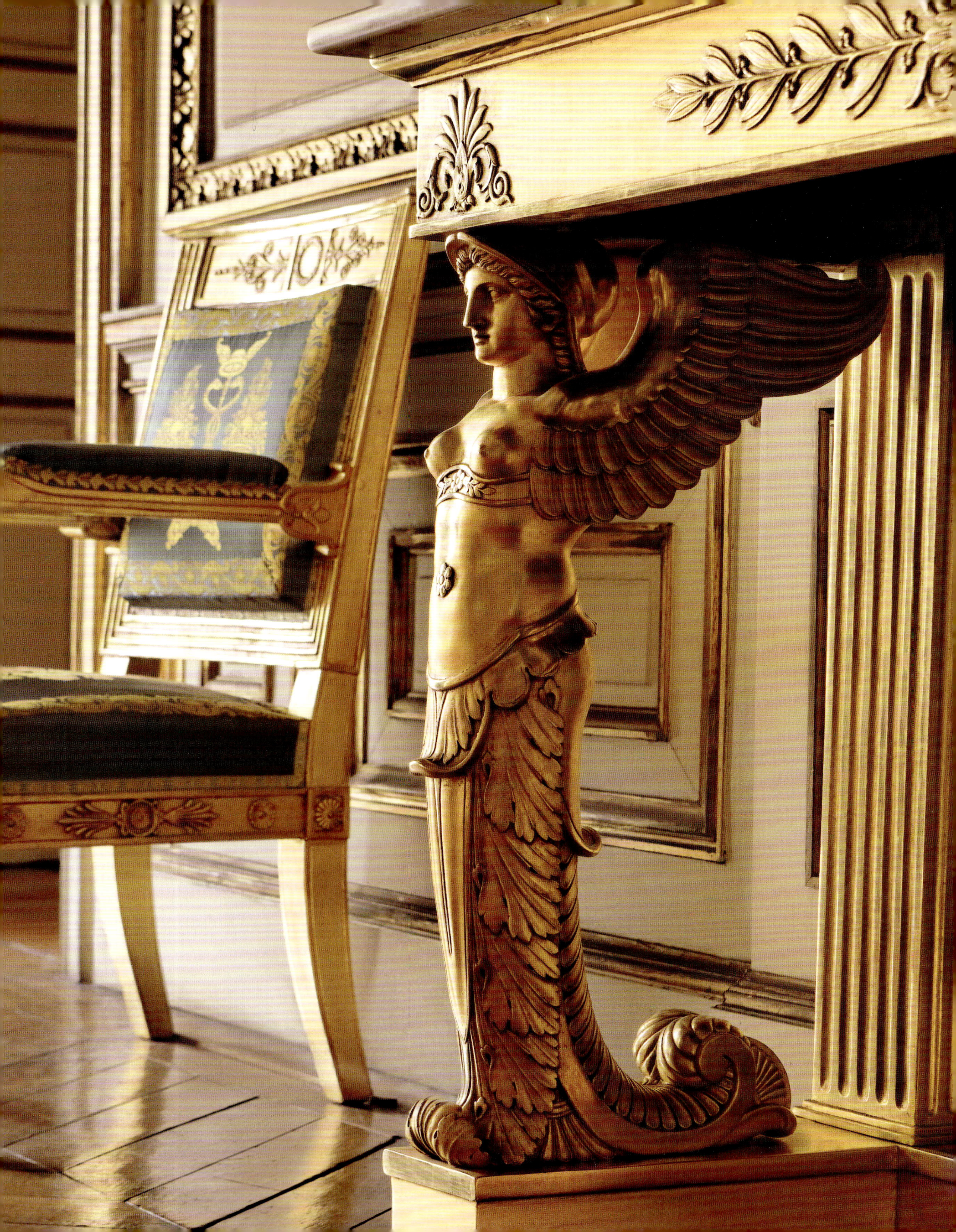

the establishments that members of the royal family had maintained during the *ancien régime*. Pauline had twenty-seven members in her household, including a grand almoner and two chaplains, a *dame d'honneur* and several ladies in waiting, seven chamberlains, four equerries, doctors and an apothecary, with many of the senior staff being members of the great families of the old aristocracy. Most of these people had apartments in the *palais*. They were, in turn, supported by an even larger staff of domestics, who also lived in the house, including those who worked in the kitchens and stables, the porters, guards and footmen, a librarian, a music master and even an in-house upholsterer. Pauline's favourite servant was her premier *valet de chambre,* Camille Paul, a black Egyptian who dressed in eastern costume and attended her every need, even carrying the princess to her bath — much to the scandal of contemporaries. Indeed, by this time Pauline was estranged from her husband and openly taking lovers. The prince, on his rare visits to Paris, was grudgingly lodged in one of the lesser apartments on the first floor. Pauline invented a host of petty rules and regulations in order to render his stay as uncomfortable as possible, often withdrawing to her country house in nearby Neuilly upon his arrival.

In 1809, an influx of funds and the need for more space encouraged Pauline to extend the Palais Borghese, commissioning Bénard to add two wings — the Picture Gallery (now the Ballroom) and a grand Dining Room (now the State Dining Room) — to the garden front. These additions were hurriedly built and extravagantly furnished; forty gilded chairs were ordered for the Picture Gallery, while the new Dining Room had sixty mahogany chairs with red morocco seats. The walls of the Picture Gallery were stocked with pictures from her husband's celebrated family collection. A few years later, in 1811, she converted the room once used as a chapel by the Charosts into a Billiard Room (today known as the Tapestry Dining Room). Pauline last saw her Palais Borghese in June 1812, but even in the

Facing page: A winged maiden supports a console table in the Salon Bleu. The gilded Empire furniture in the Residence dates from Pauline Borghese's time, but is still in regular use. *Above:* Sportive putti with bunches of grapes and drinking bowls, from an ormolu plaque on the chimneypiece in the Salon Vert et Or.

troubled last years of the Empire, she planned further improvements. A lavish jewel cabinet was ordered from the cabinetmaker Jacob-Desmalter in 1813, probably to stand between the windows of what is now the Salon Pauline. (Never delivered, it is now in the musée Marmottan in Paris.) A new portico was also proposed, as well as a laboratory for the apothecary, but neither was ever realised. On the fall of Napoleon in 1814 and the restoration of the French monarchy, Pauline stood by her brother, eventually joining him in exile on the island of Elba.

When the Allies swept into Paris in 1814, the Palais Borghese was swiftly commandeered for the use of the emperor of Austria (1768–1835). Pauline, then lying low outside Gréoux-les-Bains in Provence, issued instructions for the house to be sold. The Duke of Wellington (1769–1852) had just been appointed British ambassador to the restored Bourbon monarchy and needed a house in which to establish his embassy. Soon after his arrival in Paris in June 1814, he visited the Palais Borghese and ordered his aide-de-camp, Sir Charles Stuart (1779–1845), to negotiate its purchase. Meanwhile, Pauline was attempting to organise the transport of her furniture and personal belongings to Elba. By August 1814 her comptroller, Michelot, and Stuart's intermediary, Quentin Craufurd, had agreed on the price of 500,000 francs for the house and 300,000 francs for the furniture, with a further 61,500 francs for the stable. After the Hundred Days and the fall of Napoleon, Pauline retired to Italy, although she tried in vain to persuade the British authorities to allow her to join Napoleon in exile on St. Helena. She died in Florence in 1825 at the age of forty-four, reconciled with her long-suffering husband.

The Duke of Wellington was delighted with his purchase — a full 50,000 francs below the asking price, although 100,000 more than Pauline had paid for it, unfurnished, in 1803 — and forwarded to the authorities in London an inventory of the contents of the Palais Borghese, known from then on as the British Embassy in Paris. He entertained lavishly at the Embassy, but was less pleased in October, when his wife, to whom he had formed a great aversion, came out to join him in Paris. One commentator opined that the duchess's 'appearance unfortunately does not correspond with one's notion of an Ambassadress or the wife of a hero, but she succeeds uncommonly well in the part, and takes all proper pains to make herself and her parties agreeable.' The duke's embassy was abruptly terminated in January 1815, when he left Paris to participate in the Congress of Vienna — in all he had spent only a few months in his new home, moving in on 22 August 1814, although the sale had not completed until 24 October. Sir Charles Stuart was appointed in his place, where he shone briefly before the return of Napoleon from exile during the Hundred Days. During this time the house was placed in the safekeeping of Perregaux, the bank who had organised its purchase. With the restoration of Louis XVIII after the Battle of Waterloo on 18 June 1815, Sir Charles returned to Paris, where he was to remain as ambassador until 1824, celebrating his marriage to Lady Elizabeth Yorke at the Embassy in February 1816. Festivities at the Embassy increased under the new Lady Stuart and one of its habitués, Captain Gronow, was impressed: 'Dinners, balls and receptions were given in profusion throughout the season. In fact Sir Charles spent the whole of his private income on these noble hospitalities.' For a ball in October 1818, thrown to say farewell to the Army of Occupation, the resourceful Lady Stuart recalled how 'our supper rooms were as fete-like as could be only by dint of lighting and sticking up green and artificial flowers around the columns. I saw that the *tapissier* [upholsterer] had not a notion of it, and we stood a bad chance till I got the gardener and bid him ornament it just as he would do a fete of his own. So he whipped down some of our evergreens and twisted about the branches, and soon made it very pretty'. Stuart's successor in 1824 was the 1st Earl Granville (1773–1846), who found the

Facing page: The 1st Duke of Wellington by Alfred Guillaume Gabriel de Grimaud, comte d'Orsay (1801–1852), painted in July 1845. D'Orsay painted at least three versions of this portrait.

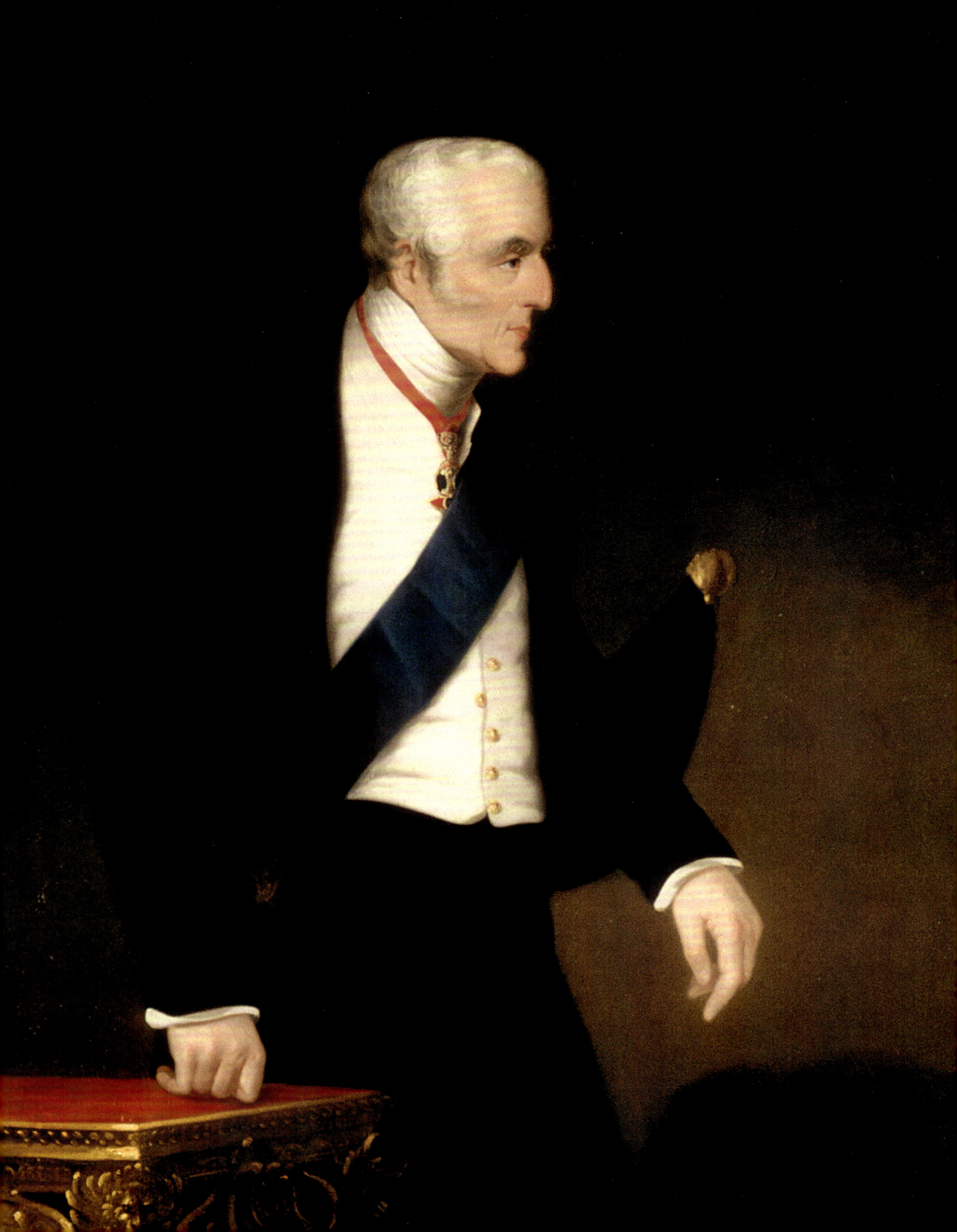

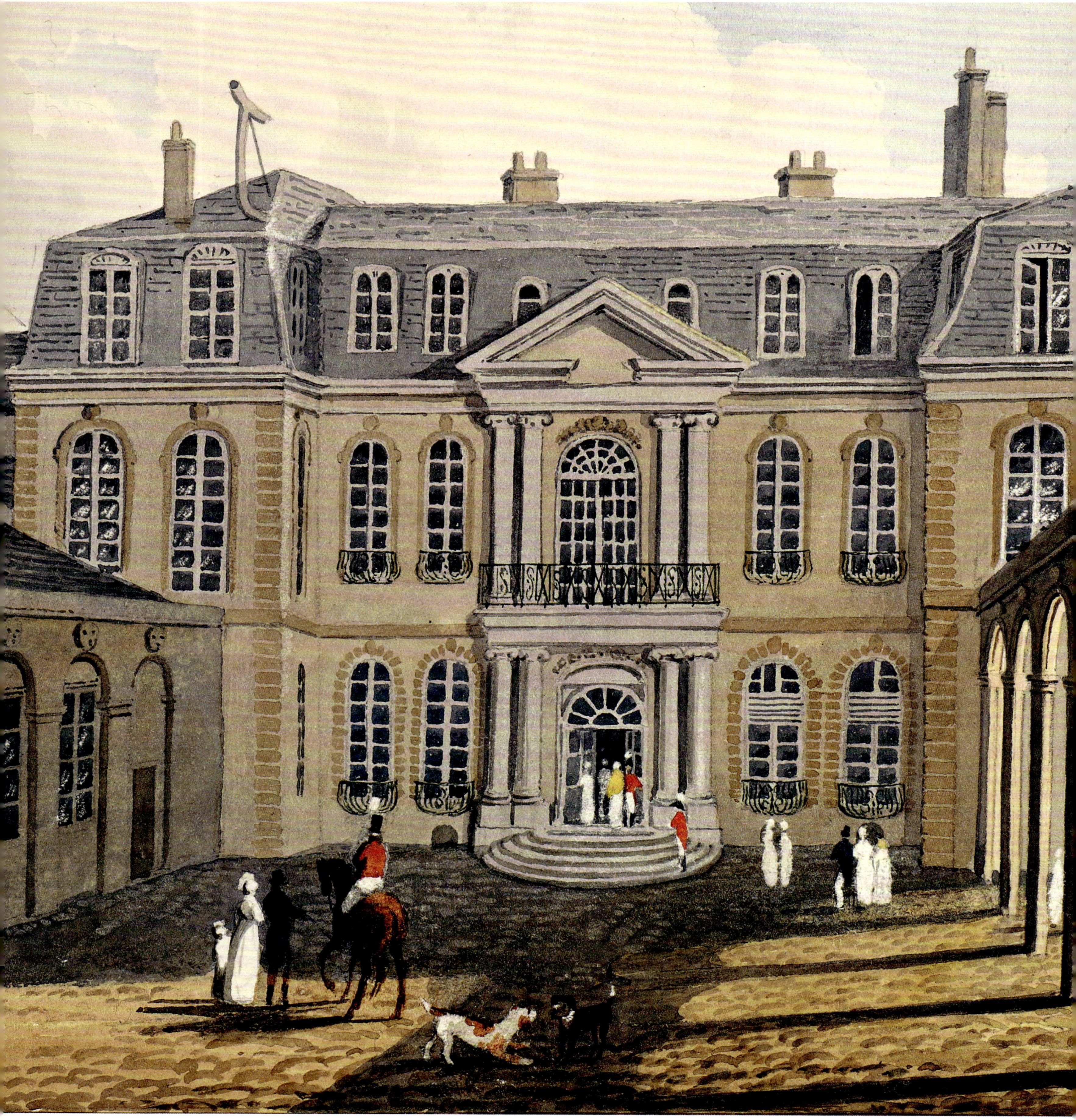

Embassy buildings dilapidated. He was the first to establish what would become a pattern with incoming ambassadors, who regularly complained of the house's disrepair upon arrival. The architect Sir Robert Smirke (1781–1867) was immediately sent out from London to report on the buildings — producing the first of many such documents that were commissioned over the next century. He found there were serious structural problems with Pauline's extensions of 1809, the Picture Gallery and Dining Room: 'The walls are light and the roofs are so injudiciously constructed that both of them are giving way', while Lady Granville wrote 'If the repair was equal to the space and beauty of this palace, it would be perfection, but there are holes in the floor big enough to let me through, props to keep them up. All this must be set to rights in the spring.' Nothing could be done until 1825, when a major refurbishment was undertaken by the Parisian architect, Louis Tullius Joachim Visconti (1791–1853), including the complete replacement of Pauline's Picture Gallery and Dining Room, and the addition of the *serre* or Glazed Galleries, today known as the Gallery, between the two wings. After its triumphant unveiling in January 1826, Lady Granville wrote to her sister 'My house looks more brilliant and enormous than I can describe ... we open the *rez de chaussée* [ground floor], the *serre* with a carpet, doubled of scarlet cloth, eighteen lustres with lamps and six divans of the same temperature as the rooms, with all the doors and windows taken off in the ball- and drawing rooms. Three salons *au premier*, five whist tables in the Salon Vert, newspapers and books of prints in the state *couleur de paille* [straw-coloured] bedroom.' The improvements cost over £18,000, well above the original estimate, and no one had given permission for the construction of the Gallery. The Foreign Office was horrified with the extravagance, and it was only after endless explanations and recriminations that they grudgingly consented to pay the bill. Stuart returned as ambassador in 1828. Now raised to the peerage as Lord Stuart de Rothesay, he hosted a famous *bal costumé* [fancy dress costume ball] at the Embassy in 1829 to celebrate George IV's birthday, which was attended by many members of the French royal family. Lady Morgan, the celebrated poetess, pronounced it to be 'the most splendid and picturesque I ever saw' and breathlessly described the spectacle:

'The most striking group was that formed by the Austrian Embassy, splendidly attired in ancient historical costumes; with a numerous group of attachés, the elite of the gay, the gallant youth of their country, in all the gorgeous pageantry of the middle-ages. When his Austrian Excellency was announced how I started! ... I did not breathe freely till his Excellency had passed on with his glittering train into the illuminated conservatory, and was lost in a wilderness of flowering shrubs and orange trees.'

Stuart and his wife were too deeply implicated in the court of the restored Bourbons to survive the fall of Charles X in August 1830 and he was recalled in 1831. An ardent Francophile, Stuart had used his time in Paris to form a fine collection of furniture and works of art. Passing through Normandy on his way home, he came across La Grand'Maison in Les Andelys, then in the course of demolition, and rescued much of its carved Gothic stonework, which was then incorporated into his fanciful seaside retreat, Highcliffe Castle in Dorset, where some of it remains to this day. The Granvilles returned to the Embassy in January 1831, staying on there — apart from a five-week interregnum in 1835 — until 1841.

Despite a major campaign of refurbishment in 1837, and the replacement of the roof of the Gallery the following year, Granville's successor, the 1st Lord Cowley (1773–1847), brother of the Duke of Wellington, was so appalled by the state of the Embassy on his arrival in 1841 that he and his family immediately moved into a local hotel. Again repairs were carried out. Their successors, the Marquess (1797–1863) and Marchioness of Normanby,

Facing page: The Ambassadorial Residence of the British Ambassador at Paris, watercolour by Lady Anne Barnard, c.1820. Lady Anne was aunt to Lady Stuart de Rothesay, whose husband served two terms as ambassador in the early nineteenth century. From an album in the possession of Lady Anne's descendants.

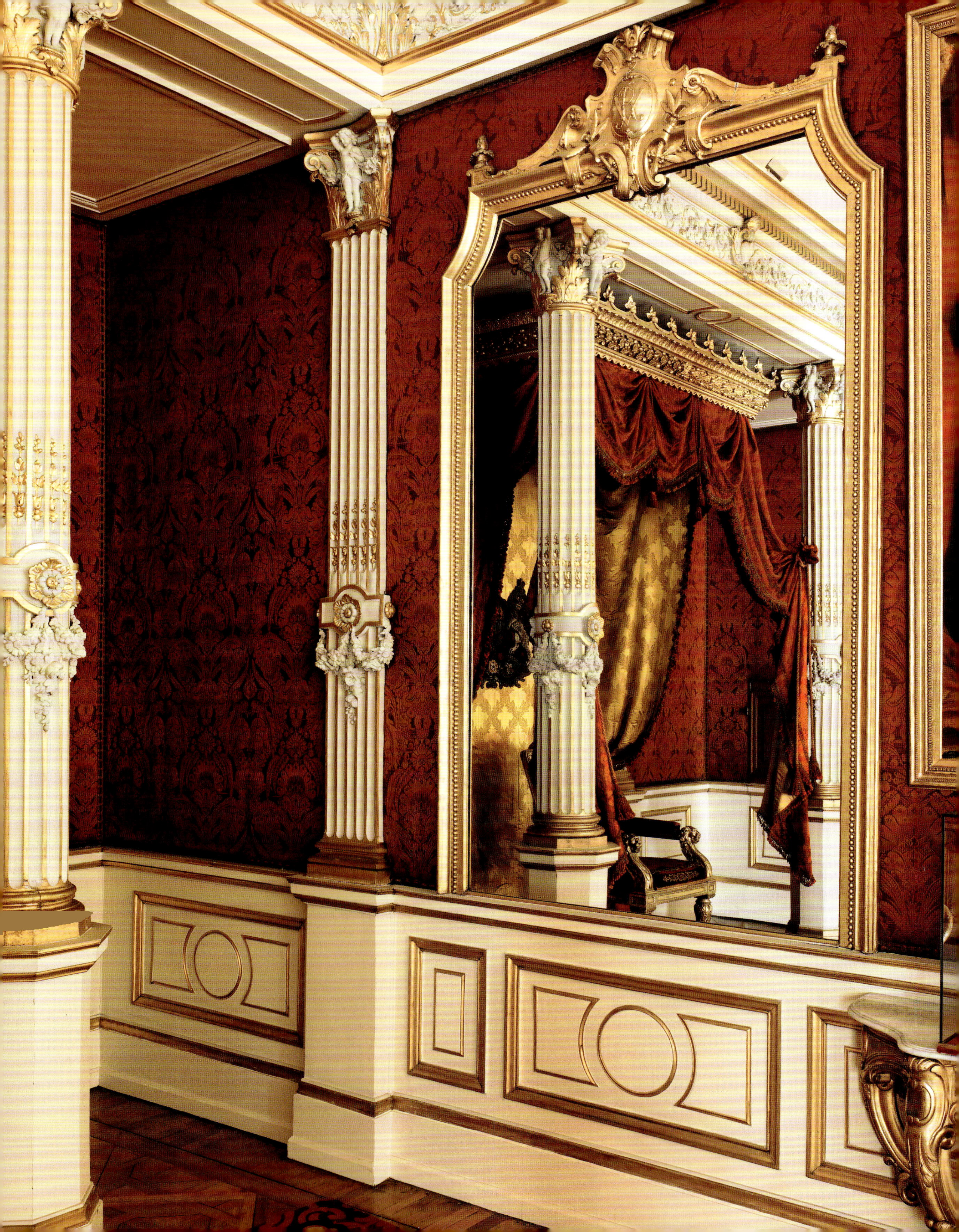

had to contend with the 1848 Revolution, which saw Louis-Philippe dethroned and the election of Louis Napoleon, Napoleon's nephew, as Prince-President (he became Emperor Napoleon III in 1852). The Embassy, defended by its high walls and strong gates, became a place of refuge for some of the neighbours during the civil unrest in the city.

In 1852, the new ambassador, the 2nd Lord Cowley (1804–84), later 1st Earl Cowley, employed another architect, Benedict Albano (1796-1881), to carry out the inevitable repairs, which included the redecoration of the Throne Room and Ballroom in an opulent Second Empire taste — the exaggeratedly rich style associated with Napoleon III and the Empress Eugenie, epitomised by the decor of Charles Garnier's masterpiece, the Paris Opera (1862–75) — and the conversion of the State Dining Room into a chapel. The other rooms in the Embassy were thoroughly Victorianised, with glazed wallpapers, busy chintz hangings and fitted carpets, while 'gas burners' were substituted for the old oil lamps and candles. Queen Victoria, who visited the house on the afternoon of 22 August 1855, noted the furnishings with approval, writing in her journal that the house was 'very pretty indeed and newly furnished'. Cowley ordered the sale of what he considered to be surplus furniture: 'several waggons full' of Pauline's Empire furniture left the Embassy and were sold at auction for a derisorily small sum. A second phase of works was undertaken by Etienne Raveau in 1858–64, after another, surprise, visit from Queen Victoria, including the demolition of the Louis XV stable arcade in the courtyard, and the erection of an iron-and-glass canopy over the front door. Visconti's Ballroom was embellished with more decorations, including trophies of musical instruments and two strapping plaster figures, known as *atlantes*, supporting the architectural elements at its north end. A second sale of furniture took place in 1860, including fifty-five mahogany chairs from Pauline's Dining Room and twenty-one sets of firedogs.

Facing page: The throne canopy reflected in a mirror in the Throne Room. The ensemble of dais, throne, and canopy of state is a rare and unusual survival. *Above left:* Queen Victoria in her coronation robes, a copy of a portrait by Sir George Hayter in the Throne Room. *Above right:* A detail of a capital in the Throne Room.

Above: Details of the Residence silver — candelabra, a tureen by Robert Hennell and a fruit basket — all of which bear the Royal Arms. *Facing page:* An urn-shaped ice pail made by John Moore in 1824, one of four ice pails in the Residence.

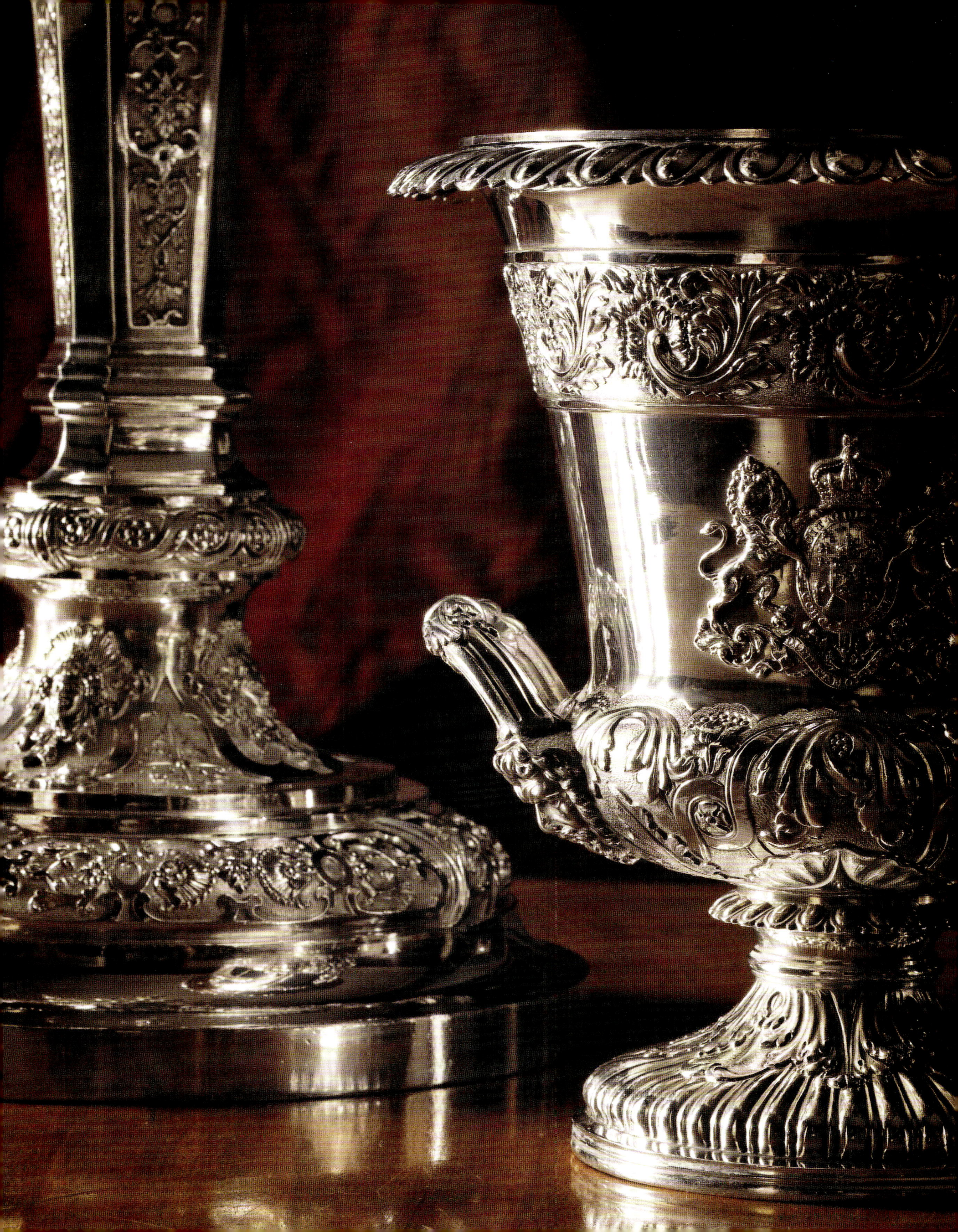

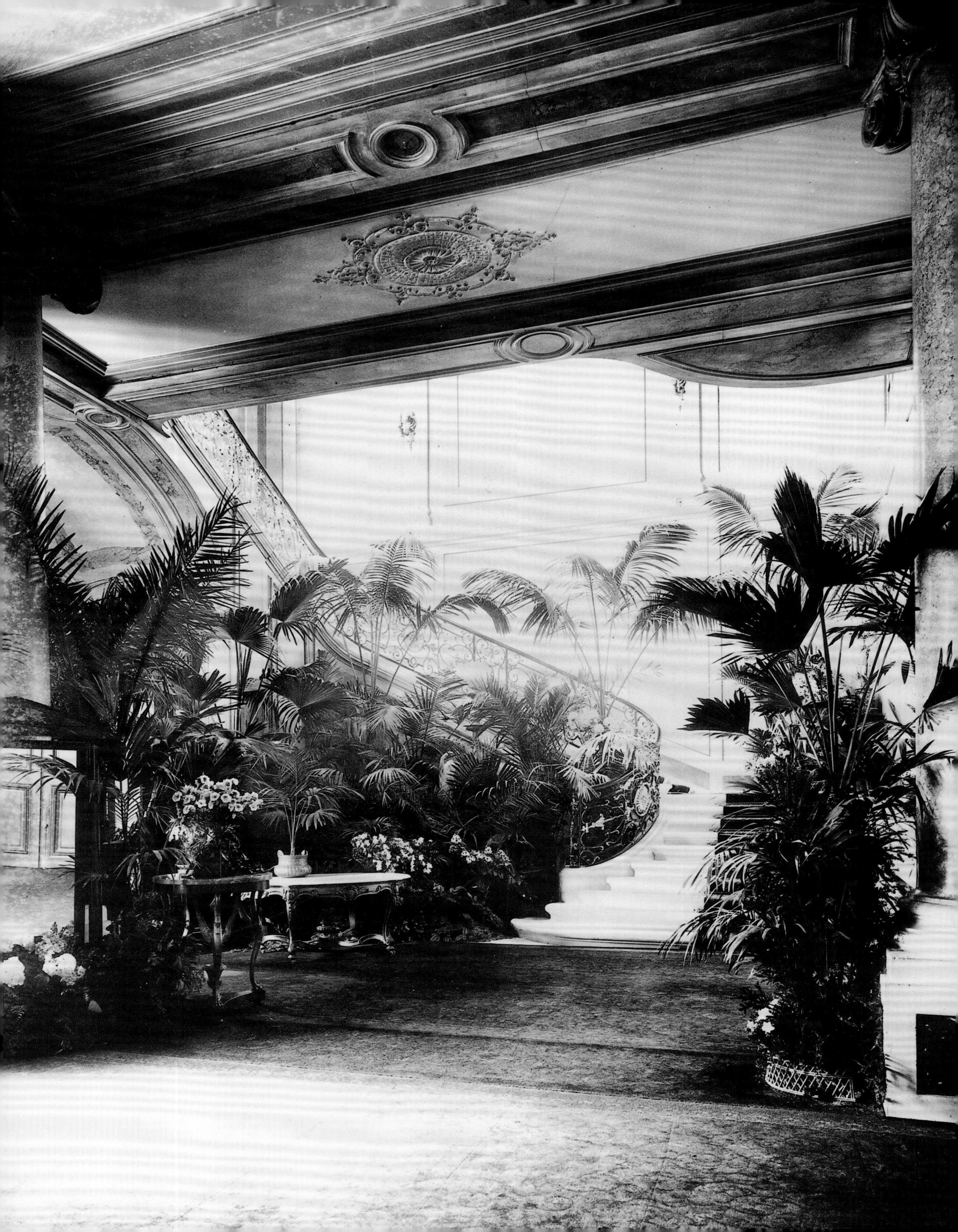

The embassy of Lord Lyons (1817–1887), the longest term of any ambassador in Paris, lasted from 1867 to 1887, and witnessed the fall of Napoleon III after his defeat at Sedan in September 1870, and the Siege of Paris by the Prussian army that followed. As the Prussians closed in on Paris that winter, Lyons joined the French government at Tours and then Bordeaux, leaving one of his staff, Edward Blount, to keep an eye on the Embassy, along with Henry Labouchère, correspondent to *The Daily News*. At first they were rather comfortable: 'I can get as much fresh mutton as I want from the porter of the Embassy', Labouchère boasted in his diary. 'There is a flock of ewes and wethers in the grounds there ... we two will have more mutton than we can eat, even if the siege lasts long. The porter knows how to grow potatoes and mushrooms in an empty cellar, so that we two have not only meat, but dainties to vary the dishes.' But the sheep were soon confiscated by the authorities to feed starving Parisians, and by the time the Siege was lifted in March 1871, Blount and Labouchère, like the rest of Paris, were reduced to eating rats and mice. More disturbances soon followed. During the rebel uprising of the Commune and Second Siege of Paris in 1871, fighting took place in the Embassy garden as French government troops struggled to gain control of a Communard barricade on the corner of the rue d'Anjou. (A pen-and-watercolour view of this incident now hangs in the Salon Vert.) During a subsequent bombardment, six shells fell on the roof of the house, knocking down a chimneystack and breaking skylights, windows and one of the Ballroom mirrors. Lyons wrote later to his superiors, commending Edward Malet, the Embassy secretary, who had 'a first rate head, and directed everything with his usual coolness and self-possession', but according to one of his clerks, William Norris, it was the Embassy servants who saved the building, 'rushing to the places where the shells fell in order to extinguish the fire', while Malet hid in the cellars. The Commune was finally suppressed in late May 1871. A small fragment of shrapnel from one of the shells is still

Facing page: The Staircase decorated for the visit of Edward VII in 1903, unknown photographer. For such important events the Embassy was transformed into a veritable winter garden, with palms and other plants hired for the occasion. *Above left:* The Gallery in 1903, unknown photographer, showing it choked with seat furniture and potted palms. *Above right:* The Ambassadress's Bedchamber (now the Cooper Bedroom) in 1905, with Pauline Borghese's psyche mirror, photograph by Frédéric Contet.

PHOTOGRAPHIE PAR E. PIROU 　11 MEDAILLES D'OR 　5, Boulevard St-Germain, PARIS
3 Diplomes d'Honneur
Médaille d'Or, Exposition Universelle 1889

Photographs of the Embassy during the time of Sir Francis Bertie, 1905. *Clockwise from top:* The Gallery on the garden front; the main entrance in the courtyard, both by Eugène Pirou. The garden view, unknown photographer.

Photographs of the Embassy during the time of Sir Francis Bertie with his Victorian furnishings, 1905.
Clockwise from top: The Ballroom; the Salon Vert; the Throne Room. Photographs by Eugène Pirou.

preserved in Ante-Room. One of the consequences of the Franco-Prussian War and the Commune was an attempt to introduce legislation declaring all male children born in France to be French citizens and therefore eligible for military service. This caused such alarm among the British expatriate community in Paris that part of the second floor of the Embassy was turned into a temporary maternity ward. One of three babies born there in 1874 was William Somerset Maugham, whose father was the Embassy solicitor. Another notable event was the marriage of Lord Randolph Churchill and Jennie Jerome, which was celebrated at the Embassy in April 1874. Their son, Winston, born the following year, was later to be a regular visitor to the Embassy. Weddings of prominent residents of Paris had often taken place in the house — for instance, Hector Berlioz to Harriet Smithson in October 1833, and William Makepeace Thackeray to Isabella Shaw in 1836. Lyons stayed on in the post until 1887, but the inaugural party thrown the following year by his successor, the Earl of Lytton (1831–1891), caused something of a sensation. A former viceroy of India, Lytton made the Embassy a showcase of imperial booty, decorating the rooms with stuffed animal heads, trophies of exotic arms and armour and Indian curios. According to *The Daily Telegraph* of 18 January 1888:

'French visitors were reminded by the decorations of the Embassy rooms that they were in the presence of the ambassador of an Empress-Queen whose sceptre sways the mightiest empire of modern times. Frenchmen of a well-balanced mind could contemplate Lord Lytton's splendid Indian trophies, thrones, and shields to-night with an admiration untinged with national jealousy. […] It is not too much to say that Lord Lytton's reception was an historical event as well as the most brilliant social gathering which has

Above: Fighting in the Garden of the British Embassy, Paris, 23rd May 1871, by William Simpson. A pen-and-wash sketch for an engraved plate for *The Illustrated London News*, showing an incident when French government troops stormed the garden of the British Embassy during the Communard uprising. The picture now hangs in the Salon Vert.

Above: View of the British Embassy in Paris from the Gardens, by an unknown artist, 1841. This charming view, also hanging in the Salon Vert, was possibly a commission from Lord and Lady Granville.

taken place in the Queen of cities since those days of scenic splendour which almost seemed to have passed for ever away with the glittering Empire of the Bonapartes.'

Charming and cultivated, the Lyttons were popular, and the Embassy, despite its strange decor, became a meeting place for actors, poets, writers and artists — Sarah Bernhardt, Alexandre Dumas and Oscar Wilde among them. Following Lord Lytton's sudden death in 1891, Paris was again treated to a display of imperial paraphernalia when another ex-viceroy of India, the Marquess of Dufferin and Ava (1826–1902), installed his Indian and Burmese trophies in Pauline's gilded salons. Dufferin managed greatly to improve Franco-British relations during his embassy, but ill health forced his retirement after only five years.

Dufferin's successor, Sir Edward Monson (1834–1909), had to contend with a surge of Anglophobia leading up to and after the Fashoda Incident (the culmination of the dispute between France and Britain over territory in Eastern Africa that brought the two countries to the brink of war), and with a series of momentous events, including the death of Queen Victoria and the signing of the Entente Cordiale. Today he is chiefly remembered for hosting a state visit to France by Edward VII in May 1903 to seal the Entente Cordiale. By this time, the Embassy, now stripped of its Asiatic weaponry and antelope heads, must have looked shabby, so Monson prepared for the royal visit by refurbishing the State Dining Room, calling in the architect Arthur Vye Parminter, advised by the French decorator and expert on eighteenth-century interiors Georges Hoentschel (1855–1915). They were responsible for converting the vast refectory into a creditable Louis XVI salon, painted several shades of grey. Lacking time to refurbish the other rooms, Monson brightened them with potted palms and other foliage. The king slept in Pauline's bed, supplemented with Empire furniture borrowed from the Mobilier National (the French state furniture repository, still responsible for furnishing government buildings today) but contemporary photographs show the state rooms choked with Monson's late-Victorian bric-a-brac. The royal visit was a resounding success, but the king, who was only too aware of the importance of keeping up appearances abroad, was privately appalled at the state of the Embassy and Monson's homely furnishings. Shortly afterwards, probably due to discreet royal pressure, the Foreign Office uncomplainingly paid for Parminter and Hoentschel to return and complete their transformation in a 'manner consonant with its history and tradition and gratifying to the artistic sentiment of the nation to which our premier embassy is accredited'. The work began in 1904 and continued after Monson's recall in 1905. The result is an architectural embodiment of the Entente Cordiale: the Entrance Hall and Staircase, the Ante-Room, the Tapestry Dining Room and the Salon Vert were all refurbished. The stables were also remodelled to provide extra accommodation for the Embassy Chancery (the section of the Embassy where diplomats supporting the ambassador worked), while the kitchens were moved to a more convenient position, from the northern to the eastern side of the courtyard.

Monson was replaced by an old crony of Edward VII, Sir Francis Bertie (1844–1919), a fascinating Edwardian conundrum. A friend of Marcel Proust, Bertie decorated the Embassy with his fine antique furniture and pictures, yet shocked contemporaries with his coarse manners and taste for erotica — the innocent framed prints that hung around the walls in his study were reputedly double-sided, so he could privately enjoy more salacious images on their reverse. Perhaps this was why he commissioned the

Above: King Edward VII by Princess Elisabeth Lwoff (Vilma von Parlaghy-Brachfeld) (1863–1923), c. 1903.

Top: Sir Francis Bertie's carriage, with coachman and footmen, in the courtyard of the Residence, c.1905, unknown photographer. *Above:* King Edward VII leaving the Residence during a state visit in 1903, unknown photographer.

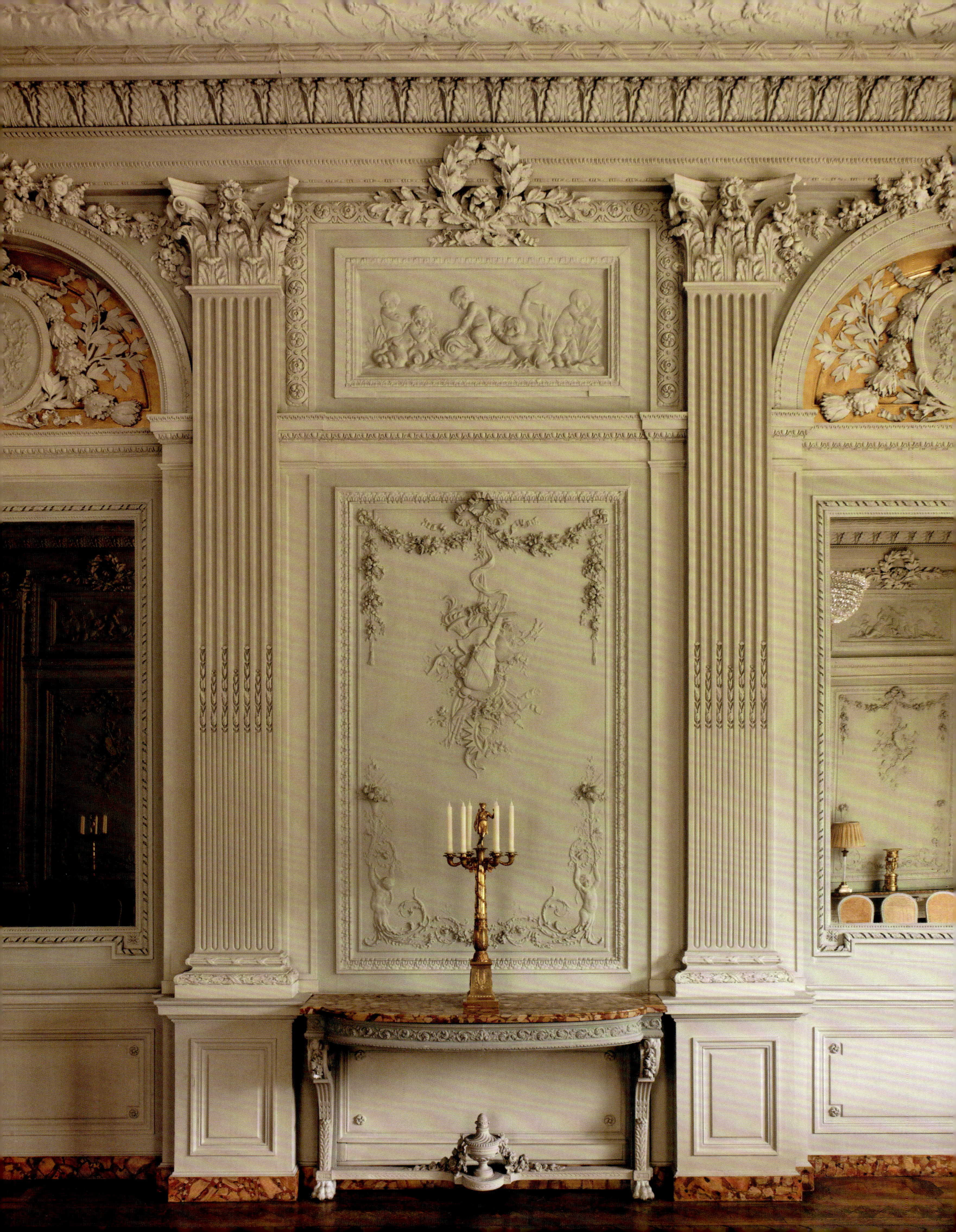

Facing page: The elegant Louis XVI-style decorations of the State Dining Room were designed by Vye Parminter and Georges Hoentschel in anticipation of the visit of Edward VII in 1903. *Above:* Detail of the State Dining Room plasterwork — a putto amidst trailing foliage — with one of the Residence's grandiose silver candelabra.

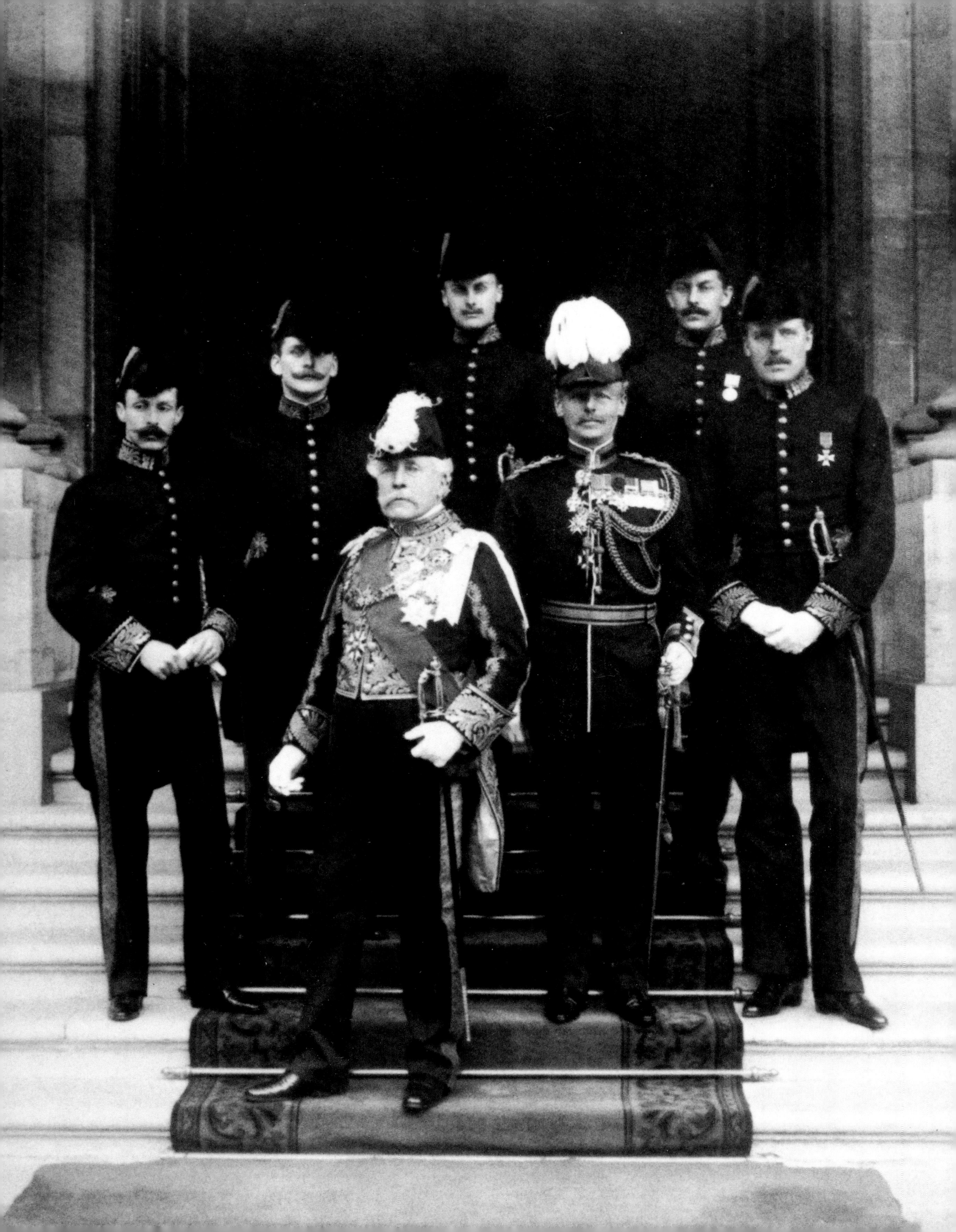

photographer Eugène Pirou — otherwise known as the maker of the world's first pornographic film — to make a photographic record of the Embassy in 1905. But there was a humane side to Bertie, who watched helplessly as France and then Britain entered the First World War in 1914, personally saying goodbye to his French manservants as they were sent to the Front. 'I have asked to be allowed to keep the French chauffeur', he noted plaintively. As the Germans advanced on Paris in early September 1914, Bertie withdrew to Bordeaux along with the French government. He later returned to Paris to sit out the war, increasingly appalled at the carnage. In 1915 he was created Lord Bertie of Thame by George V, and was recalled in April 1918, during the German bombardment of Paris.

The bombs were still dropping when the 17th Earl of Derby (1865–1948) took over, and the Germans were advancing once more on the city. Derby took the precaution of sending the Embassy silver, the *surtout de table* (an elaborate centrepiece for a dining table) and the most valuable of Pauline's clocks and bronzes for safekeeping in London, where they remained until the Paris Peace Conference in 1919. The next ambassador, Lord Hardinge of Penshurst (1858–1944), another former viceroy of India, presided over the Embassy between 1920 and 1922. Lord Curzon recalled visiting after Hardinge had been replaced by the Marquess of Crewe (1858–1945): '… it was such a pleasure to see that beautiful house without tiger-skins, the silver caskets, the elephant tusks and common photographs of Charlie Hardinge. Instead there were some quite good oil paintings, all portraits from Crewe House, not those of the first order, but quite good, including some Romneys, Reynolds, Gainsboroughs, etc.'

Embassy valuables were once again evacuated for safekeeping during the late 1930s, this time to the château de Chambord in the Loire Valley. By 1939, things were at crisis point. As the German army swept through Europe, the Embassy Ballroom was requisitioned by the Information Division and confidential papers from the Chancery files were burnt in the Embassy furnace. The ambassador, Sir Ronald Campbell (1883–1953), joined the French government as it withdrew before the advancing German forces, while Lady Campbell, the female staff and other Embassy wives were despatched to England. Campbell himself evacuated to England on 23 June 1940. When Paris fell on 14 June, only four people remained in the Embassy: the porter, William R. Chrystie, the Chancery messenger, Ernest Edward Spurgeon, and their wives. The two couples lived in the Porter's Lodge facing the rue du Faubourg-Saint-Honoré, without heating, subsisting on scant and dwindling supplies. The Americans initially assumed responsibility for Britain's diplomatic relations and assets in France, but when the United States entered the Second World War in December 1941, the Embassy was placed under Swiss protection. Several attempts by the Germans to commandeer the building were rebuffed by Chrystie and Spurgeon, including one by Hermann Goering himself. Shortly after Goering's visit, Chrystie was detained for nearly five months in an internment camp at Saint-Denis, outside Paris. When Paris was liberated in September 1944, an advance party of returning Embassy staff was greeted by Chrystie on the steps of the Embassy, resplendent in a top hat and purple frock-coat.

After the Liberation of Paris, the new ambassador was Sir Alfred Duff Cooper (1890–1954) — generally known as Duff Cooper. He was accompanied by his vivacious and beautiful wife, Lady Diana. Upon their arrival the building presented a far from welcoming sight, as Diana was to recall in her memoirs: 'The Embassy itself had been for five years the British Empire's furniture-dump; it was stuffed to its closed doors with all the paraphernalia, the treasure, the chattels and junk of Commonwealth diplomats' families and exiled Parisian residents: pianos, hatstands, bureaux, bath-mats, sponges, bottles, good and bad pictures, boxing-gloves and skates, clouds of moth, powder of woodworm. Nothing of the house's beautiful proportions or decoration could be seen.'

Facing page: Sir Francis Bertie and Embassy staff posed on the steps of the Residence, 1913. Photograph by Henri Manny. From left to right and top to bottom: Hon. Patrick Ramsay, T. Powell (Honorary Attaché), C. Michael Palairet, Percy Loraine, Sir Francis Bertie, Colonel the Hon. Henry Yarde-Buller, George Grahame.

But the Coopers soon brought the house to life, throwing open the great double doors of the state rooms to create vistas, while the gilded salons, once more graced by the returned clocks and bronzes, glittered by candlelight. Although these were difficult times, with food and fuel shortages and other privations, Lady Diana's salons became a haven for artists, writers and politicians. Her guests included Jean Cocteau, Paul Eluard, André Malraux, Louise de Vilmorin, Colette (described by Cecil Beaton as 'like an old chinchilla marmoset sitting deep in a sofa'), Christian Bérard, Charles de Beistegui, Stephen Spender, T. S. Eliot, Cyril Connolly, Harold Nicolson, Noel Coward, Laurence Olivier and Isaiah Berlin. A corps of regulars — including Cocteau, Bérard and Vilmorin — met with the Coopers night after night in the Salon Vert, and became known as 'La Bande'.

Towards the end of their stay, Duff Cooper, puzzled that the Residence had no library, offered his books as a gift for the use of his successors, on condition that the Foreign Office provided a suitable place to house them. This, after much badgering, they finally agreed to do, but no-one could have imagined the room that resulted — a perfect Empire-revival Library, designed free of charge by the Coopers' great friend Charles de Beistegui, out of 'love and respect for England', with the help of the decorator Georges Geoffroy and artist Christian Bérard. Cheaply built from pine and plaster, grained and marbled to resemble, in Lady Diana's words, a room in 'a palace in Saint Petersburg', the Library was ready in time for the Coopers' departure in 1947. Duff Cooper's other great achievement was the purchase of the next-door house, known since the nineteenth century as the hôtel Pereire, which now houses the offices of the British Embassy. Two previous ambassadors had unsuccessfully tried to persuade the Foreign Office to purchase the building for this purpose — at a far cheaper price — so it remains a monument to Cooper's tenacity and powers of persuasion. Thus, from 1947, the hôtel de Charost has been used solely as the British Ambassador's Residence, with all other Chancery functions transferred to the

Lady Diana Cooper's extravagant personality inspired Nancy Mitford's novel, *Don't Tell Alfred*, which takes place in the Residence. *Above left:* Lady Diana Cooper, photograph by Cecil Beaton, 4 December 1944. Lady Diana is shown in the Salon Jaune next to one of Pauline Borghese's candelabra. *Above right:* Lady Diana Cooper, drawing by Cecil Beaton, date unknown. The drawing hangs in the Duff Cooper Library. *Facing page:* Louise de Vilmorin, Vivien Leigh, Cecil Beaton and Laurence Olivier in the Salon Vert et Or, photograph by Cecil Beaton, c. 1945.

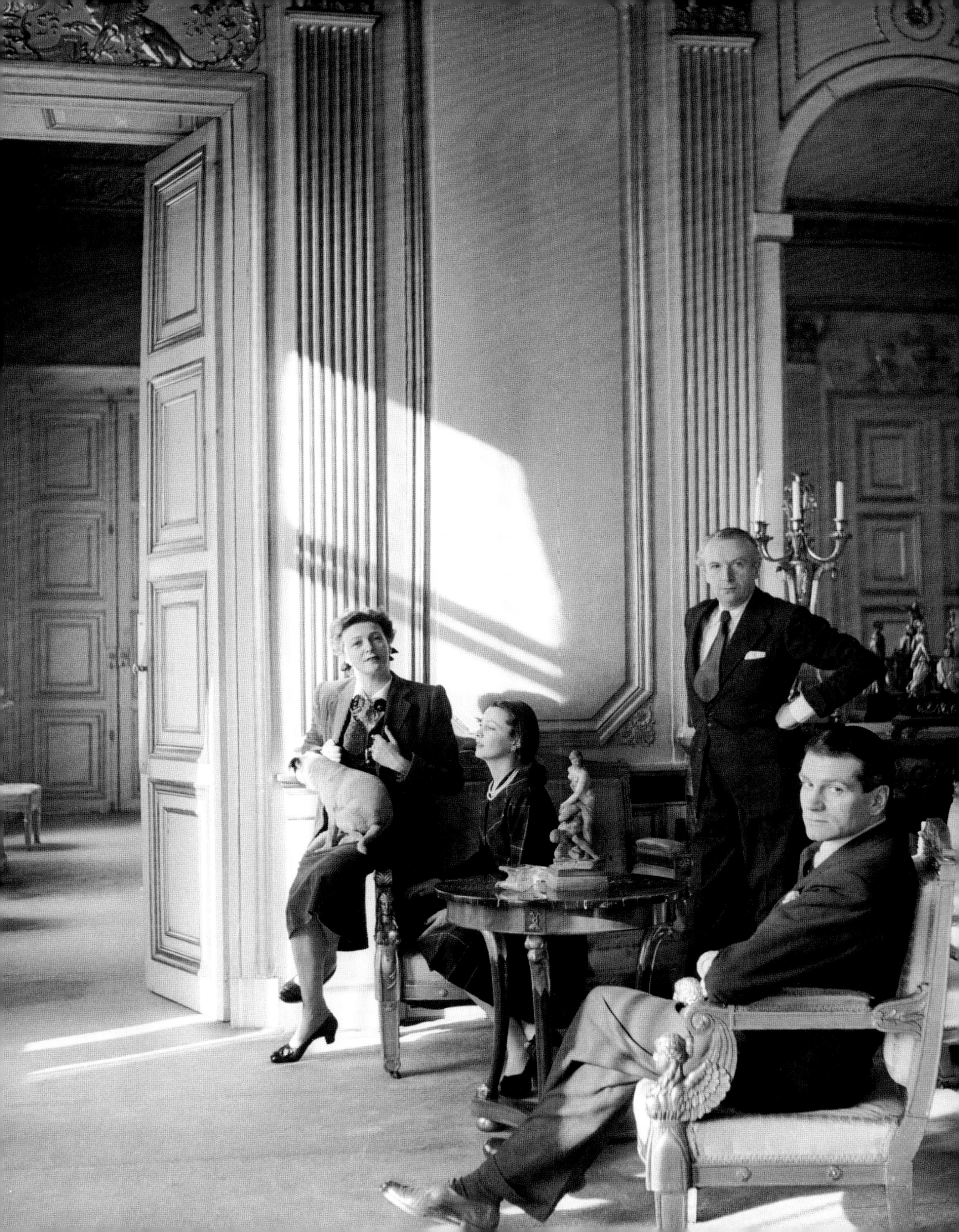

building next door. Since the Second World War, the Residence has undergone fewer refurbishments at the hands of its occupants. It is rare for a diplomat to remain in one post for longer than five years, which allows less time, or opportunity, to redecorate or make substantial changes. Indeed, since the early 1980s, the Paris Residence has been run on increasingly professional lines. Major changes to the building are now made by the Foreign and Commonwealth Office (FCO) Estates Department, particularly its interior design team, in consultation with the expert adviser on historic interiors retained by the FCO. This last position, currently held by the author of this book, was long occupied by the late John Cornforth, and was the idea of then Foreign Secretary Lord Carrington in the early 1980s. It was intended to maintain standards of presentation and furnishing in British diplomatic residences abroad.

Most of the works of art in the Residence are on loan from the Government Art Collection in London, which ensures high standards of care and conservation of the collection. It also occasionally makes new acquisitions, and changes the works on show in consultation with the current ambassador. However, most of the historic furniture and plate belongs to the Residence and is in constant use, regularly moved about as required. These practical demands require a more pragmatic approach to matters like gilding and upholstery; the Residence, above all, is a working home rather than a conventional historic house museum and as such its interiors must be hardworking as well as beautiful.

Ambassadors today still can and do leave their mark on the house. Sir Gladwyn Jebb (1900–1996) and his wife, Lady Gladwyn, rearranged the furniture and pictures in the late 1950s; while, working with the Ministry of Works, Lady Reilly, wife of Sir Patrick Reilly (1909–1999), introduced pieces of twentieth-century art into some of the rooms, a tradition that is continued today with the support of the Government Art Collection.

Between 1982 and 1987, many of the rooms were redecorated on the advice of John Cornforth and the decorator David Mlinaric, following the historical report commissioned from Joseph Friedman to inform their restoration. In 1997, the Gallery was converted into a suitable space for the display of contemporary British art. Almost every ambassador has made some improvement during his time here, and, budget constraints allowing, will continue to do so.

The British Ambassador's Residence in Paris continues to bear witness to the ebb and flow of diplomacy. Although historic and beautifully furnished, it is not a museum, but a working diplomatic mission in a setting that combines the highest achievements of French architecture and decorative arts with something of the charm and informality of an English country house. In the twenty-first century, the Paris Residence is a busy place, used and enjoyed by thousands of people every year — although today it is more likely to be the setting for a trade show, working lunch or international conference than for a magnificent ball. Thus, it is perhaps even more vital that the Residence reflects British prestige and values, and — after almost two centuries in British hands — still serves as a reminder of the many ties that bind Great Britain and France in friendship.

Above: Gilding specialist Charles Hesp restoring the water-gilding in the fluting of one of the pilasters in the Salon Bleu, 2010. The upkeep of the Residence makes constant demands on the skills of specialist craftsmen and conservators. *Facing page:* Detail of *Rorschach (Endless Column III)* by Cornelia Parker, 2006. A recent addition to the display of contemporary British art in the Gallery.

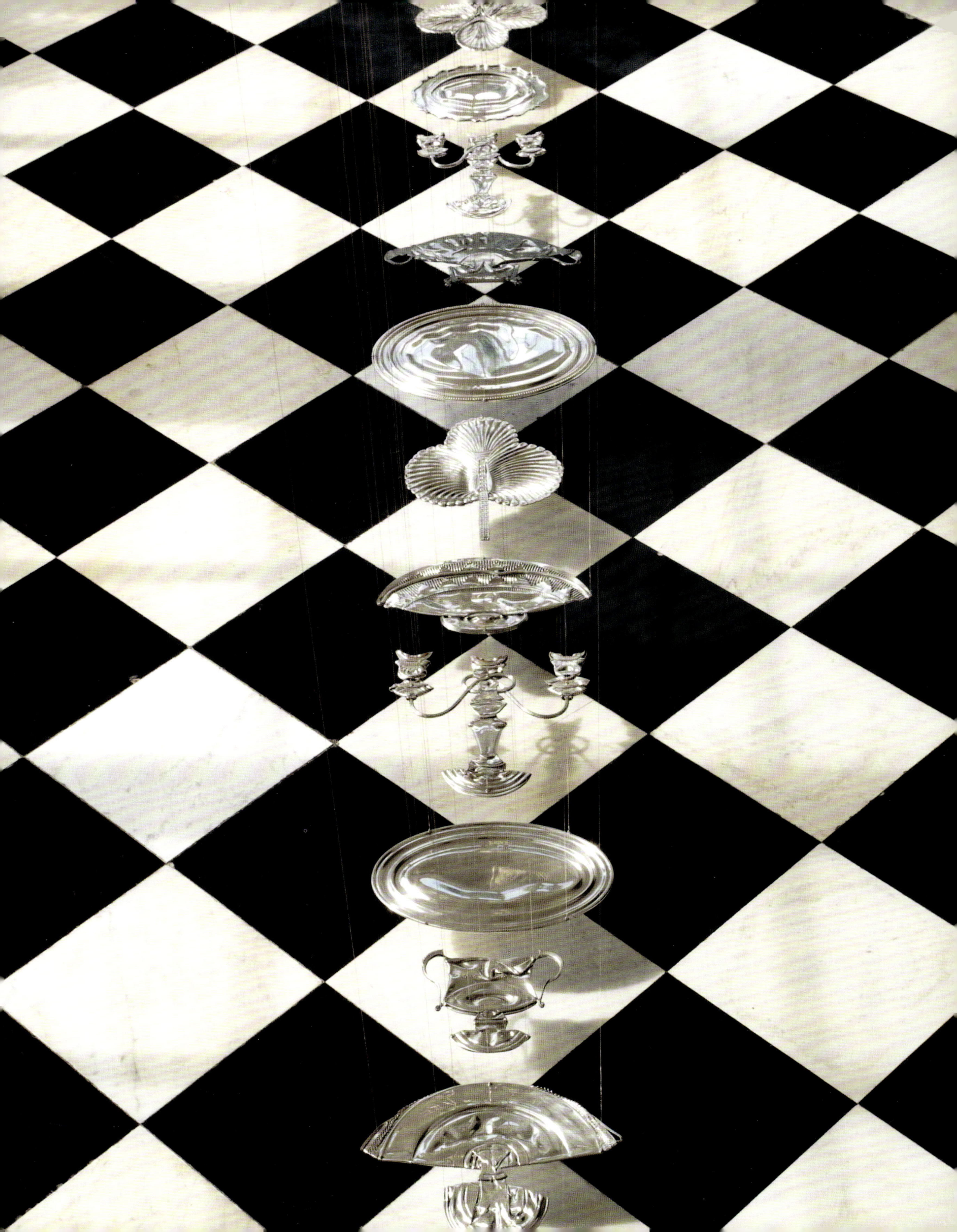

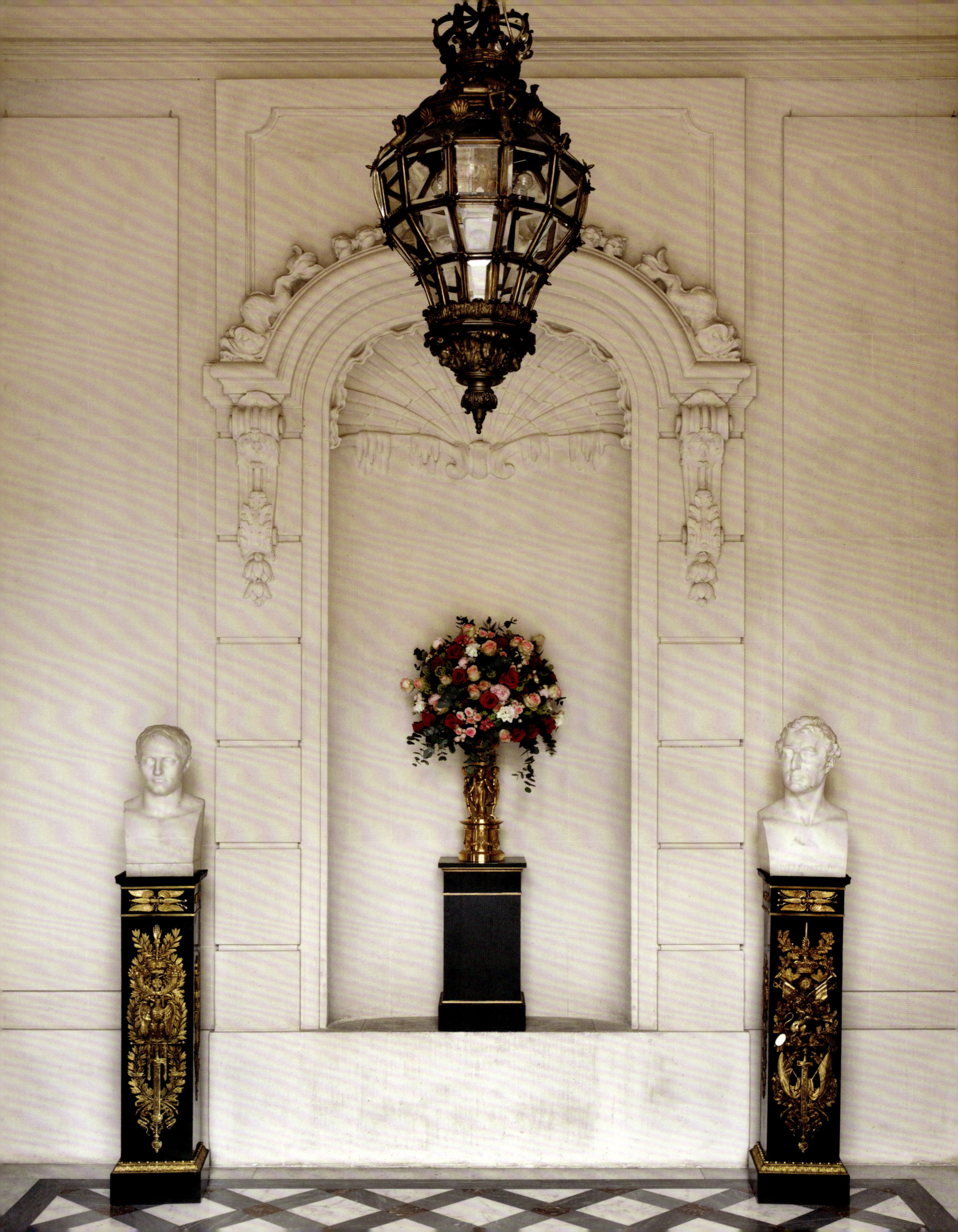

THE HOUSE
ROOM BY ROOM

Facing page: The Entrance Hall with busts of Napoleon, after Antoine Denis Chaudet, and the Duke of Wellington by Musgrave L. Watson.

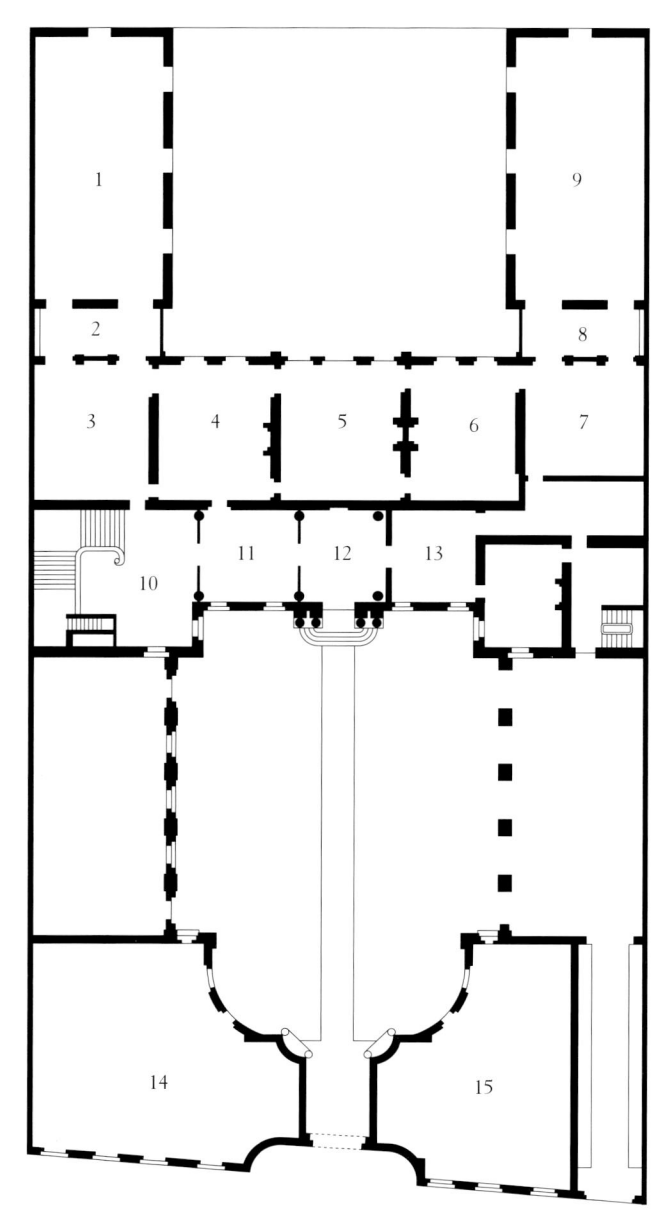

Ground floor

First floor

	Ground floor		First floor
1	State Dining Room	16	Billiard Room
2	Entre Deux	17	Salon Carmelite
3	Small Dining Room	18	Grand Salon Vert
4	Salon Jaune	19	Pauline's Bedroom / Salon Bleu
5	Salon Ponceau	20	Library
6	Chambre de Parade	21	Bathroom
7	Boudoir Violet	22	Bedroom
8	Petit Salon	23	Cabinet Vert
9	Picture Gallery	24	Salon Bleu
10	Staircase	25	Ante-Room
11	Footmen's Ante-Room	26	Staircase
12	Valets' Ante-Room		
13	Boudoir Rose		
14	Kitchens		
15	Stables and Porter's Lodge		

1814

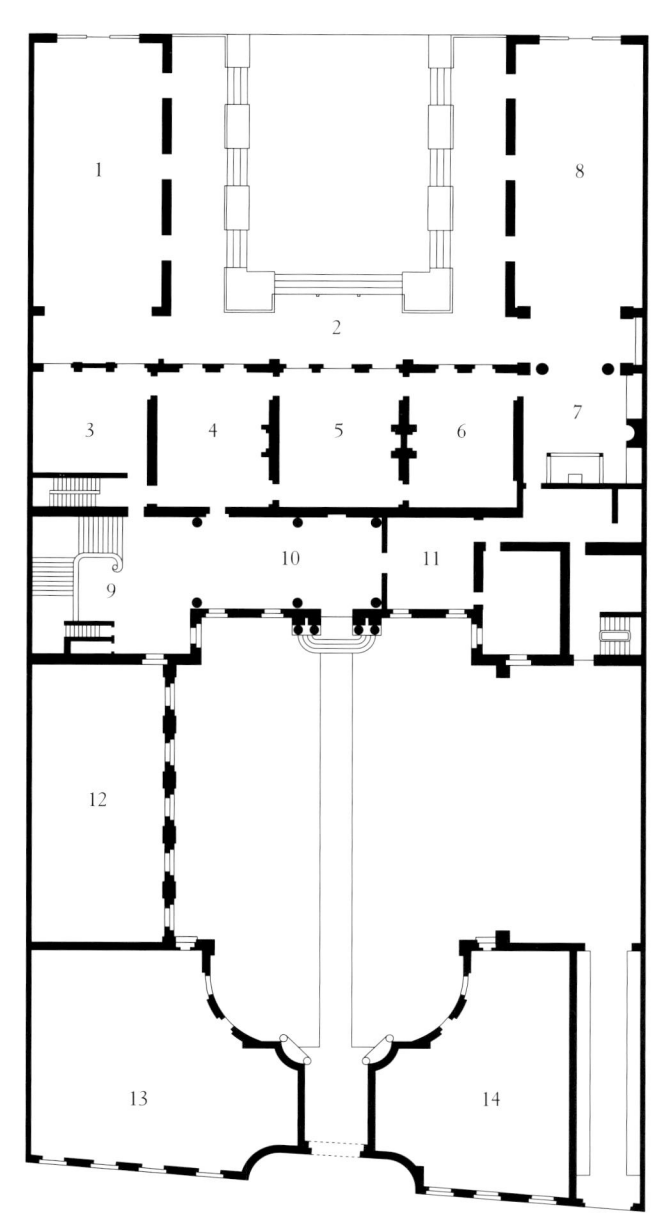

Ground floor

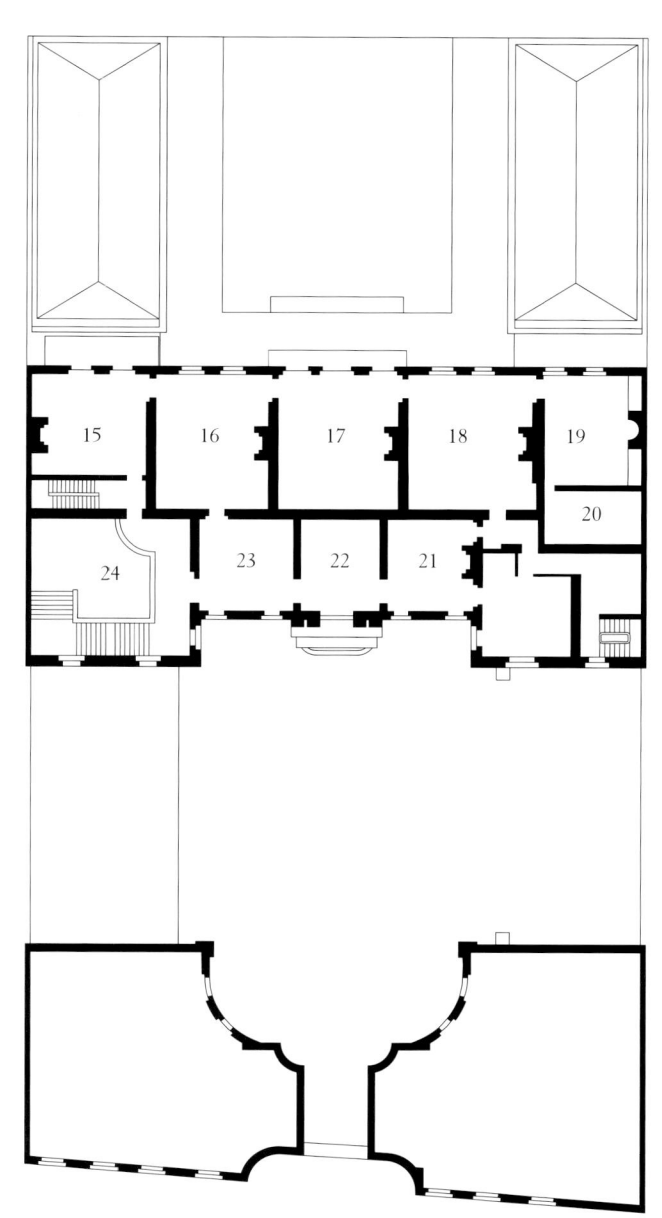

First floor

Ground floor

1. State Dining Room
2. Gallery
3. Pantry
4. Salon Rouge
5. Salon Bleu
6. Salon Pauline
7. Throne Room
8. Ballroom
9. Staircase
10. Entrance Hall
11. Cloakroom
12. Kitchen
13. Staff Offices / Dining Room
14. Porter's Lodge / Gatehouse

First floor

15. Tapestry Dining Room
16. Salon Jaune
17. Salon Vert et Or
18. Salon Vert
19. Cooper Bedroom
20. Cooper Bathroom
21. Duff Cooper Library
22. Wellington Room
23. Ante-Room
24. Staircase

2011

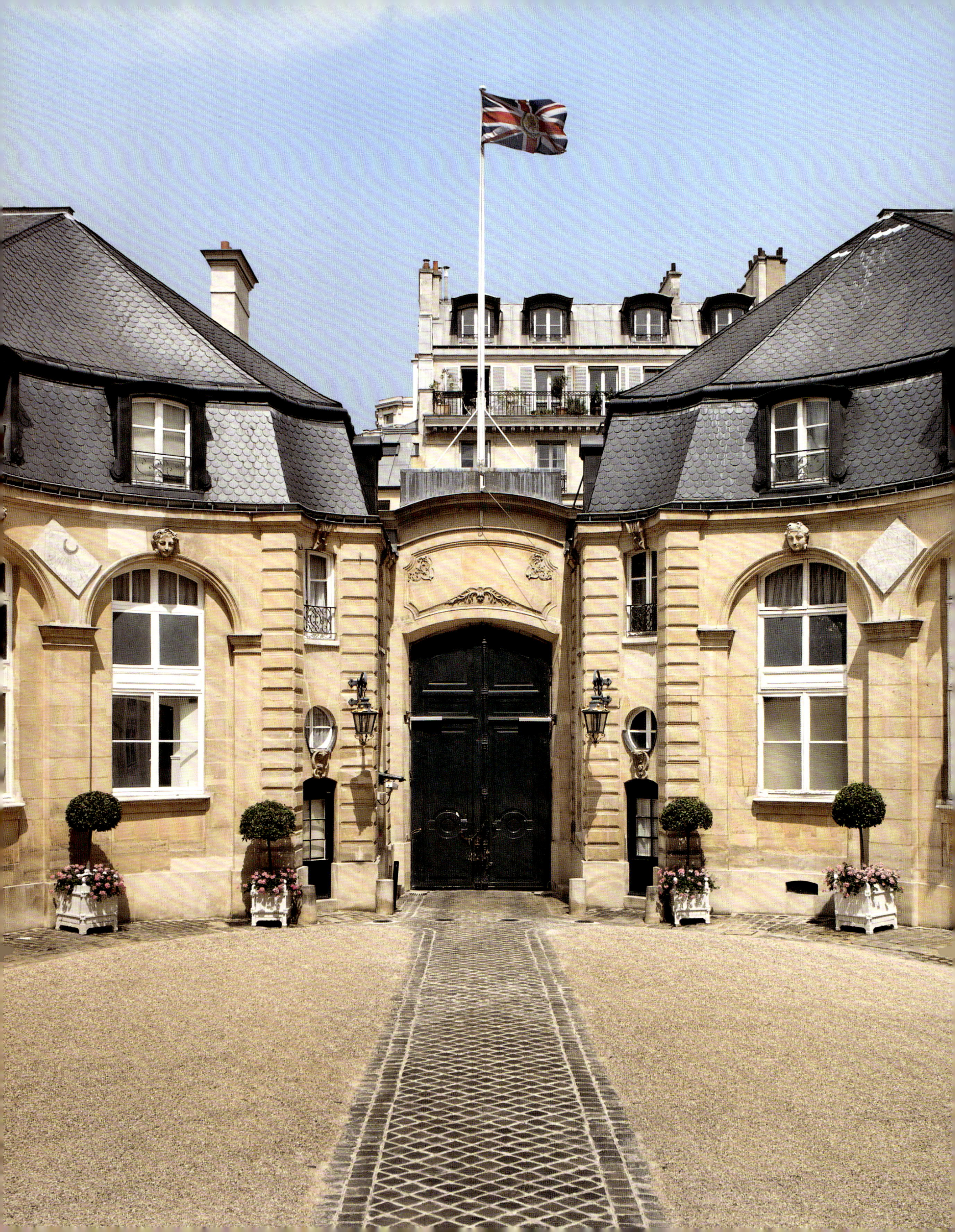

ENTRANCE FRONT AND COURTYARD

The façade which the hôtel de Charost presents to the rue du Faubourg-Saint-Honoré, with its low-flanking ranges enclosing a recessed gateway, or *porte cochère,* remains virtually unchanged since the time of its construction by Antoine Mazin. Now, as then, it provides security, as well as protection from the noise and dust of the street. In 1848, after the fall of Charles X, Lord Normanby reported that the façade of the Embassy was 'covered with placards, proclamations of the provisional government, of clubs, individuals etc, which it would not be safe at this time to disturb'.

When first built, the gateway was even more impressive than it is today, with massive carved oak doors flanked by stone pilasters decorated with military devices. Martial trophies composed of classical armour — described in the 1787 inventory as 'breast-plates, helmets and other military attributes' — surmounted each pier. Between them, in the parapet, a cartouche bore the words 'Hôtel de Charost', while above were carved in stone the arms of the house of Béthune, flanked by club-bearing warriors seated on military trophies. All these embellishments have gone, most probably destroyed during the Revolution 'as symbols of feudality', or purified during Pauline Borghese's remodelling. The façade must have looked uncomfortably bare without them, so in 1817 the present carved royal arms were installed. Earl Cowley, ordered a 'gas apparatus' (which no longer exists) from Messrs Huxley and Co. of London, in 1853 for the temporary 'illumination of the grand entrance on Her Majesty's birthday and other occasions'. According to Huxley's bill, it represented 'Her Majesty's initials supported by a wreath of roses, shamrock, and thistle, and surmounted by the English crown'.

Inside the courtyard, Mazin's elegant front rises up, symmetrical on either side of the Ionic frontispiece and portico. Originally two identical arcades linked it to the pavilions that housed the Porter's Lodge, stables and kitchens. The door surmounted by a carved relief of rearing horses led to the stables; the door with a boar and hound, to the kitchens. The western arcade was demolished sometime between 1858 and 1864 and the eastern one has been filled in. The beautiful male and female masks over the windows were originally repeated all around the courtyard — minor masterpieces of Louis XV architectural sculpture. There was also another Béthune coat of arms in the pediment, but this too has vanished. In 1858–60, Earl Cowley commissioned a replacement: the strange carving of three putti and a boat, symbolising perhaps the Union of the Crowns of England, Scotland and Ireland. The lower half of the façade still bears the scars of an enormous iron-and-glass canopy or 'marquise' that was installed here in the mid-nineteenth century to protect visitors from the rain. It was demolished by a delivery van in 1949 and not replaced.

Facing page: The façade of the gatehouse facing the courtyard, with its elegant curved arcades. The large gateway in the centre gives on to the rue du Faubourg-Saint-Honoré. The stables were located on the left, while the kitchens are sill located on the right.

ENTRANCE HALL AND STAIRCASE

When the hôtel de Charost was first built, the Entrance Hall was a columned vestibule. This led into a simple ante-room, which in turn opened into a separate compartment containing the impressive staircase. Even under Pauline Borghese this part of the house was simply furnished, with plain stone walls, and stools and benches covered in green moquette.

The rooms were knocked into one in 1852, although the Louis XV Ionic capitals of the columns survive, as does the original staircase balustrade, a splendid tour de force of ironwork by blacksmith Antoine Hallé, incorporating gilded suns in splendour, probably an allusion to Louis XIV, the Sun King, under whom the Béthune-Charost family had flourished. During Lord Lytton's embassy between 1887 and 1891, visitors entering the front door were confronted by an enormous elephant's head and other trophies — souvenirs of his time as viceroy of India. The present appearance of the room dates from an Edwardian recasting of 1904–05, when almost all the stonework — columns, walls and staircase — were renewed in artificial stone. The three-colour marble pavement also dates from this time.

Flanking the opulent Edwardian niche facing the door are marble busts of Wellington and Napoleon. They are not a pair but have been mounted on matching ebonised pedestals with elaborate ormolu trophies symbolising British and French military honours. The bust of the Duke of Wellington is by Musgrave L. Watson and that of Napoleon is after a much-copied portrait by Antoine Denis Chaudet. This example was supplied to the prefecture of Florence during the Napoleonic occupation of Italy. Sir Winston Churchill, who regularly visited the Residence, is represented by a bronze bust by Sir Jacob Epstein of 1946. Churchill's most famous visit to the Residence was on 9 June 1939, for urgent talks with Paul Reynaud and General Gamelin on the eve of the fall of Paris. At 6 o'clock the next morning the sound of singing and walrus-like splashing resounded throughout the Embassy from a second-floor bathroom, as the prime minister attended to his morning *toilette*.

The portrait of Queen Victoria in Garter robes is a copy after the famous portrait of 1843 by Franz Xaver Winterhalter, which hangs at Windsor Castle. This version was painted in 1847 by William Corden expressly for the Paris Embassy. The eighteenth-century-style table below it is in the manner of William Kent.

Facing page: The Entrance Hall and Staircase. Much of the decoration dates from Vye Parminter and Georges Hoentschel's redecoration of the Residence in 1904–05. The walls of the staircase are of an artificial stone called stuccoline. The brown marble pilasters are Edwardian, but the Ionic capitals and the carved cornice are original Louis XV work.

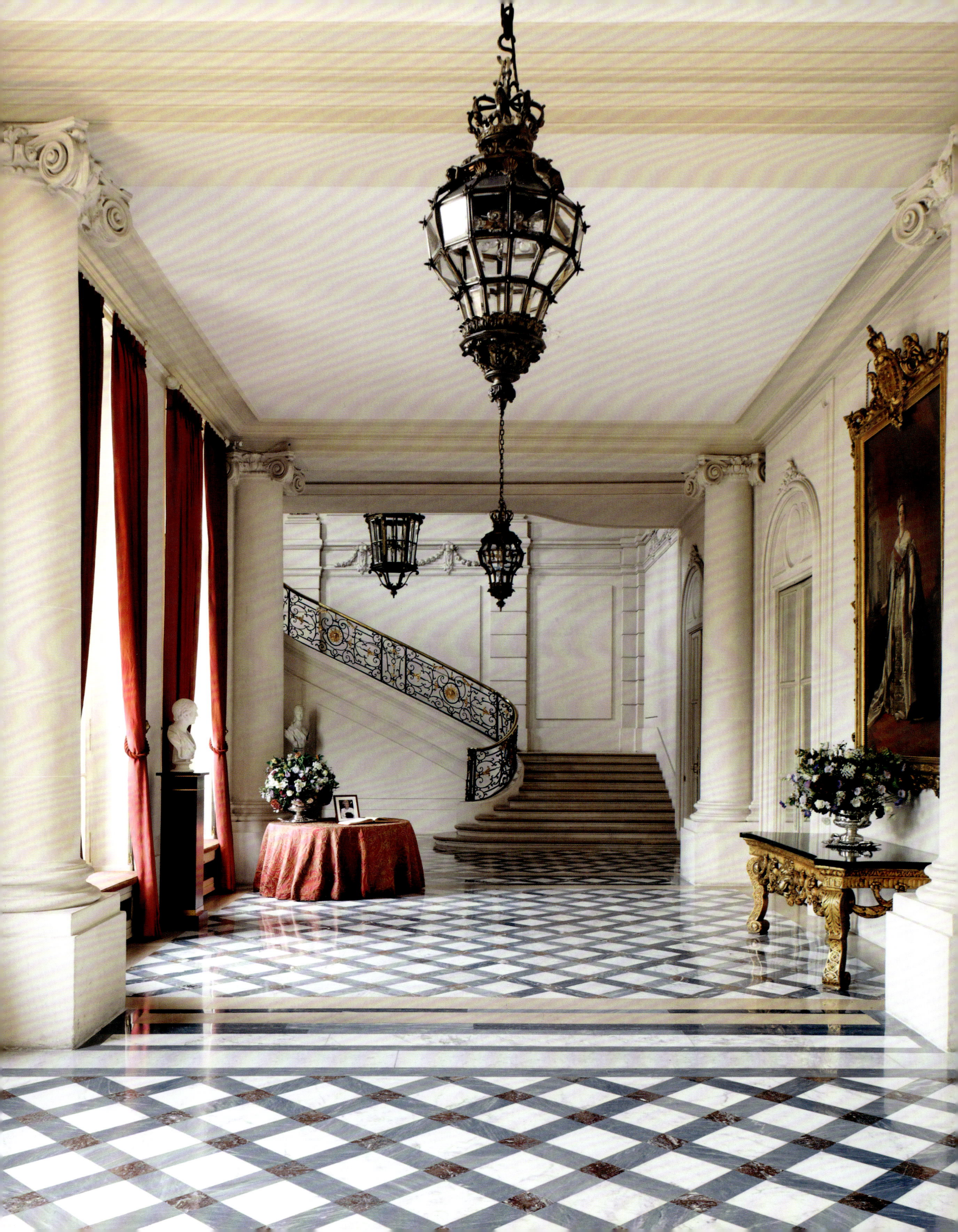

At the foot of the stairs is a bust of Queen Alexandra, wife of Edward VII, by the French sculptor Prosper d'Epinay. A chalk drawing of Edward VII, a frequent visitor to Paris, is opposite. In the nearby bay is an elaborately mounted statue, Pauline Borghese as Venus Victrix, a reduced version by Adamo Tadolini of the notorious semi-nude statue by Antonio Canova in the Villa Borghese in Rome.

Today the Entrance Hall witnesses all the comings and goings of the Residence — the Visitors Book is strategically placed to greet guests and serves as a record of their visit. It was here, on the steps to the front door, that Prime Minister Margaret Thatcher faced the press after hearing the results of the first round of the Conservative leadership ballot in November 1990. She was to resign two days later. In the Cloakroom leading off the Entrance Hall are framed photographs, copies of originals showing the Residence in 1905, during the embassy of Sir Francis Bertie.

Above and facing page: Adamo Tadolini (1788–1868), *Pauline Borghese as Venus Victrix, Original by Canova of 1805–08,* marble.

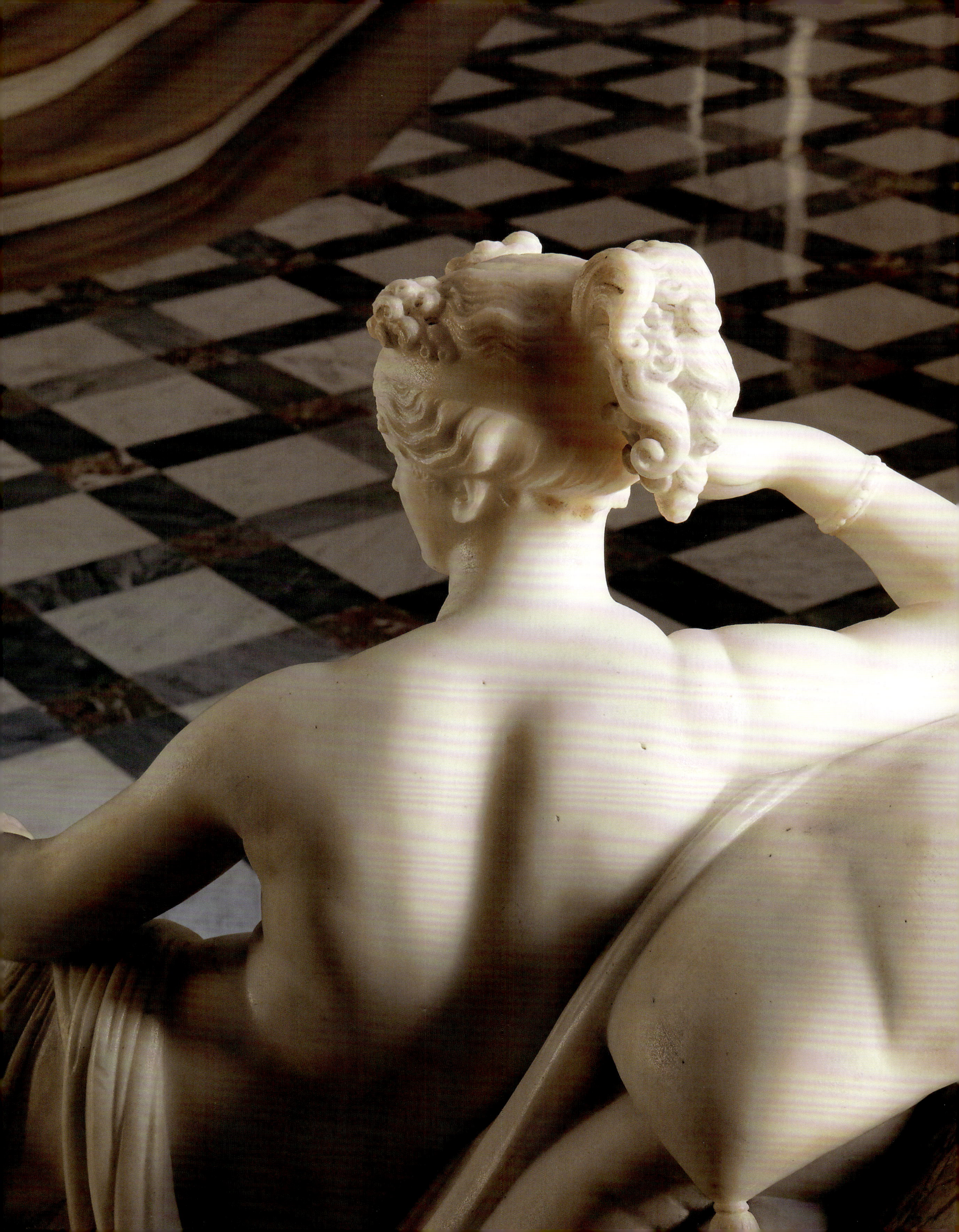

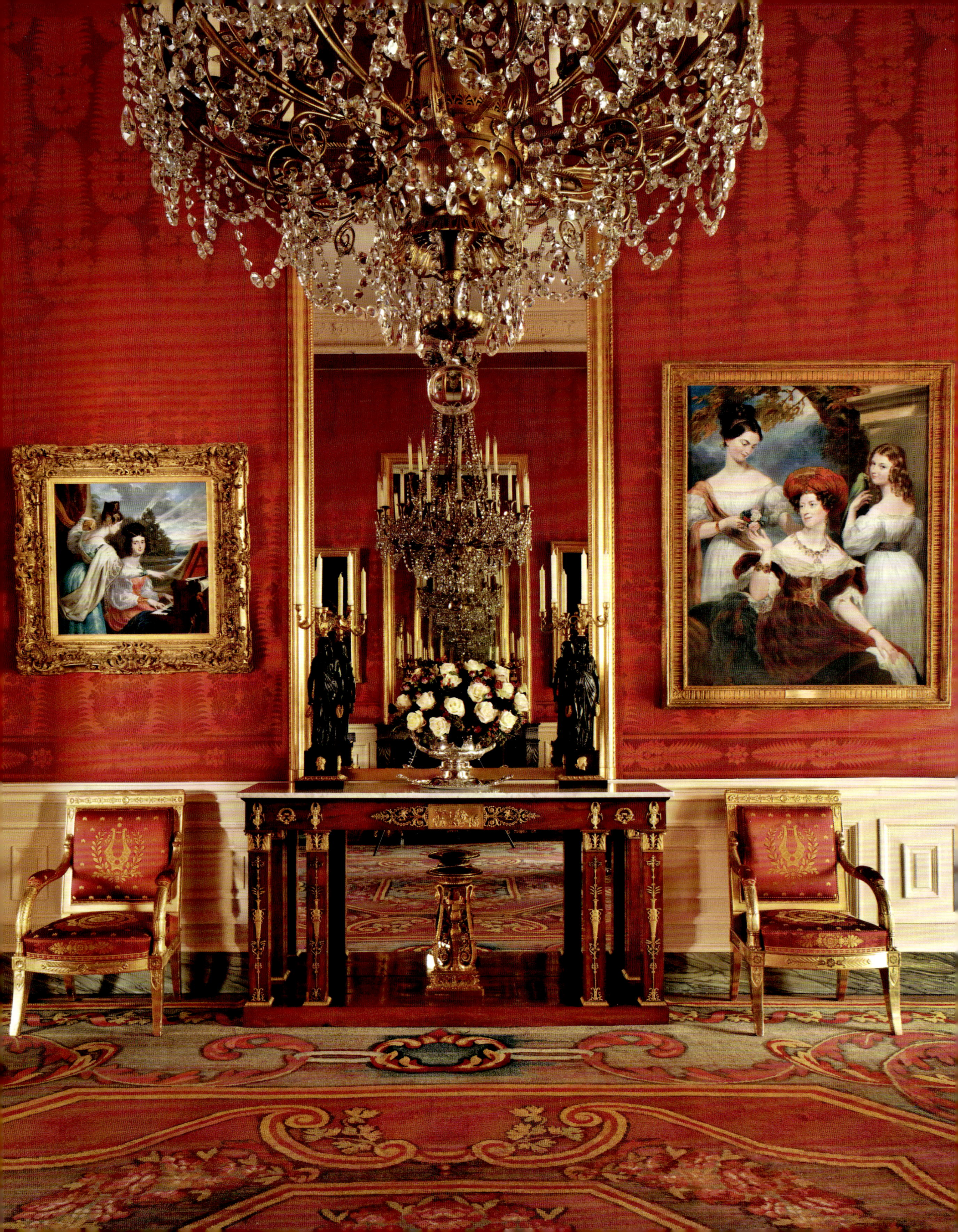

SALON ROUGE

Originally the duchesse de Béthune's dining room, the Salon Rouge was, in her day, hung with tapestries depicting the life of Scipio Africanus. The dining table and chairs would have been brought in from adjoining rooms when needed. The tapestries were still there in 1759, as well as — rather strangely — a large copper bathtub. The cornice of the room, finely wrought with female masks, pastoral figures and arabesques, is probably original and would have once been richly gilded.

Pauline Borghese hung the room with yellow silk and furnished it with white and gold seat furniture. None of this survives, and since the mid-nineteenth century the walls have been clothed with crimson damask. The current damask was hung here in 1986 and incorporates the 'Palme de Saint-Cloud' pattern, first woven in 1802 by Camille Pernon of Lyon for the First Consul's Library at the château de Saint-Cloud.

The present seat furniture is part of a large set of forty chairs, now divided among several rooms in the Residence, commissioned by Pauline Borghese from Pierre Gaston Brion (1767–c. 1841) for her now-vanished Picture Gallery, the present Ballroom. The chairs are wholly water-gilded, and upholstered in the Empire style to complement the damask wall-hangings. The massive chimneypiece of grey marble bears a striking garniture of high-quality Empire bronzes: an ormolu and griotte marble clock depicting Minerva and flanking candelabra, sprouting from marble obelisks, embellished with ormolu rostral prows and fountains. Opposite the chimneypiece is a fine Empire console table, and another pair of candelabra supported by bronze Egyptian maidens. These, and the splendid twenty-four-light chandelier, all come from the collection of Pauline Borghese. The strongly coloured and patterned nineteenth-century carpet, acquired for the Residence in 1982, came from the apartments in Palazzo Labia in Venice belonging to aesthete and collector, Charles de Beistegui. It is probably Spanish and from the manufactory of Cuenca.

Facing page: The Salon Rouge. Its crimson damask wall-hangings and opulent Spanish carpet make for a rich foil for the Empire furniture and paintings by Hayter (see pages 86–89). *Following pages:* The Salon Rouge is occasionally used for intimate dinners — here brooding portraits of the Duke of Wellington and Lord Stuart de Rothesay contemplate the richly laid table.

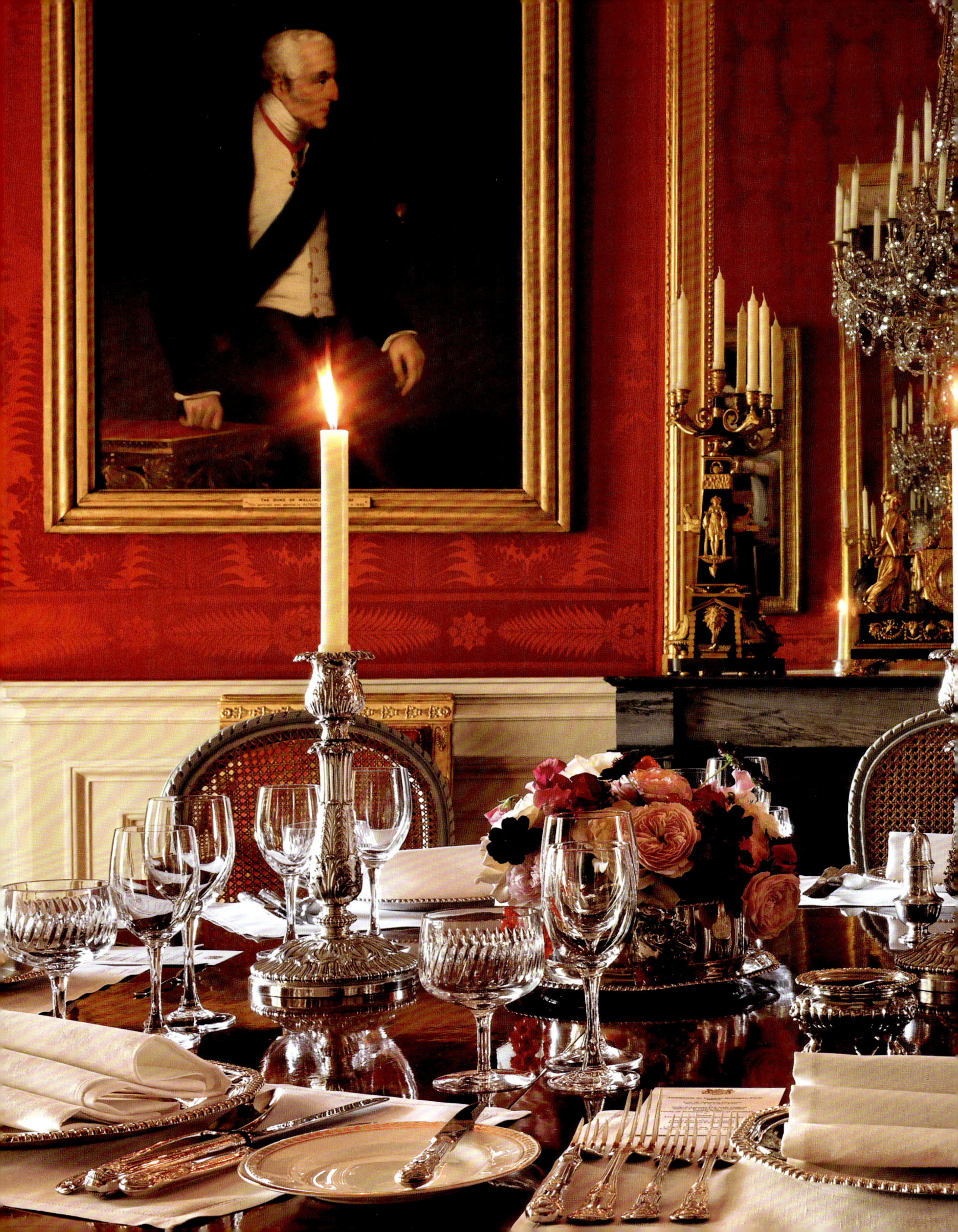

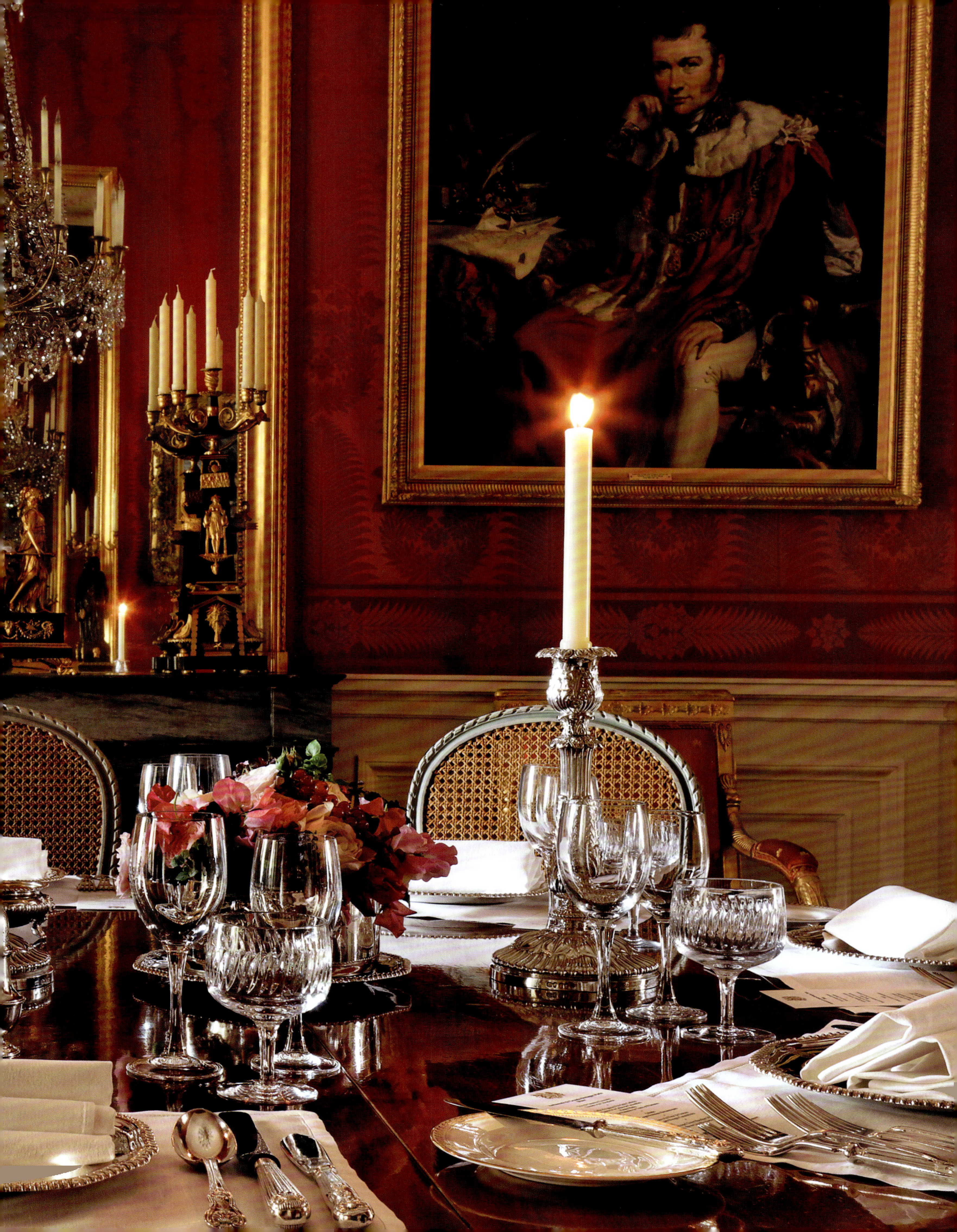

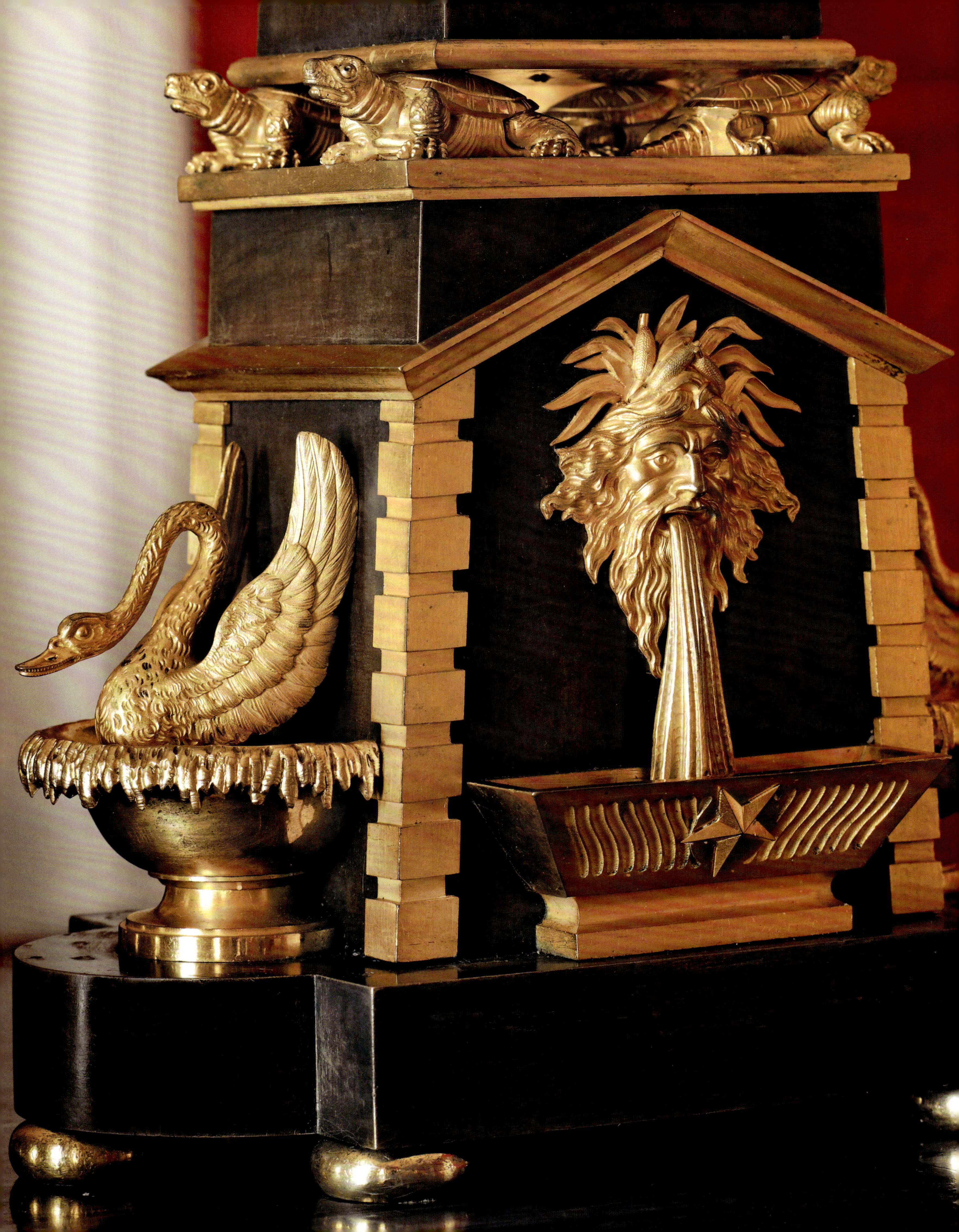

The walls are hung with portraits, including three paintings by Sir George Hayter depicting Sir Charles Stuart, later Lord Stuart de Rothesay, his wife and daughters. Almost as an antidote to the showy dresses and jewels of Lady Stuart and her daughters is the comte d'Orsay's sombre portrait of Stuart's predecessor as ambassador, the Duke of Wellington, painted in July 1845. Wellington hated sitting for his portrait, but the painter Benjamin Robert Haydon, on seeing the painting at the Royal Academy in London, pronounced this one 'Capital, just like him when dressed for dinner.' Haydon was not alone in judging the portrait a success: d'Orsay went on to paint at least three versions of it.

Strategically embedded in the heart of the house, the Salon Rouge is constantly in demand, especially for intimate winter dinners enclosed by the red damask curtains, which keep out the cold from the Gallery.

Facing page: Empire aquatic motifs in ormolu — a spewing river god, swans and tortoises — adorn the base of one of a pair of candelabra, described in the 1814 inventory. *Above left:* One of a pair of bronze candelabra by Thomire representing a vestal holding wreaths of flowers. *Above right:* One of the elements of the elaborate *surtout* by Thomire used in the State Dining Room (see pages 118–119).

LORD STUART DE ROTHESAY, LADY STUART DE ROTHESAY AND THEIR DAUGHTERS
THREE PORTRAITS BY SIR GEORGE HAYTER

Charles Stuart, Lord Stuart de Rothesay, grandson of former prime minister Lord Bute, was serving a second term as ambassador to France when he commissioned George Hayter to paint his portrait. Stuart is depicted in his privy counsellor's uniform, over which are his peer's robes and collar, indicating membership of the Order of the Bath. Agnes Berry (sister of author and diarist Mary Berry) wrote of the painting in October 1829 'They have got our English painter Mr. Hayter here, who is in great vogue in Paris, and has made a good picture of Lord Stuart, the strongest likeness imaginable, and downright handsome.' Berry probably saw the work at Hayter's studio in Paris which, according to a British newspaper, was 'thronged with admiring visitors'.

Hayter also painted Stuart's two daughters. Titled *The Music Lesson*, the work is dated 1830, the year Louisa (later Marchioness of Waterford) turned twelve and Charlotte (later Countess Canning) turned thirteen. Charlotte is depicted playing a piano, while Louisa turns the music pages. Their features have been matured by the artist.

Hayter's final work for the family is a group portrait of Lady Elizabeth Stuart with her daughters. The heads were painted in Paris in 1830 and the painting completed in London the following year. Lady Stuart is sumptuously dressed in a crimson velvet gown, a turban and lavish gold jewellery. By contrast her daughters are in plain white dresses — Louisa holding a parrot and Charlotte a posy of flowers.

Lord Stuart was recalled from his post in 1831. After his return to England he built Highcliffe Castle on a family estate in Dorset, where his portrait and that of Lady Stuart and her daughters were displayed flanking a door within the dining room. Hayter also returned to London in 1831 and, in the following year, sent the portrait of the former ambassador to the Royal Academy exhibition, along with a portrait of another of his patrons, John Russell, 6th Duke of Bedford. Both were singled out for praise in the press, with one journalist describing them as 'among the best portraits in the exhibition'.

More than a century after the death of Lord Stuart, in 1949, the contents of Highcliffe were sold through Christie's. All three Hayter paintings of the Stuart family were dispersed to separate collections until the Government Art Collection gradually reunited them. The portrait of Lady Stuart and her daughters, and the double portrait of Louisa and Charlotte, were purchased in London in 1987 and 2005 respectively. That of Lord Stuart was bought in 1998 from a New York-based dealer, having formerly been on display in an upstairs suite of the Essex House Hotel, Manhattan. The works are now reunited in the city where they were created and are displayed together in the Stuart family's former home.

Text by Philippa Martin

With thanks to Barbara Bryant for her expert guidance on George Hayter.

Facing page: Charles Stuart, Lord Stuart de Rothesay (1779–1845) Diplomat, 1830.

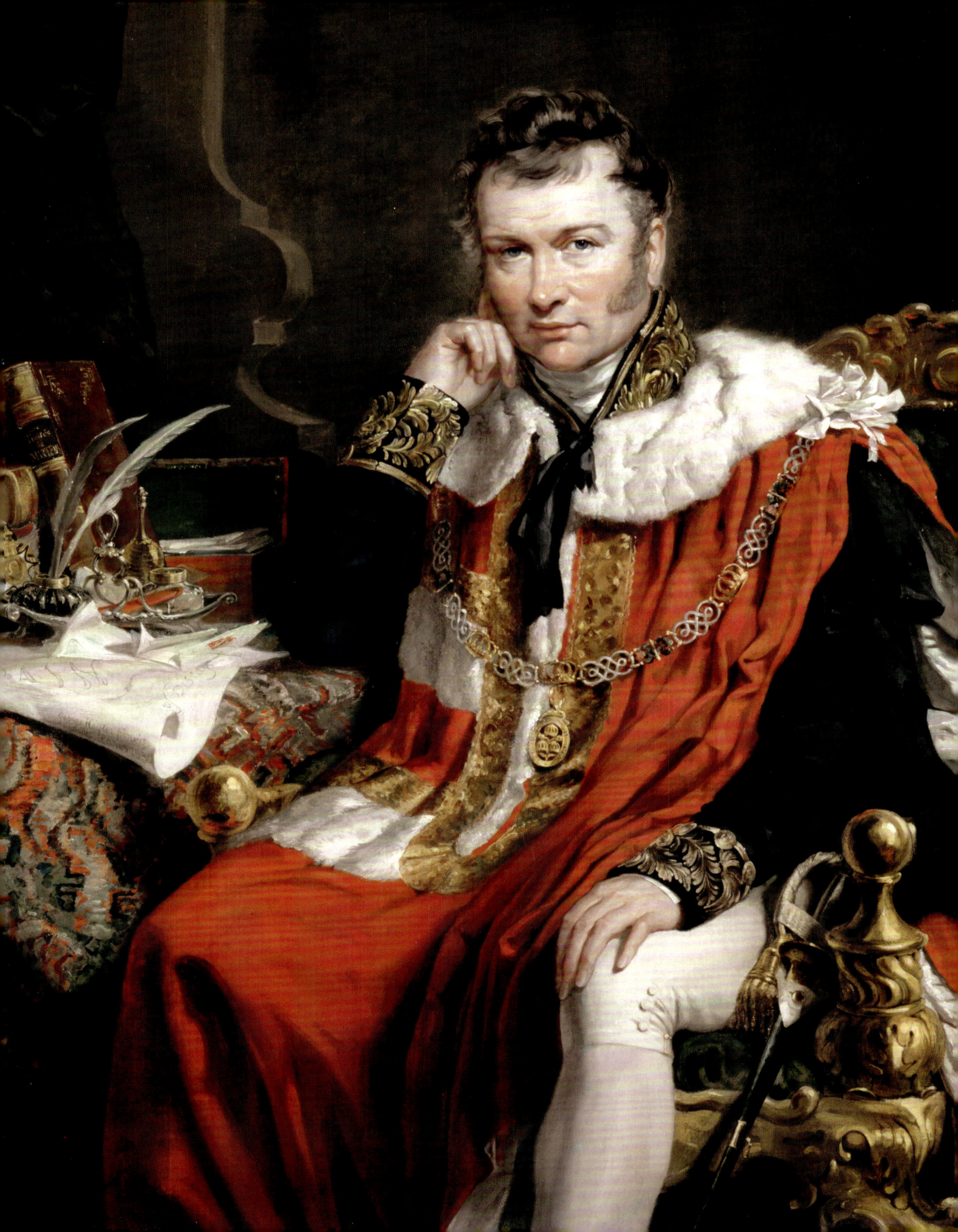

Above: The Hon. Charlotte Stuart (1817–1861) and the Hon. Louisa Stuart (1818–1891), 1830. This double portrait shows Charlotte Stuart (seated at the piano) and her younger sister, Louisa. They were the daughters of Charles Stuart, Lord Stuart de Rothesay, British ambassador to France from 1815 to 1824 and from 1828 to 1831. Charlotte and Louisa were born at the Embassy and spent part of their childhood there. This double portrait of the two sisters was painted in Paris in 1830. Charlotte married Charles Canning, son of the prime minister George Canning, in 1835. She became a Lady of the Bedchamber to Queen Victoria and accompanied her husband to India when he was made governor general in 1855. Louisa married Henry de la Poer Beresford, 3rd Marquess of Waterford, in 1842. She was an artist and philanthropist, and counted John Ruskin and George Frederic Watts among her friends.

Facing page: Elizabeth, Lady Stuart de Rothesay (died 1867) and her Daughters Charlotte (later Countess Canning) and Louisa (later Marchioness of Waterford), 1830–31.

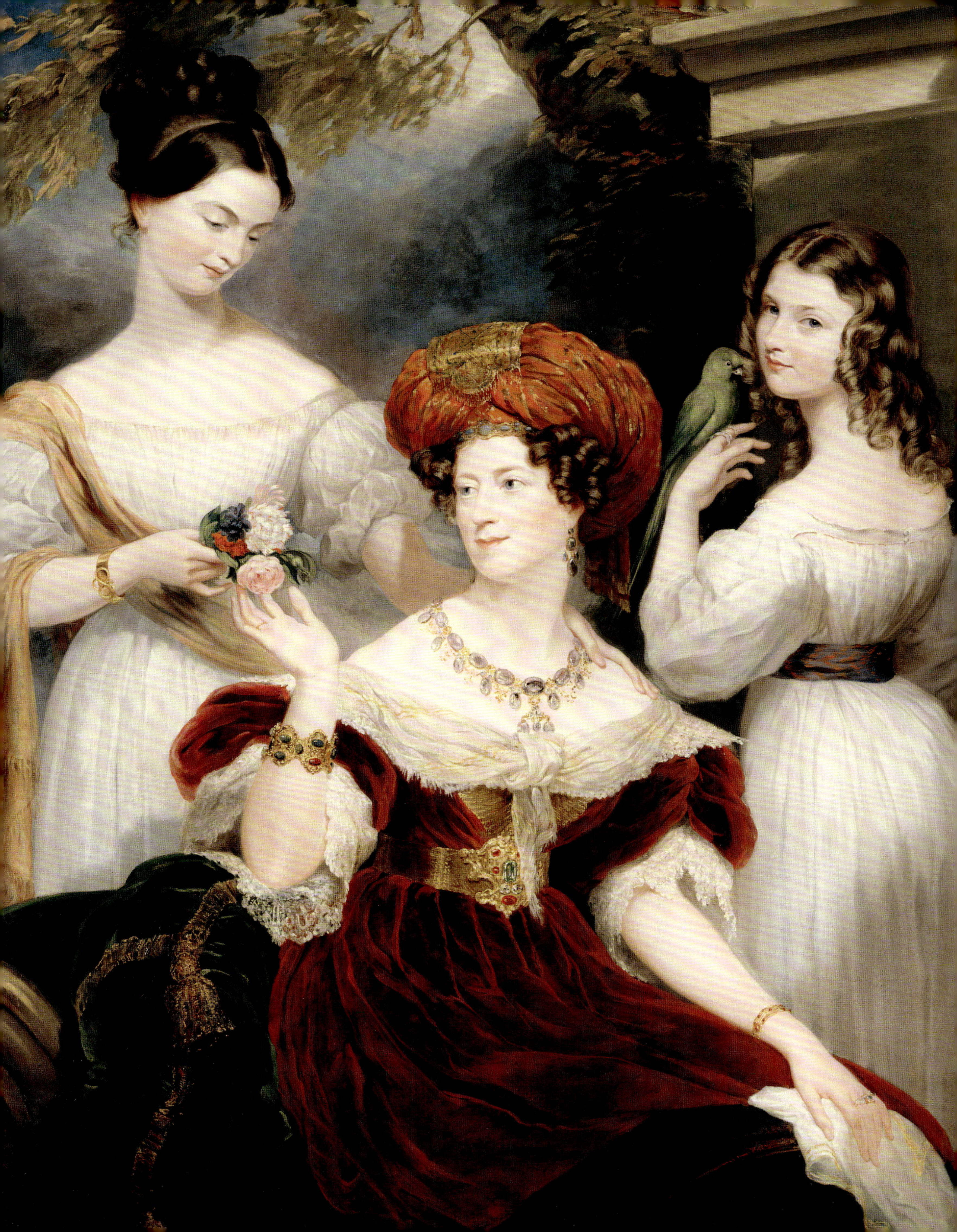

SALON BLEU

The duchesse de Béthune used this room as her salon, and in 1737 the walls were hung with Gobelins tapestries, with crimson silk and velvet curtains at every door and window. It also contained a gilt sofa and twelve armchairs that were upholstered with crimson velvet, and another set upholstered with watered yellow silk with crimson flowers and a fringe of gold thread.

This old-fashioned decor was swept away by the comte and comtesse de La Marck around 1790, when they fitted up the room with *boiseries*, or panelling, in the form of an arcaded colonnade of giant Ionic pilasters, with sprays of laurel and oak leaves in the spandrels. The overdoors have reliefs depicting music-making maidens flanking flaming braziers. These, and the lyres on the doors, suggest that this was intended as a music room. Its designer is unknown, but Joseph Friedman, who conducted extensive research into the history of the Residence, creates a convincing argument that this is the work of Jacques Denis Antoine (1733–1801), who used comparable motifs in the interior of the hôtel de la Monnaie. The rich gilding on the panelling may have been introduced by Pauline Borghese, and has recently been restored. It is worth noting that the overmantel 'mirror' is in fact a clever window looking into the Salon Pauline; during Pauline's day it is said that this was a two-way mirror, allowing her to survey the company in the room next door before making her entrance.

What is left of Pauline Borghese's suite of gilded seat furniture for this room is displayed elsewhere in the house, and the present chairs are from the large set of forty chairs ordered for her Picture Gallery. The clock, by Manière (movement) and Héricourt (bronze case) from about 1810, depicts Father Time and illustrates the motto *Ars Longa, Vita Brevis*. Both this and the incense burner, supported by ormolu maidens yoked with wreaths, have been recorded in this room since before 1814. The impressive gilt-bronze chandelier also dates from this time, although the mouldings on the ceiling were added in the nineteenth century. Lady Granville boasted that her entertainments here in the mid-1820s were 'brilliantly lighted'.

The Salon Bleu remains an important room today and is often used for dinners and receptions. The continual wear and tear proved too much for the room's magnificent mid-nineteenth-century Aubusson carpet, adorned with the lilies of France, the insignia of the Ordre du Saint-Esprit and the crossed 'Ls' of Louis Philippe, said to have been at Hamilton Palace and then Derby House, London. This has been replaced by a near-identical replica, woven in China in 2006.

Facing page: The Salon Bleu. The magnificent decoration composed of *rinceaux* and laurel branches largely dates from c. 1790, the time of the comte and comtesse de La Marck, but the gilding was probably introduced later by Pauline Borghese. On the floor is a recent copy of an Aubusson carpet bearing the lilies of France and the insignia of the Ordre du Saint-Esprit.

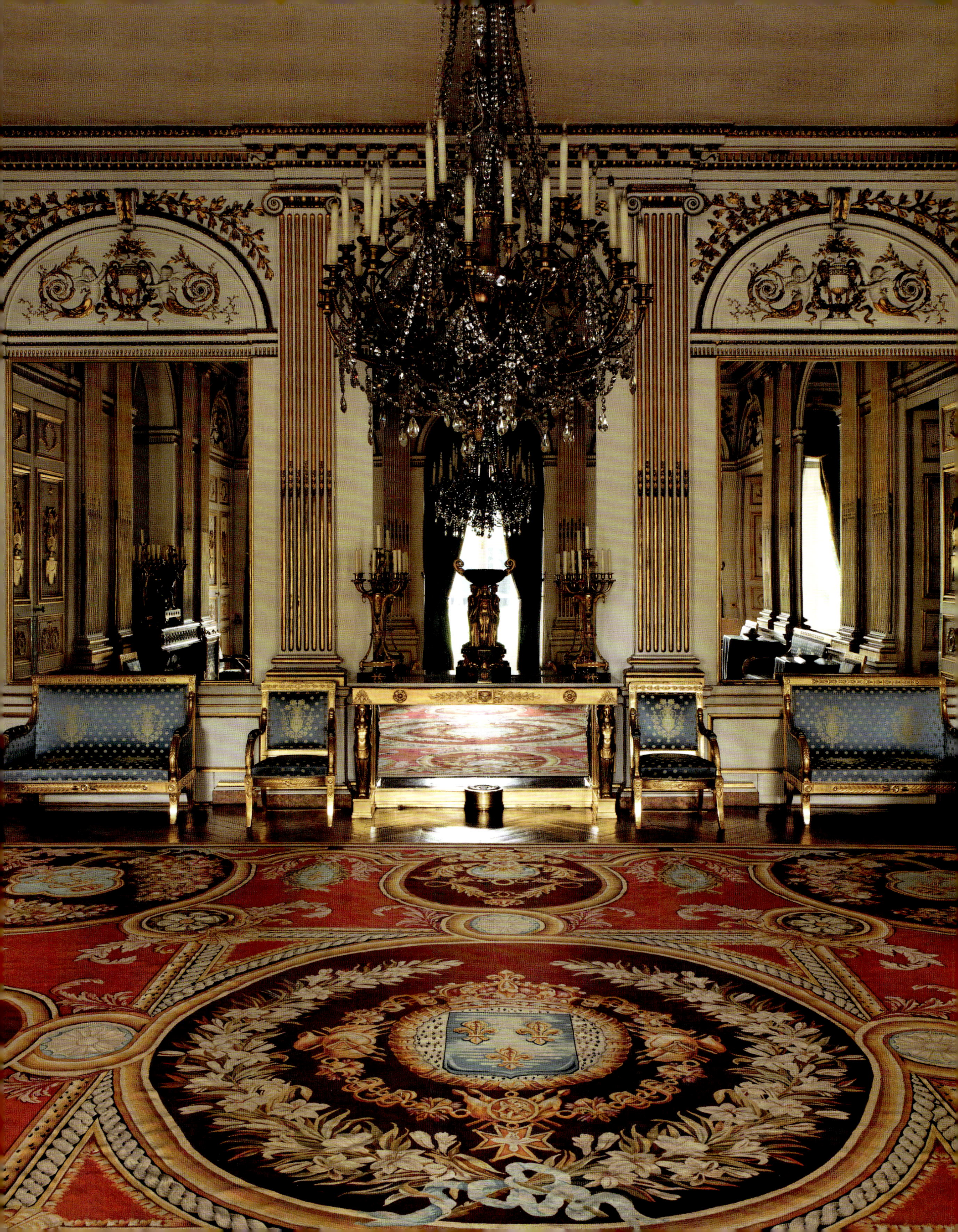

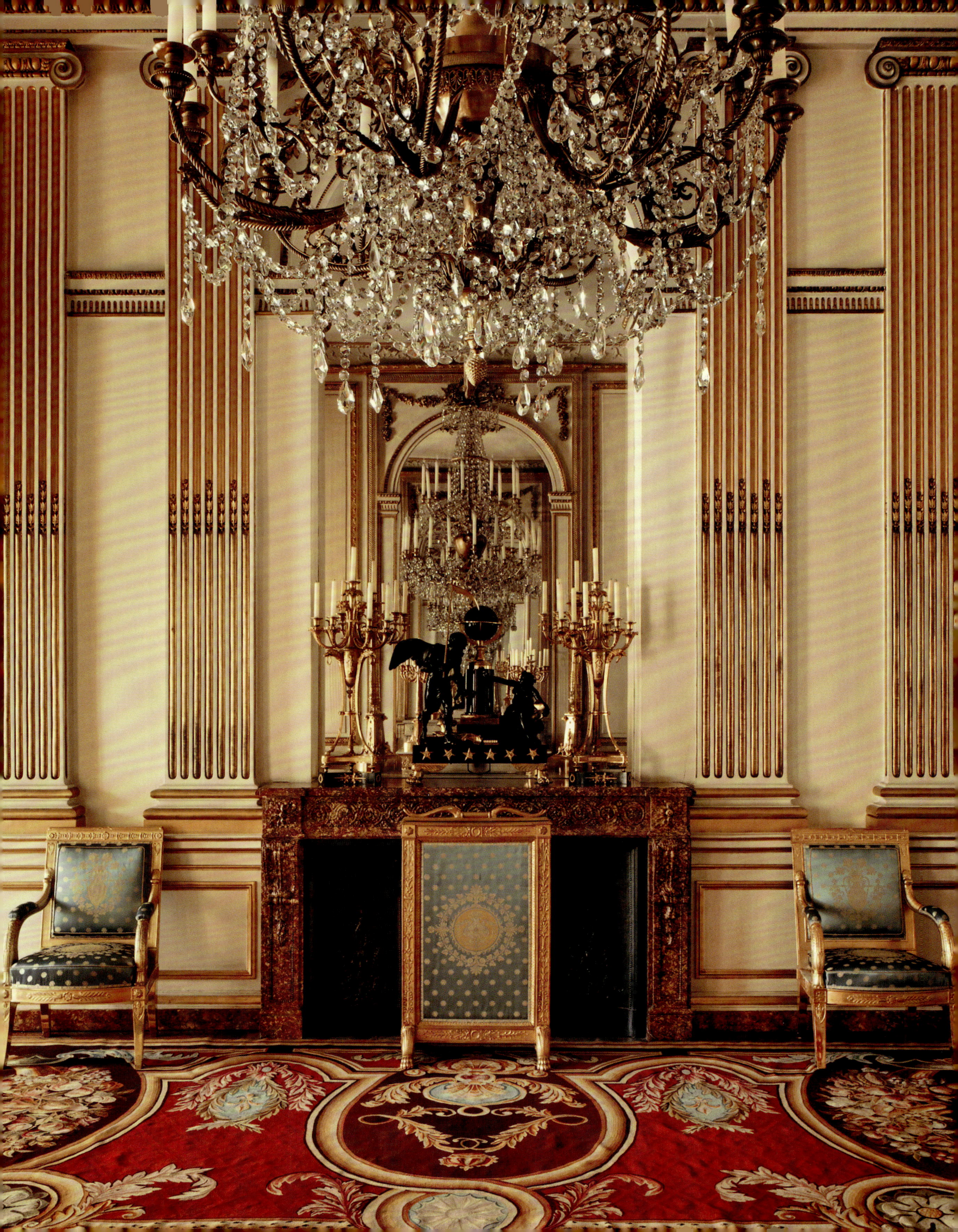

Facing page: The chimneypiece in the Salon Bleu supports an impressive bronze and ormolu clock depicting Father Time. The thirty-light crystal chandelier is one of those originally supplied to Pauline Borghese and is one of the most magnificent in the Residence. *Above:* The Salon Bleu displays a set of chairs that were part of a set originally made for Pauline's Picture Gallery.

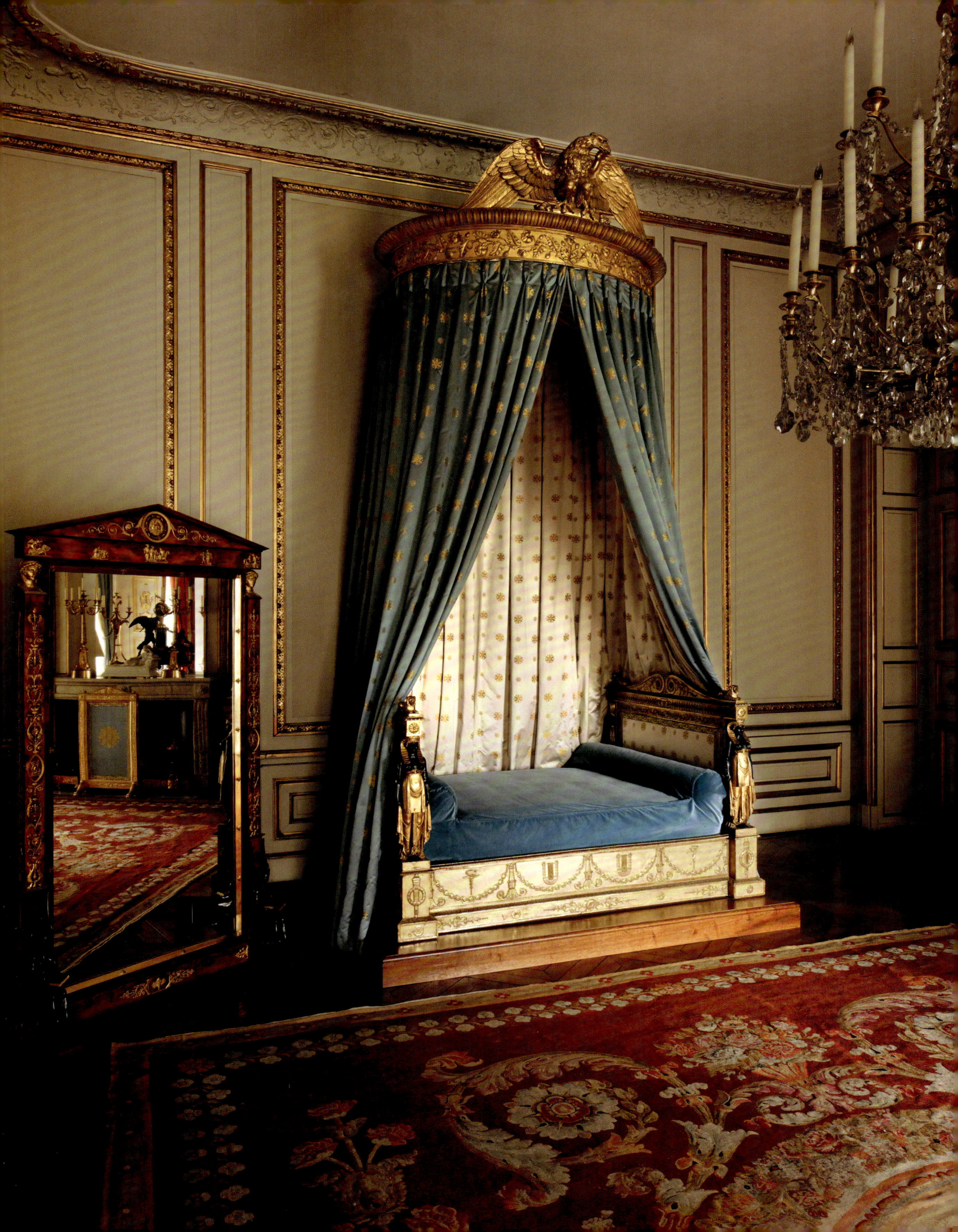

SALON PAULINE

Appropriately dominated by an imposing eagle-topped bed, this room was originally the duchesse de Béthune's bedchamber. Pauline Borghese used it as a room for repose and intimate receptions for important visitors — her *chambre de parade* — over which she regally presided from a sort of sofa bed (not the magnificent bed displayed here today), surmounted by a canopy of blue silk embroidered with gold. It was only the British, in the mid-1820s, who turned this room into a drawing room. Later known as the Salon Victoria, the huge portrait of the queen now in the Entrance Hall hung here. The white-and-gold panelling dates from 1904–05, although the cornice and the panel depicting Venus and Cupid amid arabesques between the windows are precious survivals of the elaborate Louis XV carving that once decorated these apartments.

The imposing bed now in the room was only brought here in 1985. It was originally in the princess's principal bedroom upstairs, now the Salon Vert. After 1841, it was moved to the Ambassadress's Bedroom, today known as the Cooper Bedroom, where it was used by successive ambassadresses and, occasionally, visiting royalty. King Edward VII slept in it in 1903 and 1907, and Queen Elizabeth The Queen Mother in 1956 and 1982. However, not everyone wanted to spend the night under such a towering confection or in so public a room, and it hasn't been used since its careful restoration in 1986, when it was reupholstered in pale blue silk, with a white silk lining, both powdered with golden rosettes. The gilded bed frame, with its bronzed maidens and miniature lions, is a tour de force of neo-Egyptian Empire taste, as is the bed canopy, with its carved eagle — symbolising Jupiter, king of the gods, who occasionally took this disguise on his amorous adventures. According to the inventory of 1814, behind it originally sprouted a *panache* of twenty-six large white ostrich feathers, sadly not yet reinstated.

The other notable item of Empire furniture is the psyche, or full-length mirror, its frame enriched with ormolu mounts of the highest quality, including Napoleonic bees. This, too, belonged to Pauline Borghese, who kept it in her Boudoir Rose — what is now the Cloakroom. The Italian aesthete, Mario Praz, in his book *Neoclassical Taste* (1940) described the mirror as an 'altar' dedicated to vanity. The set of chairs, upholstered in blue silk to match the bed, may have once been intended for the Salon Bleu, while the four gilt-bronze candelabra have been in this room since 1814. The firedogs in the form of winged sphinxes guarding tripods are probably by the master craftsman Jean André Wallner (active 1780–1815), while the carpet is mid-nineteenth-century Aubusson.

Facing page: The Salon Pauline is dominated by the imposing Empire bed which once belonged to Pauline Borghese. Originally, it was surmounted by a gilded eagle decorated with twenty-four white ostrich feathers. Pauline also admired herself in the psyche, or full-length mirror, with its splendid ormolu mounts and winged bronze maidens reading books.

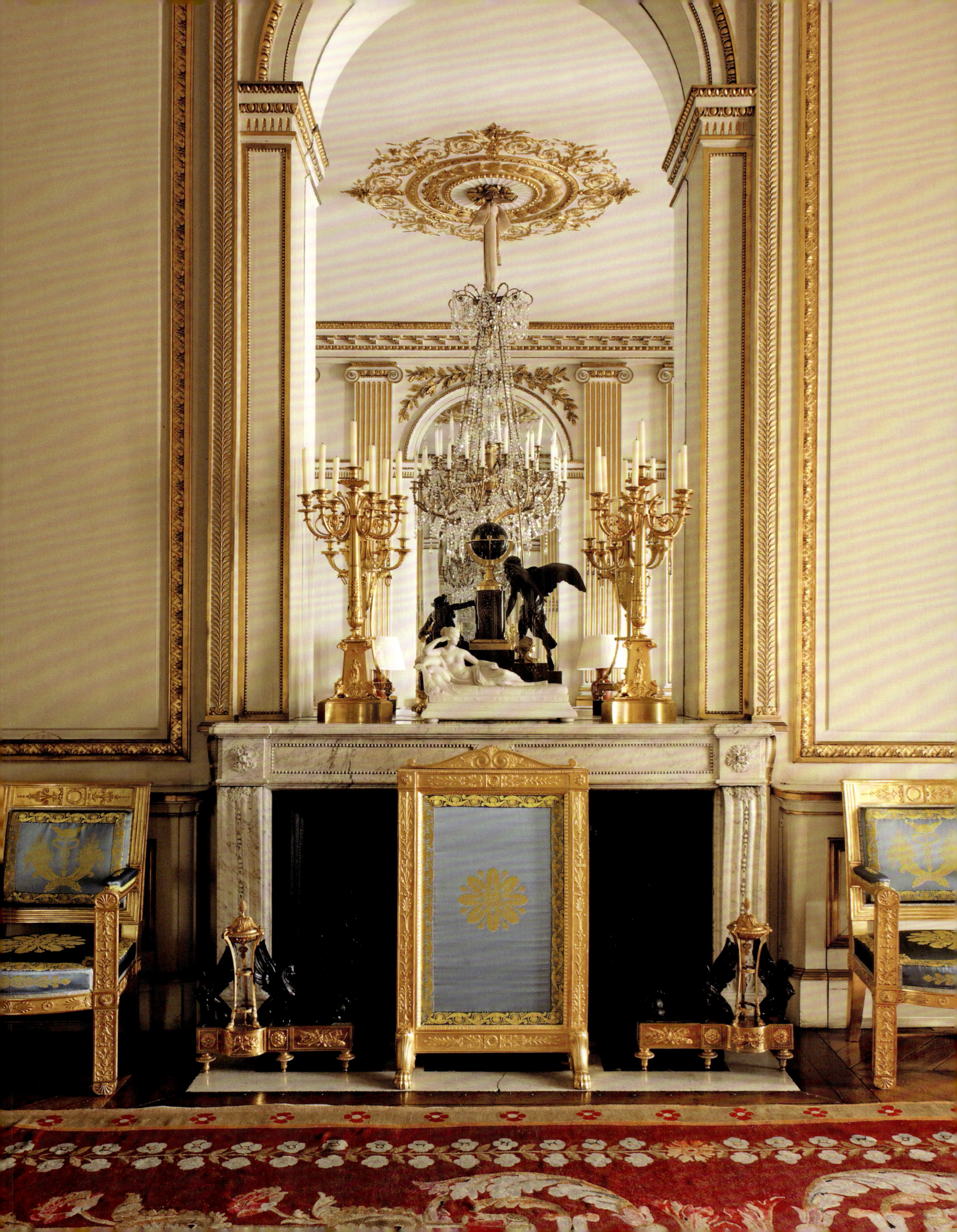

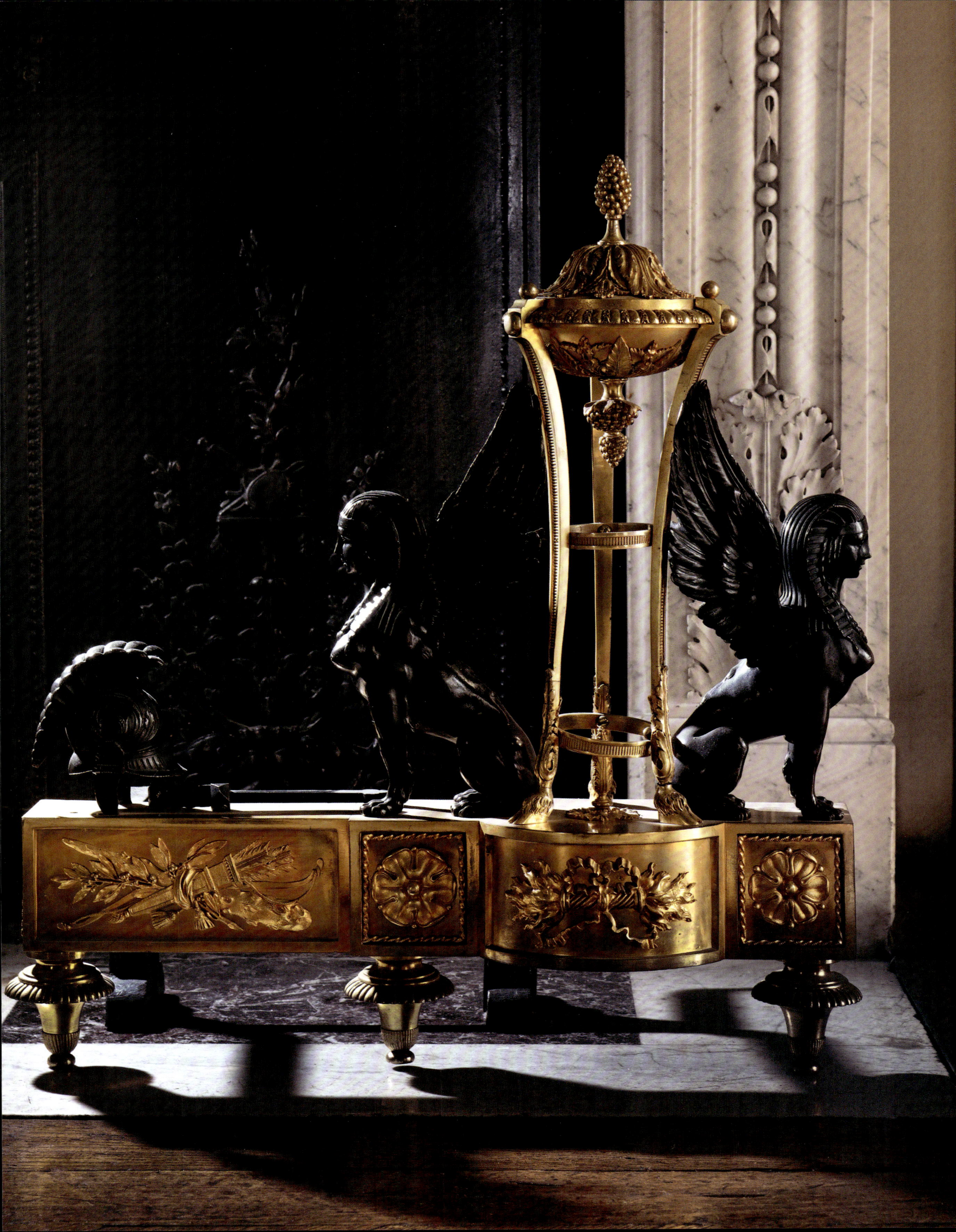

The furniture in the Salon Pauline reflects the vogue for Egyptian motifs as a result of Napoleon's Egyptian campaign of 1798–1801, made popular by the publication of the drawings in Dominique Vivant Denon's 1802 *Voyage dans la Haute et la Basse Égypte*. *Page 96:* The chimneypiece in the Salon Pauline. The overmantel is a sheet of glass, looking into the Salon Bleu. In Pauline Borghese's day, this was a two-way mirror, allowing her to review unseen the courtiers waiting to see her in the salon next door. *Page 97:* The firedogs in the Salon Pauline are among the finest Empire bronzes in the house. In the form of tripods flanked by winged sphinxes, they attest to the richness of every detail of Pauline Borghese's furnishings. *Above:* A stern Egyptian maiden guards the magnificent bed of Pauline Borghese. *Facing page:* Another view of the bed, showing the rich hangings of blue and white silk, powdered with golden rosettes.

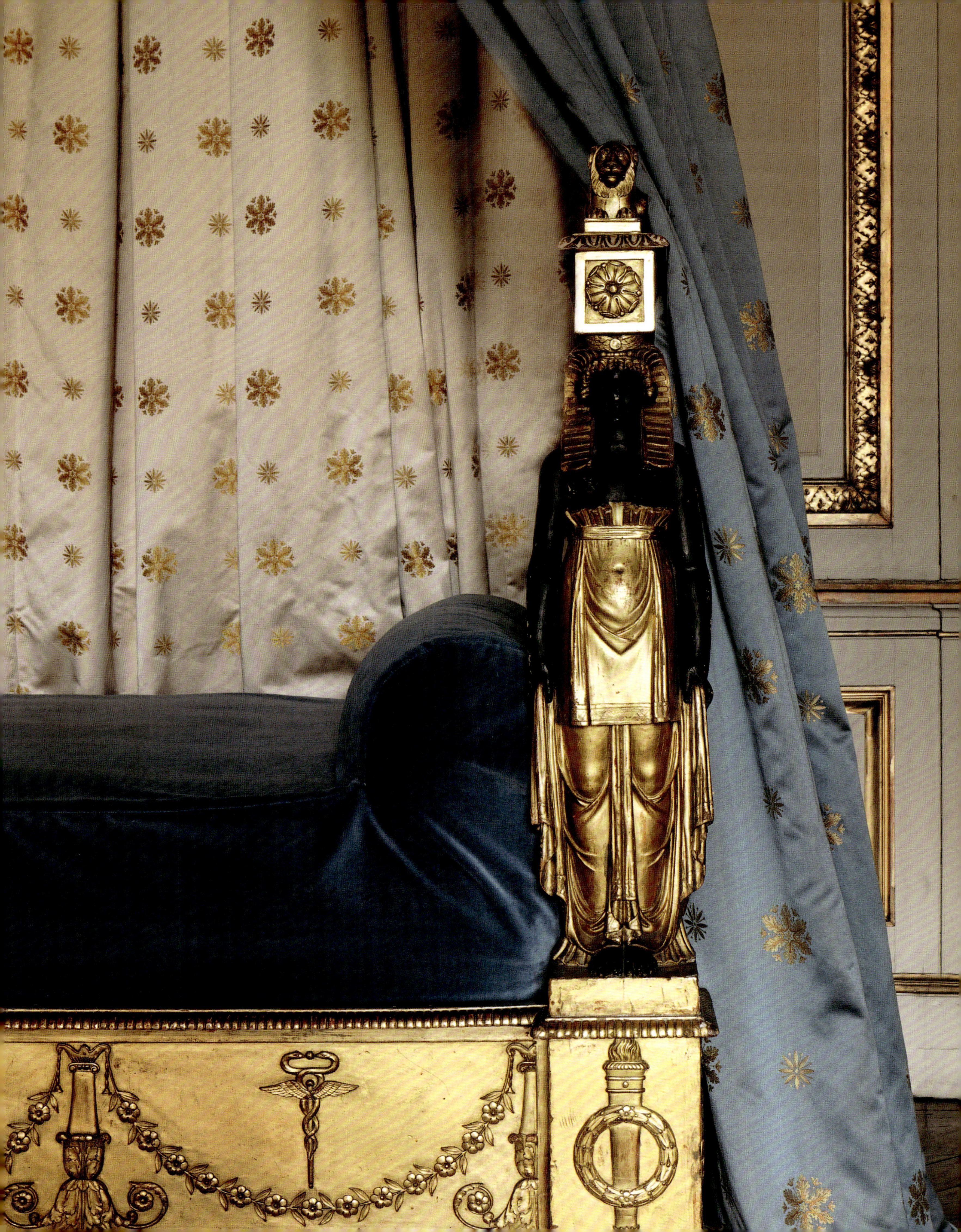

THRONE ROOM

Now part of the Ballroom, in 1737, the Throne Room was described as the 'Cabinet doré à la niche' with a bed in the alcove. The 1787 inventory describes the alcove as being embellished with *rocaille*, or grotto-work, surmounted by a mosaic of garlands of flowers. There were also two large, arched pier glasses, over nine feet tall, in three parts, decorated with clusters of rods, garlands of flowers, palm leaves surmounted by horns of plenty and scrolling foliage. Above the doors, set in rich gilt frames, were mythological scenes painted in the manner of François Boucher.

All this must have been swept away by Pauline Borghese, whose Boudoir Violet occupied this part of the house. It became the Throne Room in about 1834, but the present decoration must date from the same time as Etienne Raveau's remodelling of the Ballroom, during the embassy of Earl Cowley in 1862. The columned screen, with elaborate garlanded columns — of a composite order unknown to the ancients — occupies the site of the original bed alcove.

Within the alcove sits a gilded throne on a stepped dais. The throne was bought in 1842 from an upholsterer in Old Bond Street, London, to replace a chair that the previous ambassador, Lord Granville, had removed as being his own property. The canopy of state is later, but incorporates an earlier embroidered coat of arms that may be eighteenth century. The complete ensemble of dais, throne and canopy is a survival of the ancient tradition of equipping ambassadors with a cloth of state, along with a throne, two stools and a foot stool, as symbols of the monarch they represent. The room is still used for investitures on behalf of the monarch.

The crimson brocatelle wall-hangings date from 1904–05 and are the oldest wall coverings in the house, while the worn Aubusson carpet incorporates the royal arms of Queen Victoria, who is also represented by a portrait of her in coronation robes by Sir George Hayter, a plaster bust by Edward Onslow-Ford, and by the 'VR' monograms on the mirrors and furniture.

The silver-gilt communion plate in the glass case was made by Joseph Angell in 1825 and supplied to the Embassy Chapel in that year. Its fitted travelling trunk is still preserved, bearing the label 'His Britannick Majesty's Embassy at the Court of France. Chapel Plate.' The set includes a pair of flagons, two communion cups and four paten, as well as '1 spoon to take the flies out of the wine'. The plate is still used on special occasions at St Michael's, the local English church in Paris.

Facing page: The gilded throne, bought in London in 1842, sits beneath its original canopy of state in the Throne Room. The empty throne represents the absent monarch at state occasions and investitures.

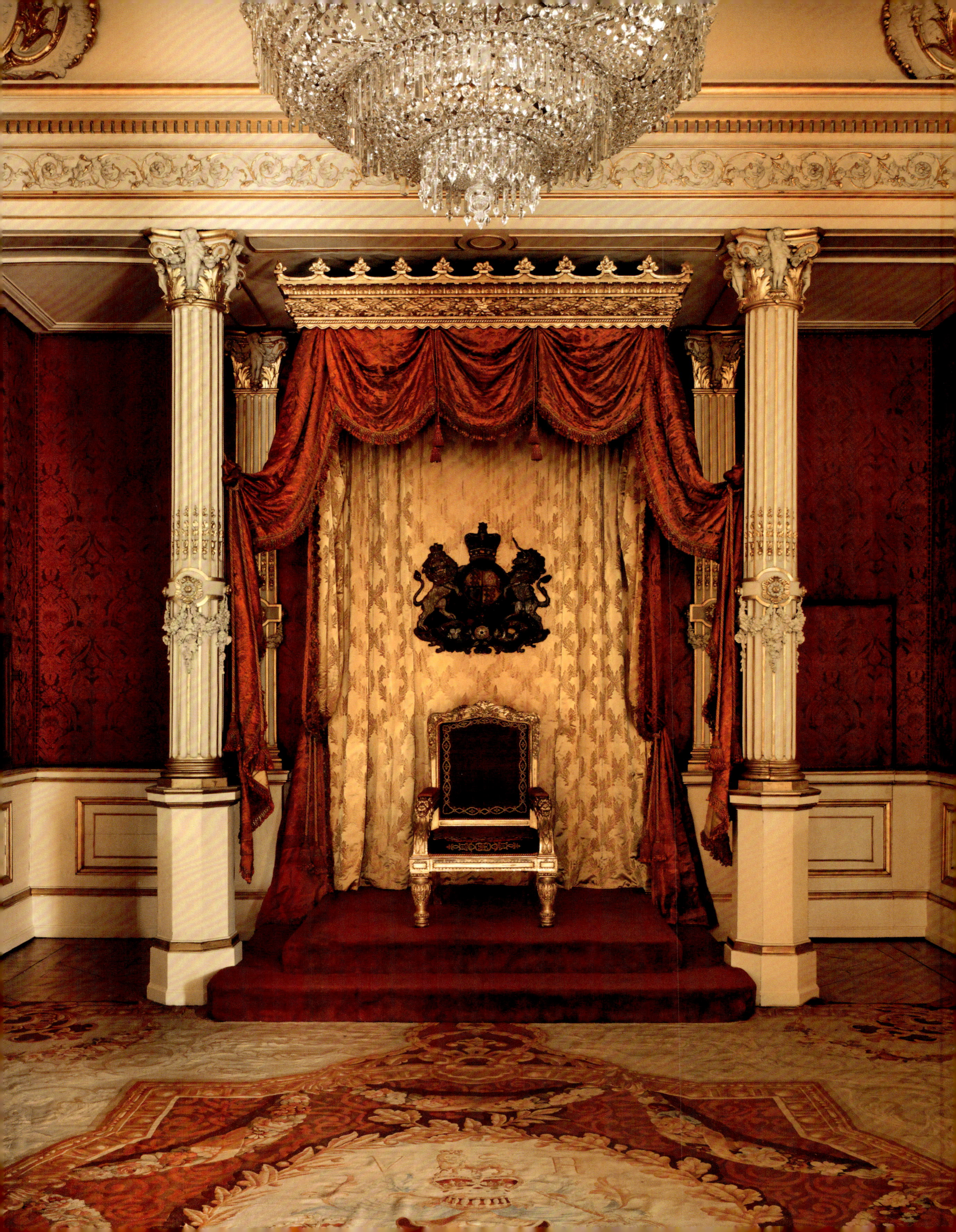

Above: Detail of the elaborate braid or passementerie of the canopy of state in the Throne Room. The canopy is a mid-nineteenth-century creation, possibly incorporating an earlier royal coat of arms. *Facing page:* The screen of columns in the Throne Room dates from Earl Cowley's improvements of 1862. This is a detail of the garlanded feature adorning the shaft of the column.

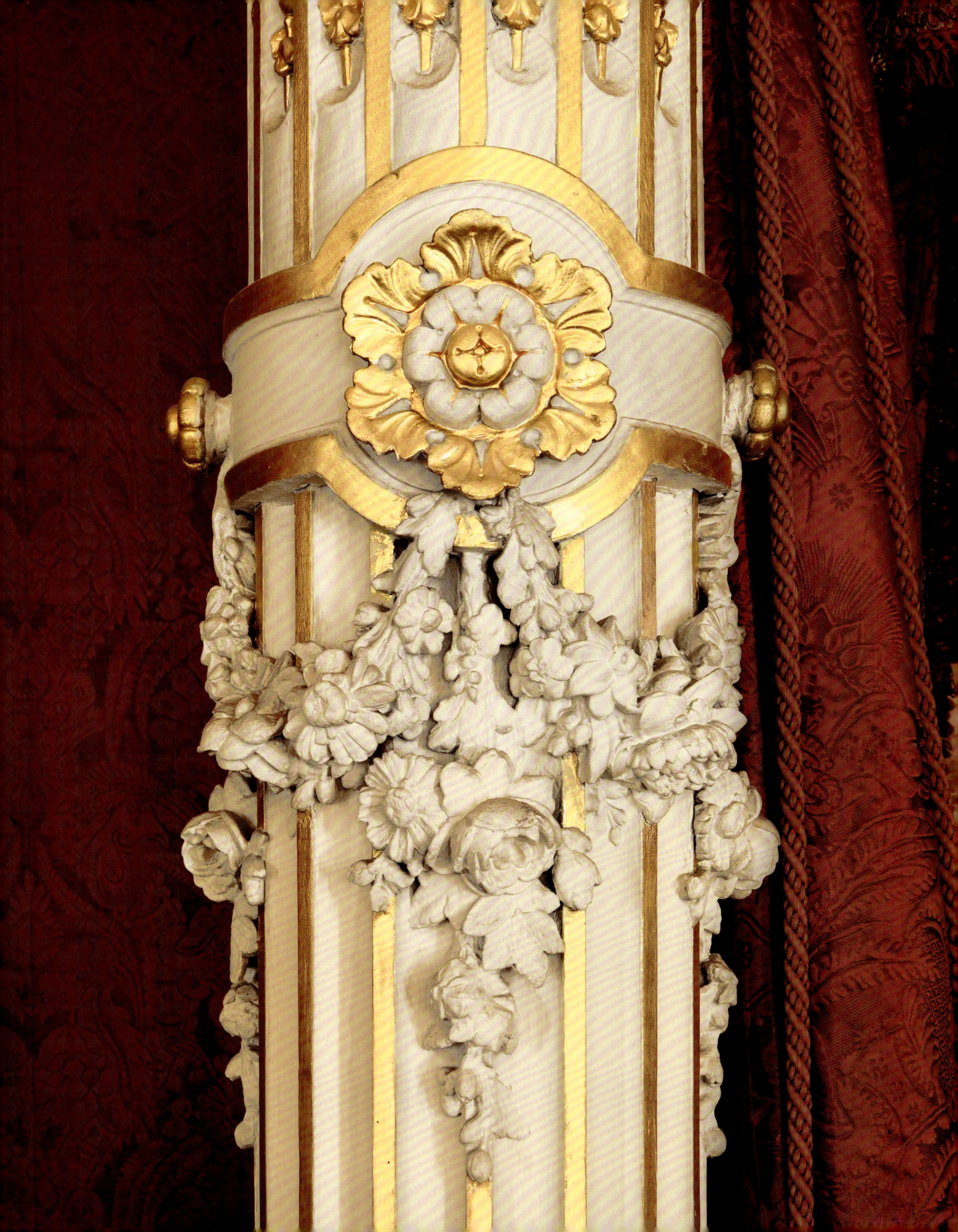

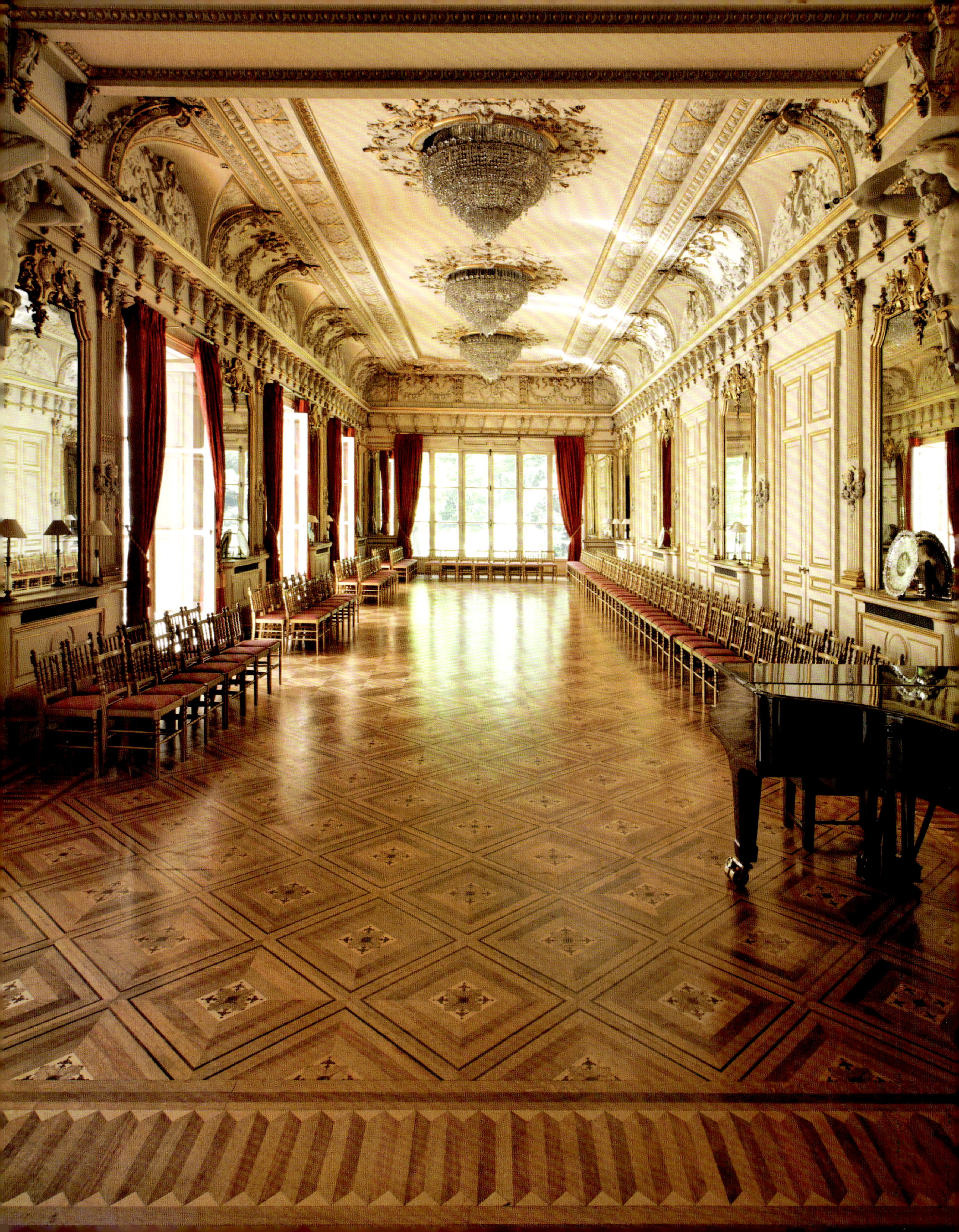

BALLROOM

One of the showiest rooms of the house, the Ballroom stands on the site of the Picture Gallery and Petit Salon, erected here in 1809 by Pauline Borghese's architect, Bénard. Little is known of the princess's collection of pictures, other than that it housed a collection of 175 Old Master paintings she had borrowed from the Borghese collection in Rome. The Picture Gallery was partly top-lit and tented with cotton cambric, while below were green velvet *portières*, or door curtains, and forty giltwood chairs upholstered to match, some of which still survive, reupholstered, in other parts of the house. The Petit Salon, which acted as an ante-room to the Picture Gallery, was lined with orange silk.

Both rooms, which had been hurriedly built, were already dilapidated by 1824, so were replaced by a ballroom, erected in 1825–26 by Louis Visconti for Lord Granville, who needed more space for the entertainments of his vivacious wife. One of her balls, Lady Granville recalled, lasted from two to six in the afternoon, and then, after a 'rest and refit … they came flocking back, set to and danced until twelve when I was obliged to drag them out of the ballroom to supper where they sat eating, drinking, shouting, till half past one'. Not much is known of the appearance of Granville's ballroom, other than it was hung with crimson silk and had a partly coffered ceiling. At a ball given by Lady Granville in the spring of 1839 in honour of Queen Victoria, all the guests, 'dowagers included', wore only pink and white.

By 1842, the Ballroom was damp and again showing its age, its crimson hangings faded. The architect Jacques Ignace Hittorf (1792–1867) (who built the Gare du Nord station) improved the ventilation and created the large windows at the north end, overlooking the garden. The Ballroom was regularly used as the Embassy Chapel in the time of Lord Normanby, but this combination of sacred and profane use was thought immoral by his successor, Earl Cowley. In 1862 he had the room remodelled by Etienne Raveau in an opulent Napoleon III style, the walls divided up by the sixteen miniature pilasters, which enclose mirrors, once placed against a foil of white-and-gold patterned brocatelle. Above lay an elaborate coving, with festoons, trophies of musical instruments and symbols of the arts. The chandeliers are by the firm of F. and C. Osler and Company in Birmingham, who specialised in producing grandiose cut-glass light-fittings, exporting many of them to maharajas' palaces in India. Among the room's most notable features is the superb parquet floor of coloured woods, which does wonders for the acoustics. Today, the room is constantly used for receptions, conferences, dinners and concerts, as well as the annual Christmas pantomime put on by Embassy staff. This is a continuation of an old

Facing page: The Ballroom was remodelled in 1825–26 by Louis Visconti during the embassy of Earl Granville, but most of the decoration was added in 1862 by Etienne Raveau for Earl Cowley.
Following pages: The Ballroom decorated for Christmas dinner.

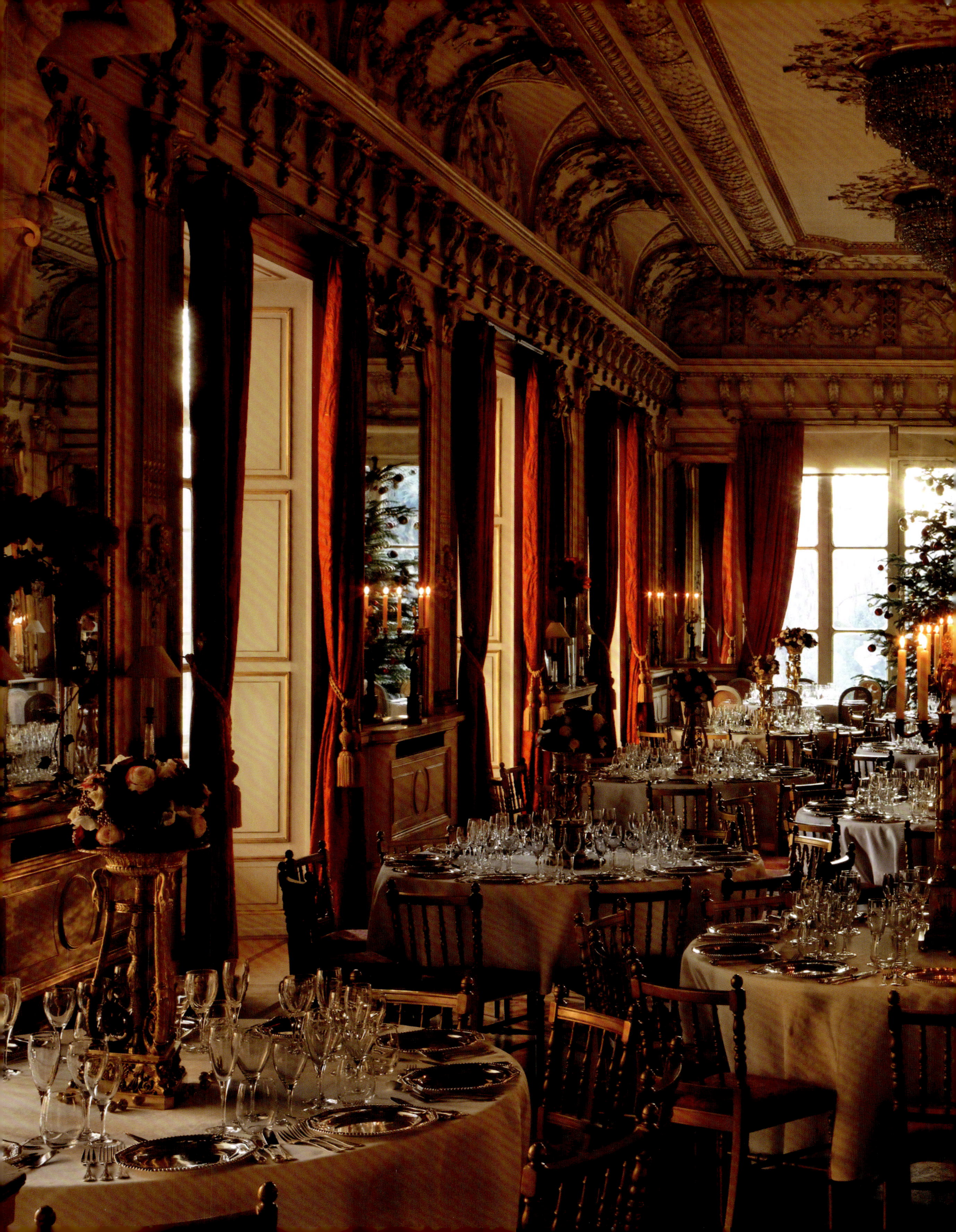

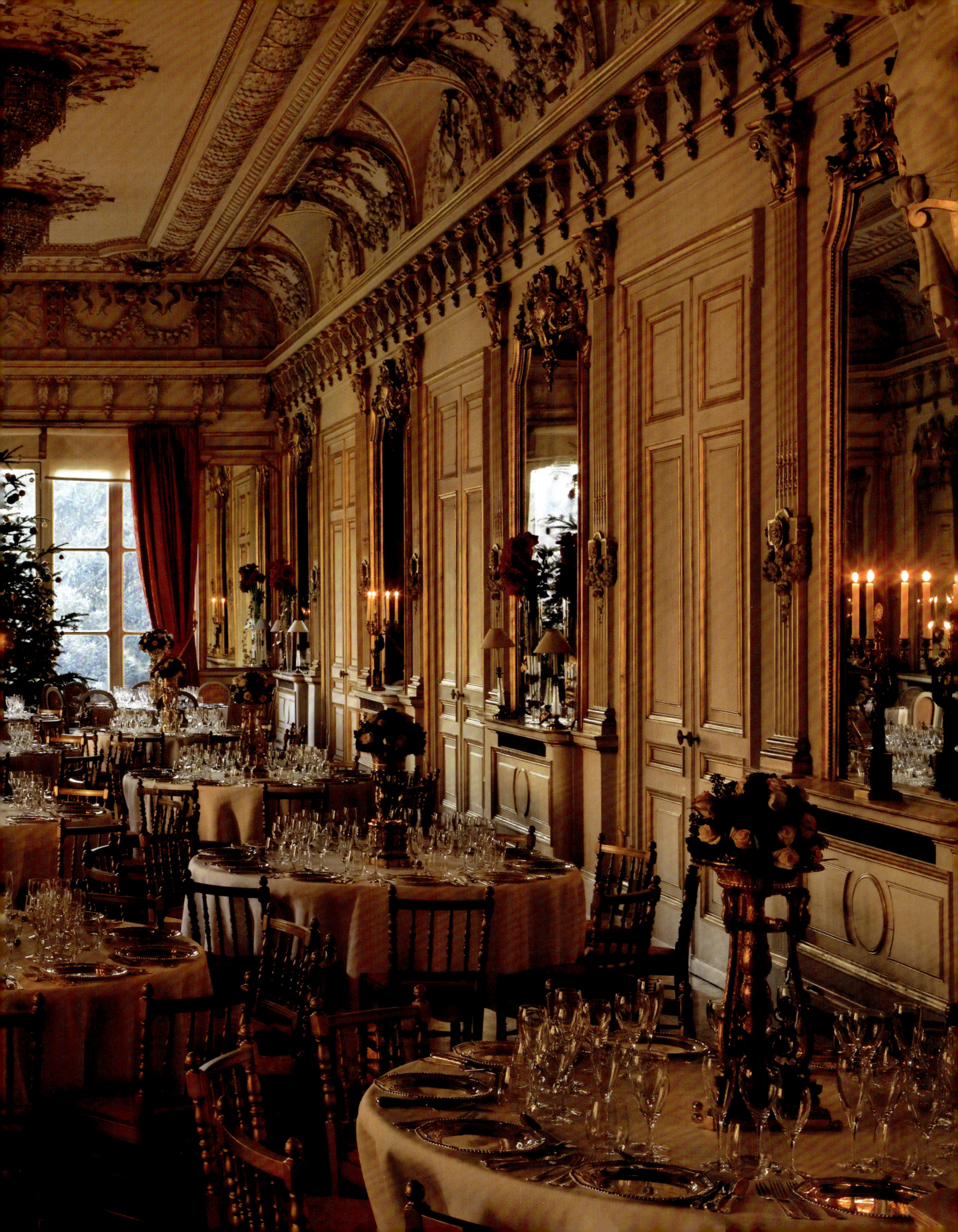

tradition: in December 1840 the ballroom was transformed into what was described by a contemporary as the 'prettiest little theatre you ever saw' for two performances of *The Wreck Ashore,* a popular play of the day. Charles Dickens gave public readings here from *Little Dorritt* and *The Pickwick Papers* to benefit the British Charitable Fund in 1863, and in May 1891, Lord Lytton organised a private performance by the Comédie-Française. The Ballroom was put to still stranger use by Sir Oliver and Lady Harvey, who arrived at the Embassy in 1948. When it was discovered that they had marked out a badminton court in white paint on the parquet floor of the Ballroom, Lady Harvey was rebuked and the damage made good.

Above: The north end of the Ballroom — where it joins the Throne Room — is embellished with consoles in the form of *atlantes*, or brawny male architectural supports. *Facing page:* The endlessly reflected mirrors in the Ballroom, which bear Queen Victoria's cypher, 'VR', on their cresting. *Following pages:* A detail of the Ballroom ceiling, showing Etienne Raveau's elaborate plasterwork, and one of the three chandeliers by Osler.

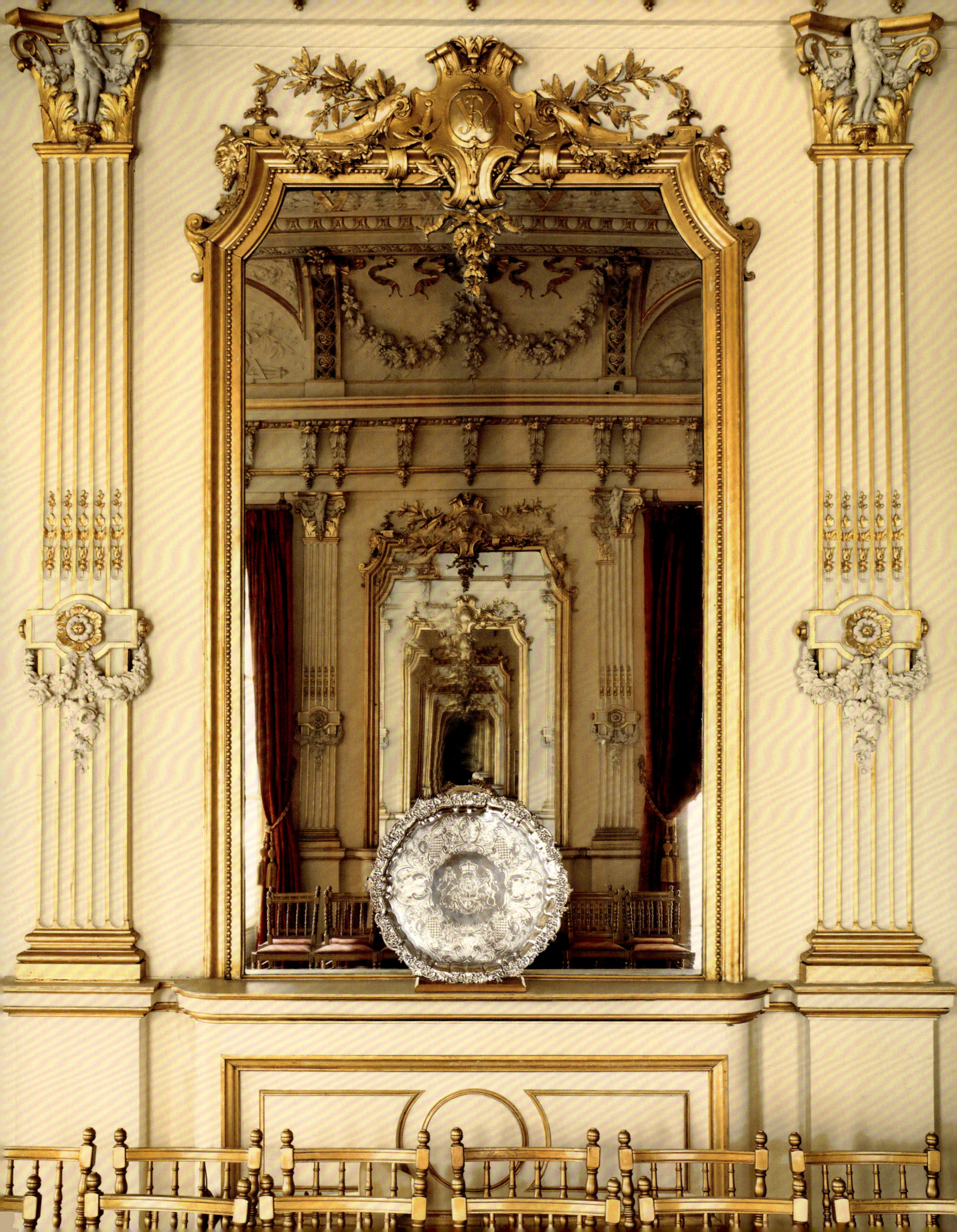

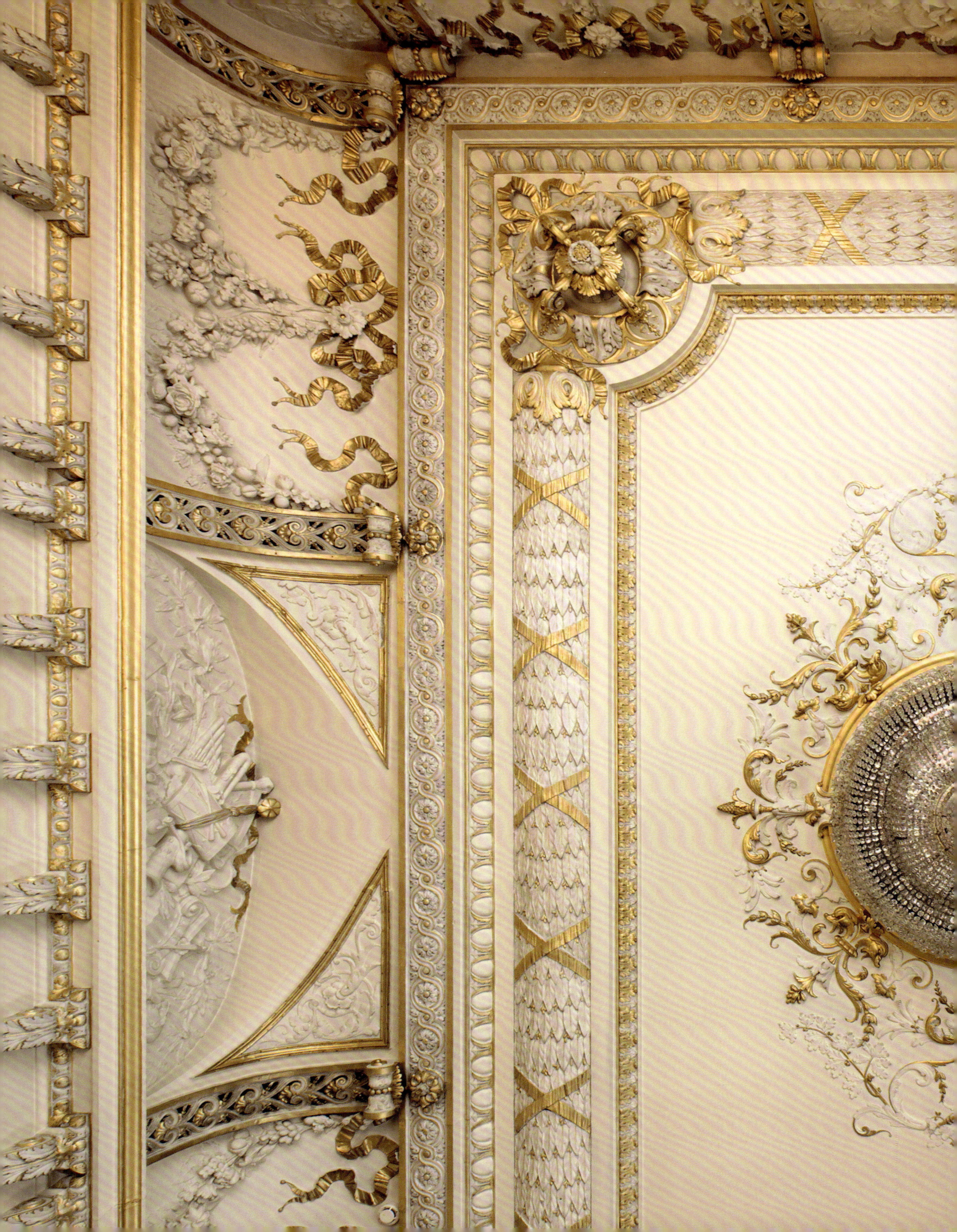

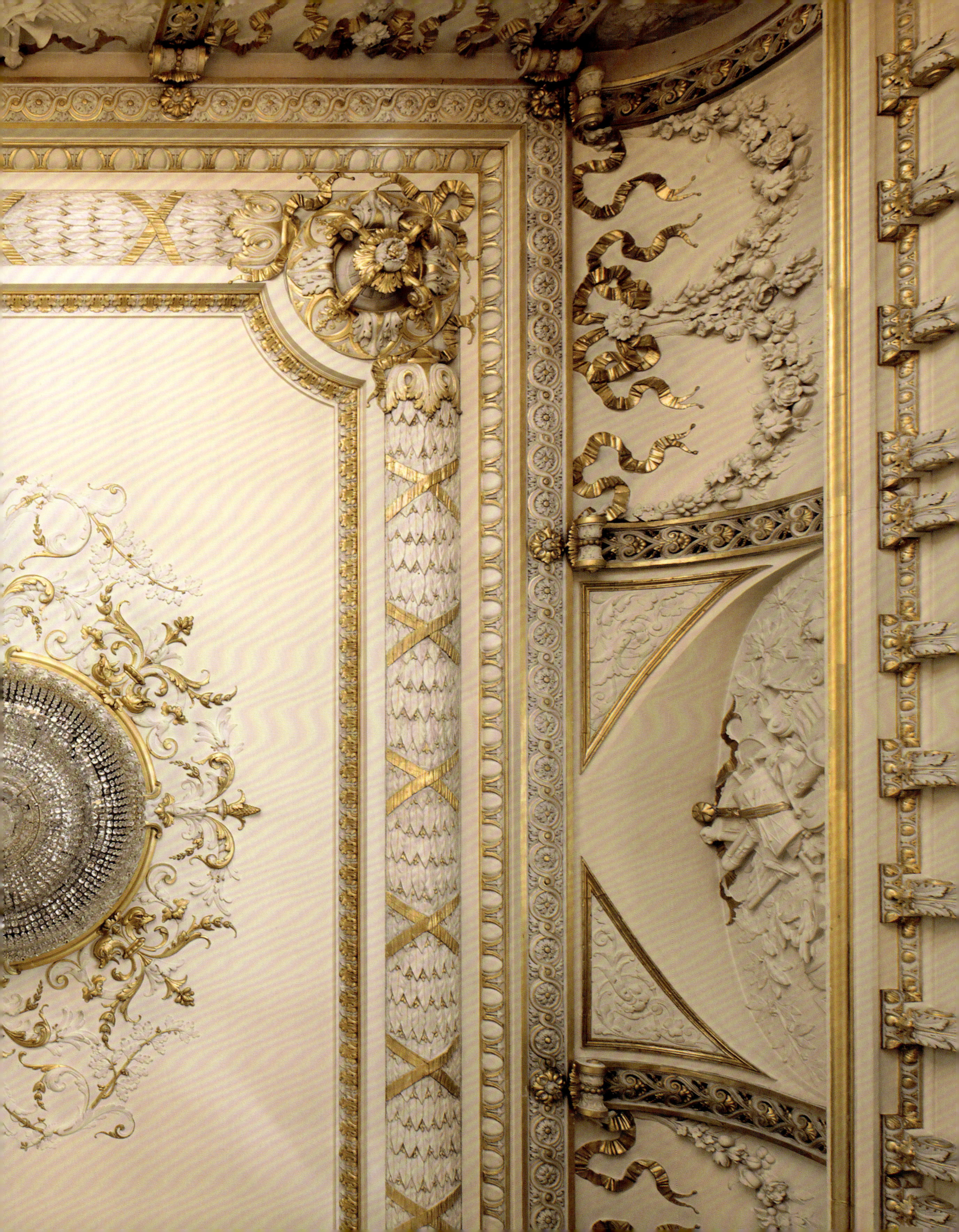

GALLERY

The Gallery that runs around the garden front of the house, between the wings containing the Ballroom and State Dining Room, is another addition of Lord and Lady Granville. Built to designs by Visconti in 1825–26, without permission from the Foreign Office (which blenched at the expense), it was an immediate success, with Lady Granville writing to a friend: 'The conservatory is quite beautiful. Antoine has brought oranges and fastened them among the orange trees, the effect of this little contrivance is quite enchanting. The conservatory now it is finished with its divans and carpet looks exactly like a very comfortable gallery.' Lady Granville filled it with plants — 'a little grove of orange trees and lilacs, a large basketful of moss and violets on the table, and all along the gallery I look down, every flower of the Spring' — but for grand balls the windows were taken out of the Ballroom and salons and the Gallery was treated as part of the house, accommodating 'five or six hundred, even when half open'. Photographs taken in 1903 show the Gallery lined with urns containing citrus and palms, and crammed with gilded and upholstered furniture.

Today the furnishings and decoration of the Gallery are more restrained. Since 1997, it has been kept as a light-filled setting for a rotating display of works by contemporary British artists from the Government Art Collection. This is part of its mission of promoting British art in government buildings in the UK and abroad. Temporary exhibits have included pieces by Damien Hirst, Julian Opie and Rachel Whiteread. More permanent residents include *Embassy I* and *II*, a pair of light-boxes by Catherine Yass commissioned in 1998–99, with backlit colour transparencies of the Residence garden by day and evening. Just as in Lady Granville's time, the Gallery is in constant use for receptions and other functions. In summer and autumn, its huge French windows provide easy access to the magnificent Residence garden.

Facing page: The Gallery. Rachel Whiteread's *Monument*, a model for her installation on the Fourth Plinth in Trafalgar Square in 2001.

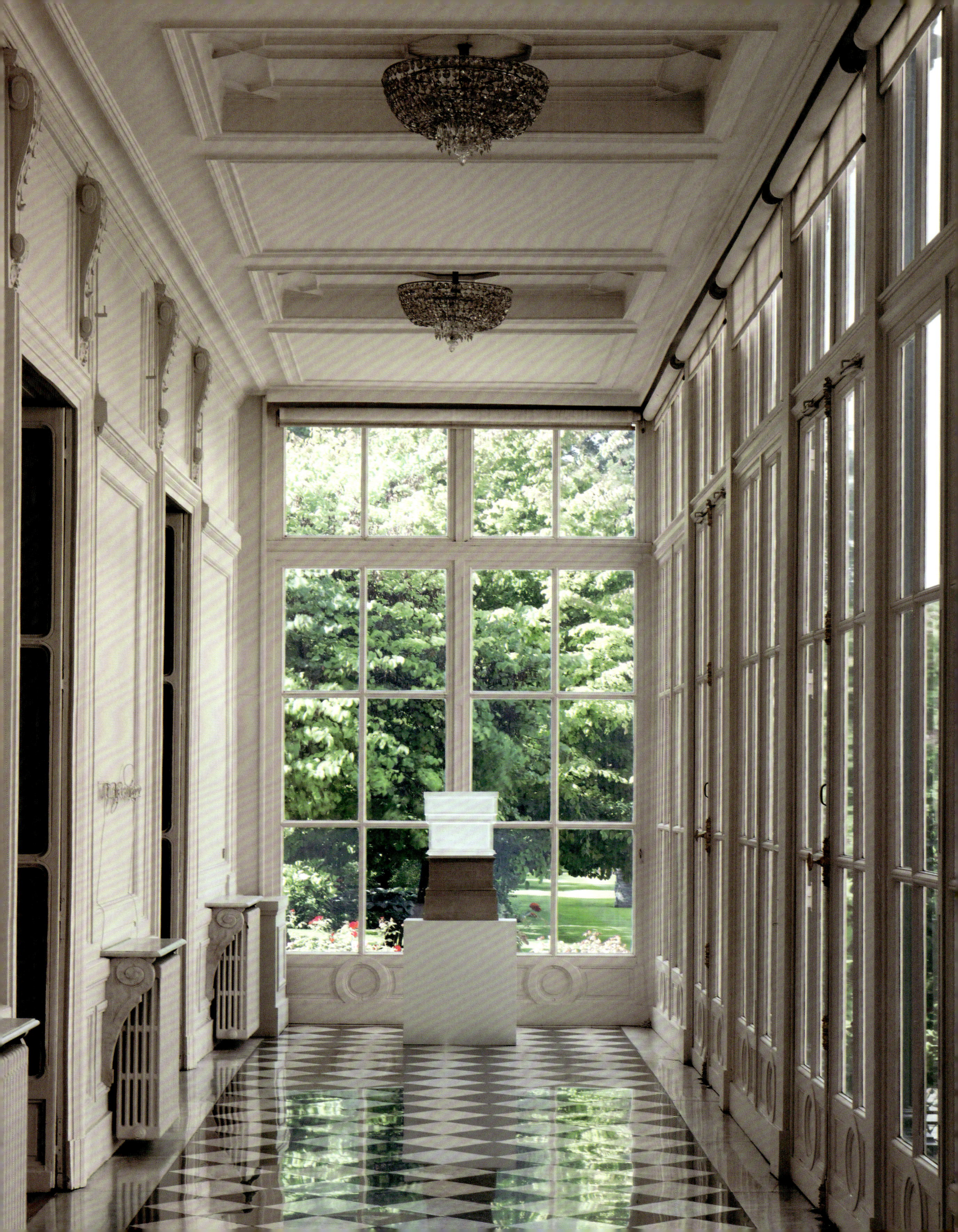

CATHERINE YASS
EMBASSY (DAY) 1999, EMBASSY (EVENING) 1999

Playing with our sense of time and space, *Embassy (day)* and *Embassy (evening)*, by Catherine Yass (b. 1963), depict the back of the Residence, including the Gallery, as viewed from the garden. Framed by the foliage of a mature tree, the neo-classical façade is a ghostly apparition set against a vivid blue sky. Rising from the lawn in the mid-distance of each image is *The Extended Shadow* (1994), a sculpture by Shirazeh Houshiary.

In 1998, the Government Art Collection, in collaboration with the British Embassy, Paris, commissioned the artist Catherine Yass to produce two light-boxes of the garden and rear façade to complement *British Embassy in Paris from the Gardens*, a mid-nineteenth-century painting by an unknown artist, already displayed at the Residence. Yass spent a few days photographing the Residence, at different times of the day and in different weather conditions. She set out to produce twilight images of the garden, to capture a fleeting moment between day and night, in which a blue sky and an illuminated building interior co-existed. In the winter of 1999, a fierce storm destroyed the large overhanging trees depicted in the light-boxes, thereby making Yass's images important historical records of what had once been there sooner than anticipated.

Yass creates photographic light-boxes using a particular artistic process that she has explored in her work since the early 1990s. She photographs a subject twice, often mere moments apart. Two colour transparencies, one positive and one negative, are then superimposed on to a light-box. In *Embassy (day)* and *Embassy (evening)*, this results in startling, even unnerving, images of what are otherwise faithful depictions of the building's grandeur. Despite the stillness of each scene, the superimposition of transparencies creates subtle ripples of movement. In *Embassy (day)*, the leaves of the overhanging tree seem to shift slightly in the breeze, while dappled shadows shimmer on the lawn. In both works, Yass suggests the dual relationships between what we see and what we feel, by pondering on the relationship between reality and illusion.

Above and facing page: Embassy (evening) and Embassy (day), 1999. Text by Chantal Condron

115

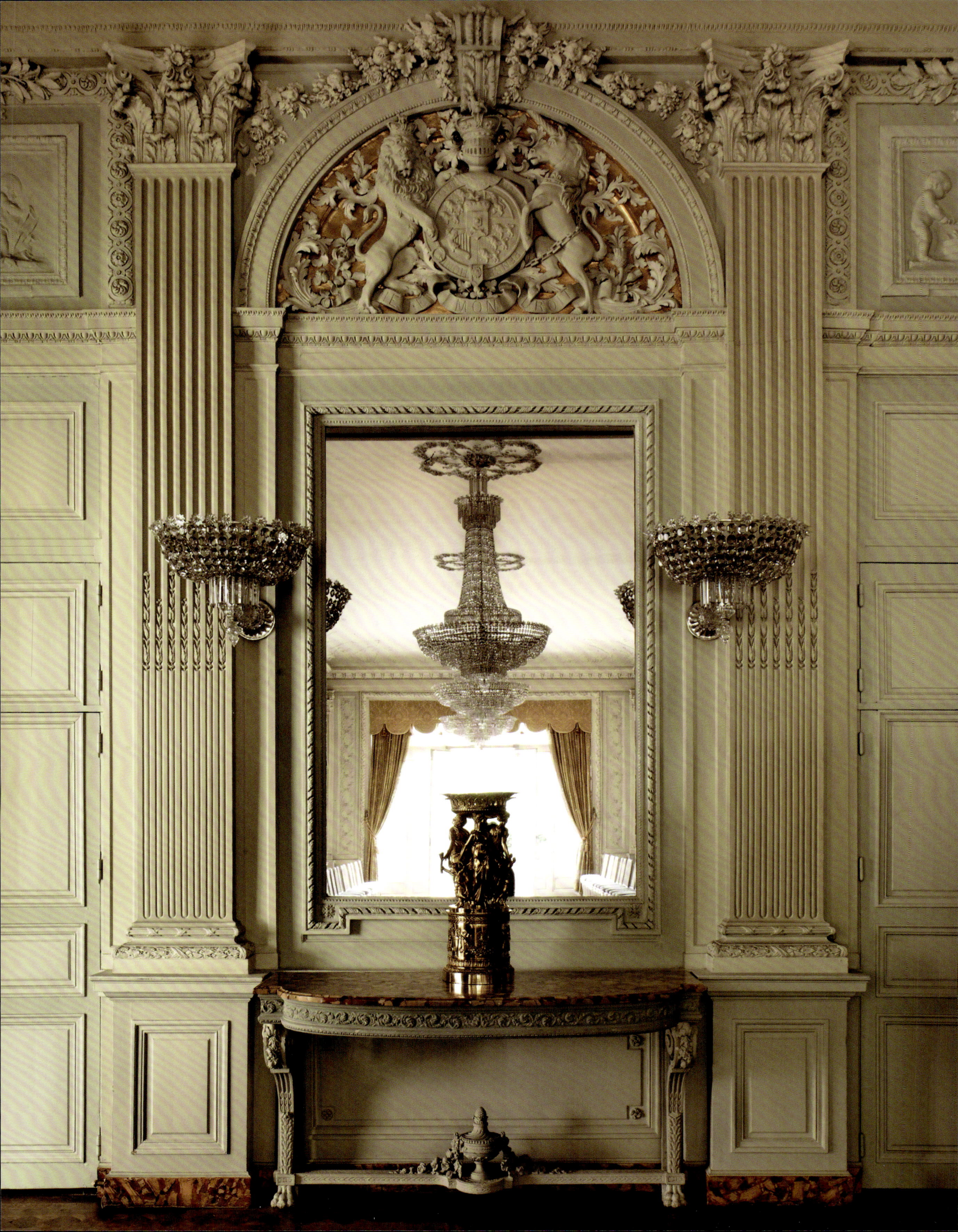
MON

STATE DINING ROOM

One of the additions made by Bénard in 1809, the State Dining Room, was used for the same purpose by Pauline Borghese. Like her Picture Gallery, it was top-lit and hung with cotton cambric like a tent. Of the original furnishings, the long mahogany table and sixty mahogany chairs with red leather seats have disappeared, as have the fourteen mahogany *servantes* or 'dinner wagons' and three matching armchairs. Gone, too, are the thirty-two round cushions with speckled velvet-pile covers and four pairs of candelabra borne by bronze Egyptian figures. Only one of the two original gilt-bronze chandeliers survives, now hanging in the Salon Vert.

The State Dining Room was entirely rebuilt by Visconti in 1825 as a long room with full-length windows down the west side, opening onto the Gallery. To the north lay the Small Dining Room, now the Pantry. In 1852, at the behest of the pious Earl Cowley, Benedict Albano converted both dining rooms into the Embassy Chapel, capable of accommodating five hundred people, with the altar on a velvet-covered dais between them and the congregation split on either side on benches. The ambassador and his family sat in a screened-off corner of the Small Dining Room. Later, between 1860 and 1864, after a visit from Queen Victoria, the State Dining Room was returned to its original purpose. The work was entrusted to Etienne Raveau, who covered the walls with a combination of imitation marble and panels of crimson silk, with matching curtains. Three Victorian lustres by F. and C. Osler and Company supplanted Pauline's gilt-bronze chandeliers.

The present decoration of the State Dining Room dates from about 1903 and was prepared for the visit of King Edward VII in May that year. The architect was Vye Parminter, assisted by Georges Hoentschel of Maison Leys, who installed plasterwork in the style of a Louis XVI panelled salon, possibly incorporating some earlier elements, such as the royal arms on the north wall. The greenish-grey paintwork is a near-replica of the Edwardian scheme, reinstated in twelve subtly differing tones, with gilded grounds to the trophies over the windows and doors.

The State Dining Room is best appreciated when in use for receptions or dinners, when it can accommodate up to one hundred twenty guests. On rare state occasions the magnificent ormolu centrepiece or *surtout de table* is used, a long mirrored plateau with gilt-bronze enrichments on which

Facing page: The north end of the State Dining Room with the royal arms of George III in gilded plaster puzzlingly incorporated into the Edwardian decor of the State Dining Room. *Following pages:* The State Dining Room. The dining table can accommodate fifty-eight people, and is laid with the magnificent Empire *surtout de table* which has been at the Embassy since the early nineteenth century. The table is laid as for a State Dinner for display on Patrimony Day.

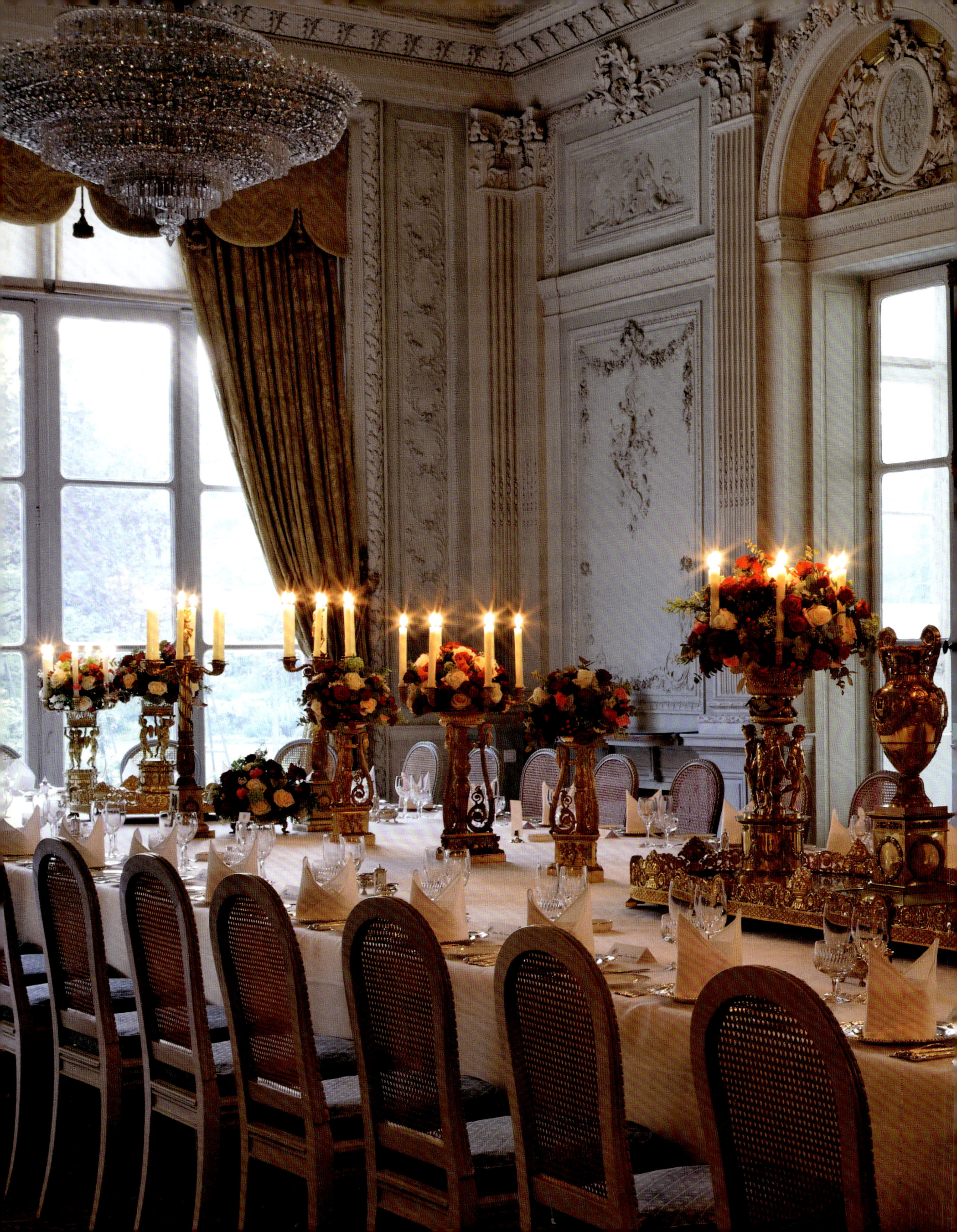

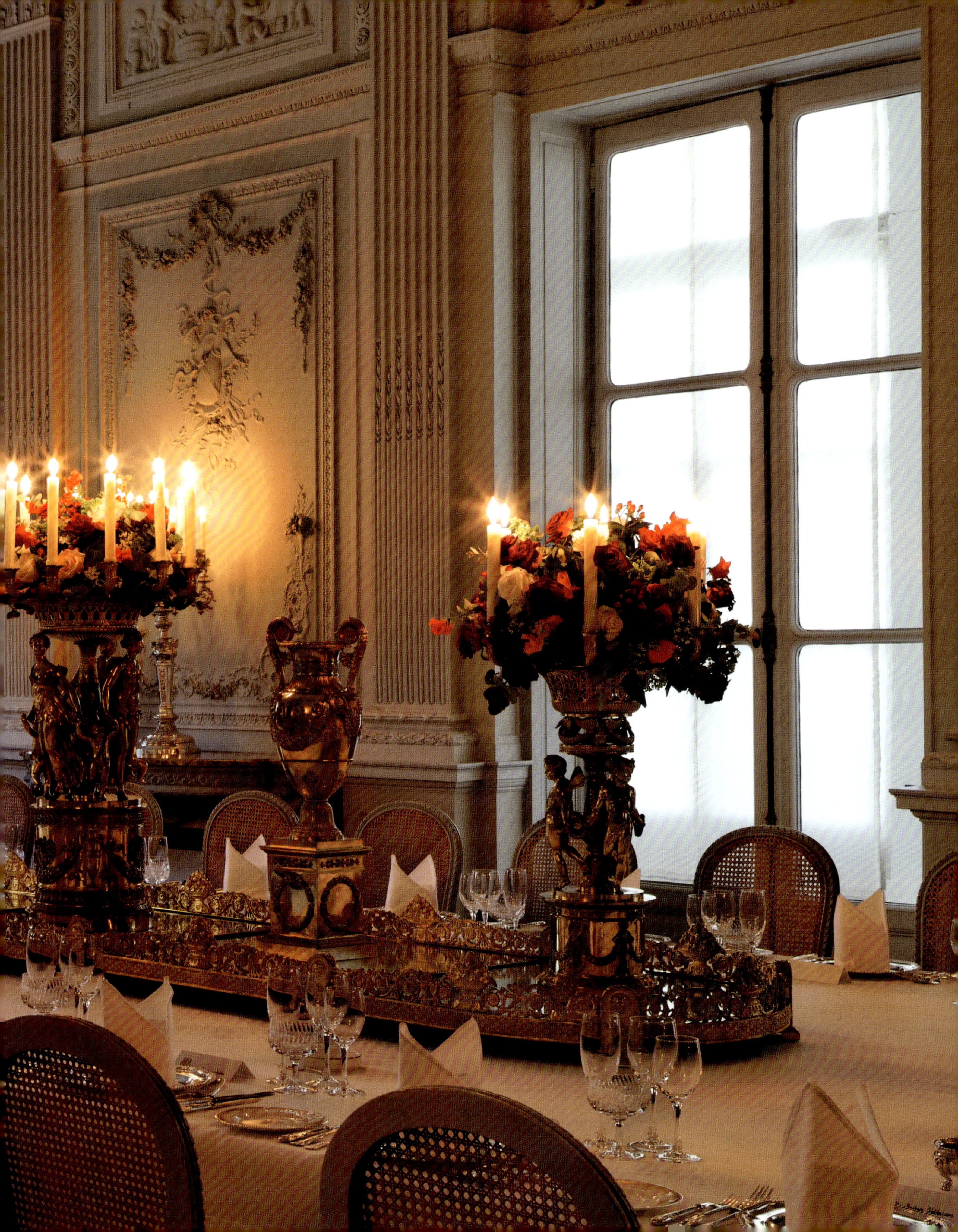

stand a garniture of ormolu candelabra and vases, incorporating baskets for flowers or fruit, upheld by figures of the seasons or dancing zephyrs. Although contemporary with Pauline Borghese and of high quality — parts of the *surtout* are by the great Pierre Philippe Thomire (1751–1843) — it must have been acquired for the Embassy later, by one of the early ambassadors, such as Lord Stuart de Rothesay or, more probably, Lord Granville. Nor is it a complete set, for it includes stands from another dessert service and several later pieces.

The dazzling centrepiece is supplemented by the Embassy silver, much of it supplied in 1825 to Lord Granville by P. R. Gilbert, goldsmith to the king, at a cost of about £8,000. The service includes two massive tureens made by Robert Hennell in 1824, who also made a silver-gilt salver and one of the two pairs of ice pails — the other pair is by Craddock and Reid. There are also silver fruit baskets by John Moore. The larger pieces bear the royal arms and are engraved with the words 'His Brittanick Majesty's Embassy at the Court of France'. Additional plate was supplied in 1867 by Garrard and Co.

Above: A detail of the plasterwork in the State Dining Room. This clever Edwardian pastiche of a Louis XVI salon was installed in 1903 to celebrate the state visit of King Edward VII. *Facing page:* A flower stand from the *surtout de table*. This impressive ormolu casting, with its dancing zephyrs and swans holding garlands in their beaks, is one of several flower stands in the garniture — masterpieces by Thomire.

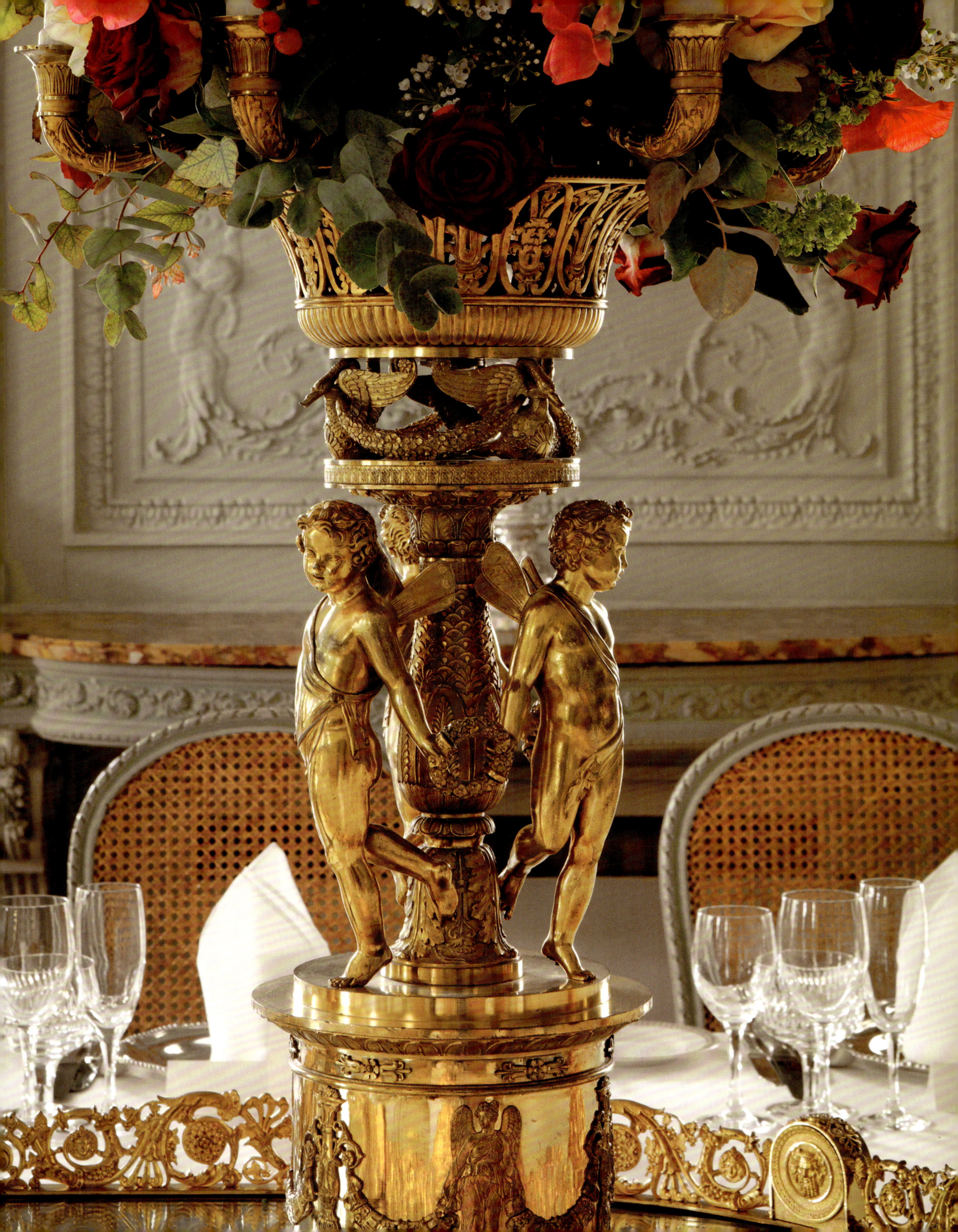

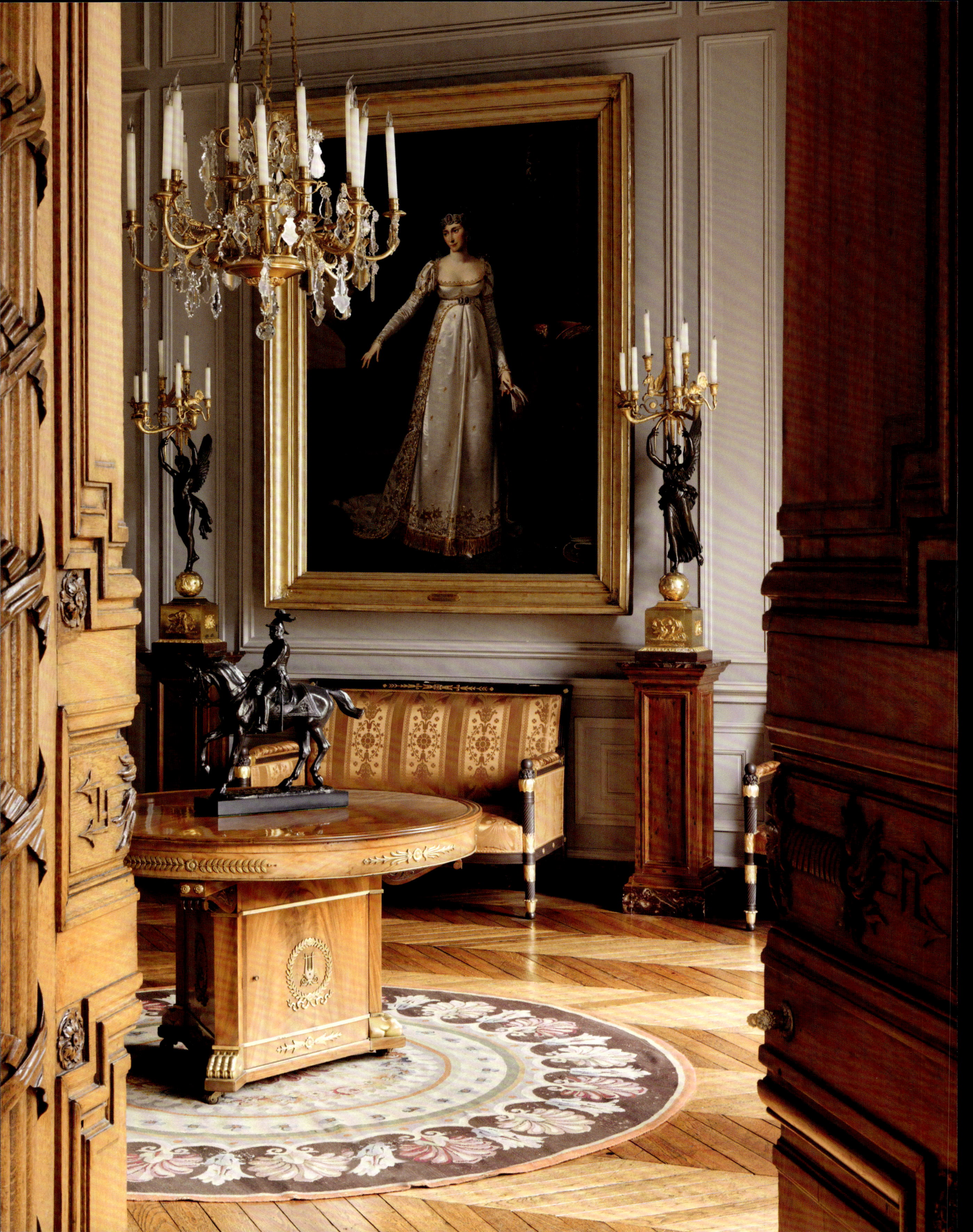

ANTE-ROOM

The Ante-Room is located at the top of the grand Staircase. It is entered through a gigantic oak door, carved with a bundle of javelins surmounted by a helm, flanked by wreaths of laurel and winged thunderbolts, and which remains exactly as described in the 1787 inventory. The martial trophies were appropriate, for this was the front door of two sets of apartments on the first floor, those of the head of the family and his eldest son, although after the marriage of the 5th duc de Charost in 1760, these upstairs apartments were largely abandoned until the house was let to the comte de La Marck and his family in 1785.

In the eighteenth century, the Ante-Room was a simple room that led to the duc's apartments overlooking the garden, and his son's overlooking the courtyard. Even Pauline Borghese furnished it with plain mahogany furniture, such as the console table presently between the windows. The wall panelling must date from the 1904–05 remodelling, when the chimneypiece was removed and the stone floor replaced by parquet.

The room was redecorated in 1985 on the advice of David Mlinaric, who painted the Edwardian panelling in shades of grey, combined with curtains and upholstery of brown damask, woven to an Empire pattern of 1802 used at the château de Saint-Cloud. The set of seat furniture, with supports in the form of a thyrsus, or Bacchic wand, was once entirely gilded and is probably the suite, upholstered with blue silk, recorded in the bedchamber of Pauline Borghese on this floor — now the Salon Vert. The suite was probably designed by Pierre Gaston Brion; similar suites can be seen at the château de Fontainebleau and the Grand Trianon. The two pairs of ormolu candelabra supported by balletic figures of Apollo and Aurora stand on griotte marble bases decorated with gilt-bronze reliefs of Jupiter and Ganymede and Jupiter and Leda, with Gallic cockerels attacking the serpent candle branches. Another cockerel, flanked by upright torches symbolising the dawn, decorates the plinth of the clock, *L'Étude* ('Study') by Vaillant, which also belonged to Pauline. This originally stood in her *chambre de parade*, (now the Salon Pauline) on the ground floor. The English writing desk and the centre table supporting William Goscombe John's bronze statuette of Edward VII on horseback are later introductions. The table stands on the central medallion cut from a large Savonnerie carpet.

The room is dominated by Robert Lefèvre's 1808 full-length portrait of Pauline, depicted looking wistfully at a marble bust of her powerful brother. A version of a portrait by Lefèvre in the musée de Versailles, it appears to be one of a group of portraits of the imperial family acquired by Field Marshal Blücher after the looting of the château de Saint-Cloud by Prussian troops during the occupation of Paris after the Battle of Waterloo. On the adjacent wall is an 1814 portrait of the Duke of Wellington by Baron Gérard. A pupil of Jacques Louis David, Gérard was a favourite portrait

Facing page: The Ante-Room on the first floor of the Residence. Its comparatively sober decor is compensated for by this imposing full-length portrait of Pauline Borghese, appropriately displayed surrounded by furniture and bronzes from her collection.

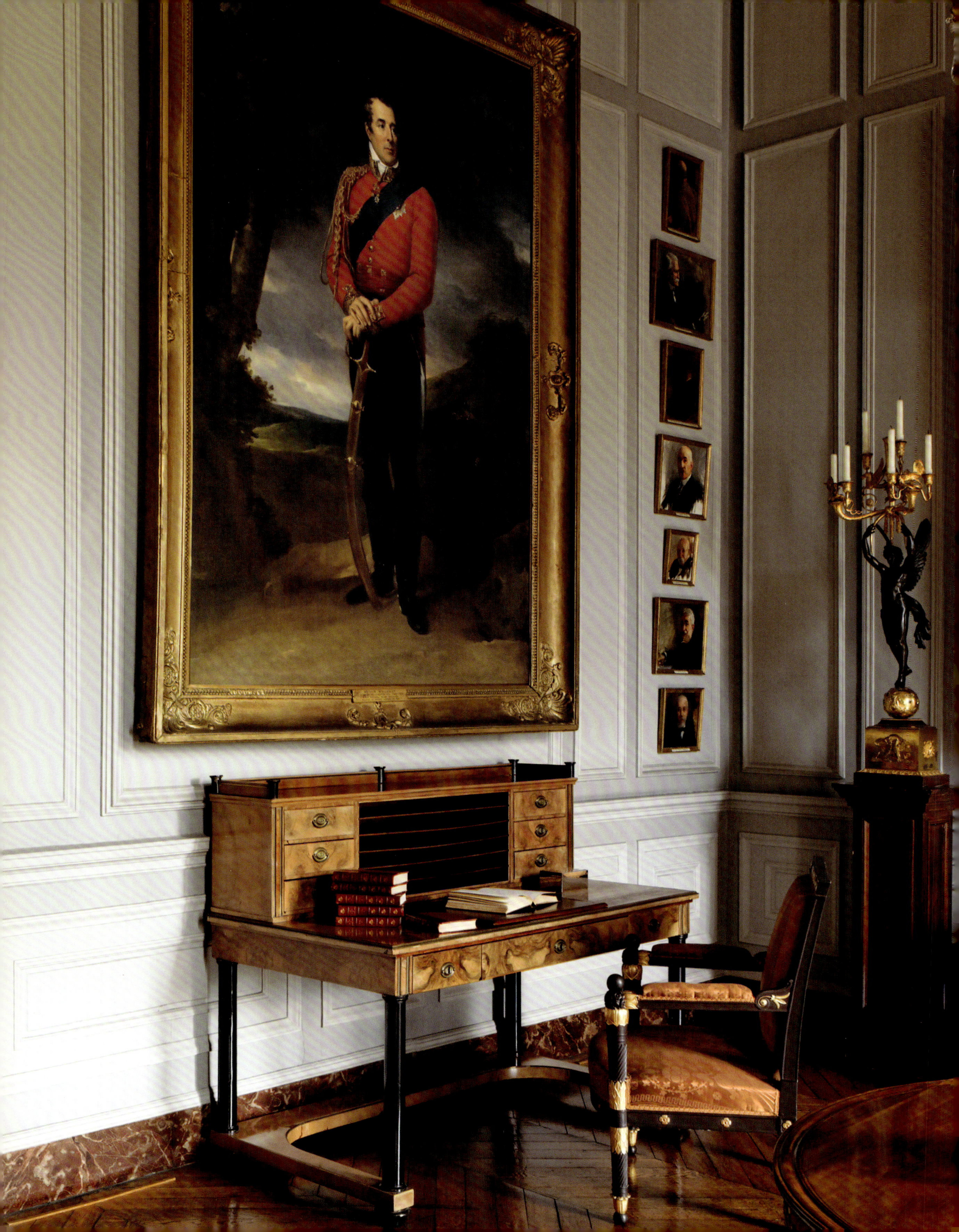

painter of the court of Napoleon, who transferred his allegiance to the Bourbons during the Restoration, becoming official painter to Louis XVIII. Wellington probably sat to Gérard in late 1814, shortly after taking up his post as ambassador. He is shown wearing the star of the Order of the Garter and the Order of the Golden Fleece, although Gérard has not made the most of the duke's famous aquiline profile. Since it was the Duke of Wellington who acquired the house from Pauline, it seems appropriate that the two portraits should be hung together here, as if warily sizing each other up, almost two centuries after striking the bargain.

The narrow panels around the room are presently hung with 'drops' of forty small oil sketches by Herbert Arnould Olivier (1861–1952), a series of portraits entitled *The Representatives, Delegates and Supporting Staff at the Supreme War Council Meetings, Versailles 1918–19*. These sketches, rapidly painted from life, are on loan to the Paris Residence from the artist's family.

Facing page: Baron Gérard's full-length portrait of the Duke of Wellington hangs over a fine Empire desk in the Ante-Room. The small oils flanking it are portraits of delegates at the Versailles Peace Conference by Herbert Arnould Olivier (see page 176). *Above:* Details of a pair of candelabra in the Ante-Room. Supported by figures of Apollo and Aurora, they belonged to Pauline Borghese.

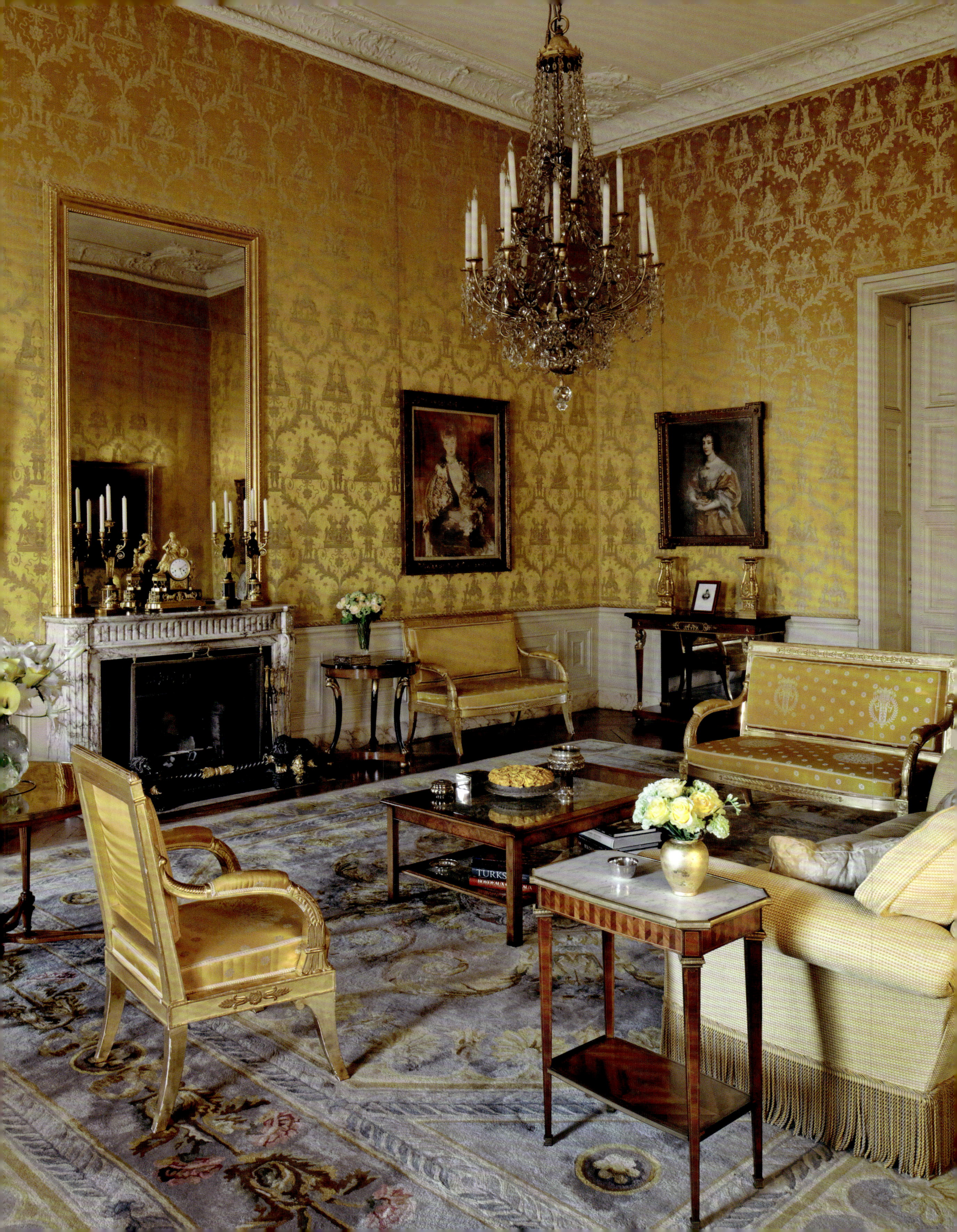
TURKS

SALON JAUNE

This room was the ante-room to the 3rd duc de Charost's apartment, hung with tapestry. Today it retains its original Louis XV sculpted cornice, although its detail is now obscured by layers of paint. By 1762, these rooms were unoccupied, but the very detailed 1787 inventory notes that a full-length portrait of Maria Leczinska, queen of Louis XV, hung here, in a grand frame surmounted with the arms of France — a relic of the Charost family's close ties with the court. Pauline Borghese changed all of this when she took on the house in 1803, creating an upstairs drawing room here, known as the Salon Carmelite for its brown hangings, piped with blue silk, tassels and fringes. The only survivor of her furnishings is the gilt-bronze chandelier, of two tiers and eighteen lights, which still hangs in its original position. Other Pauline furniture has also come to rest here, including chairs from the Picture Gallery. The clock, *Le Messager d'Amour,* with its charming tableau of a girl receiving a love letter from a dove, was originally either in the Ante-Room or what is now the Salon Rouge (known as the Salon Jaune in Pauline's day) downstairs.

At first the British used the Salon Jaune as a first-floor dining room. One visitor, Simeon South, who dined at the Embassy in February 1832, recalled how Lady Granville's dining room 'has a carpet of the very best Gobelin [sic] fabric, the identical one made for Pauline, with the Imperial eagle still distinguishing it; to remove which would spoil the carpet. Lady G. therefore prudently lets it remain.' Sadly, this carpet does not survive. The Salon Jaune was hung with yellow silk in 1904–05 as part of the refurbishments following the visit of Edward VII. The room is now used as a drawing room by ambassadors, and in 1986 the old damask wall-hangings were replaced by a silk lampas of the pattern '*Aux Quatre Continents*' (The Four Parts of the World), originally woven in Lyon in 1784 in blue and silver for Marie Antoinette's private drawing room at the château de Rambouillet. Also in the room are an interesting series of tables, including a circular mahogany table for *bouillotte*, a card game resembling poker in which chips are used, which were stored in the 'pot' under the removable central section of the table. This beautiful table is probably by the cabinetmaker Adam Weisweiller (1744–1820). The two marble-topped *guéridon* (tripod) tables are supported by curved legs terminated by eagle heads. The firedogs with recumbent lions in front of the chimneypiece are part of a group of such fittings that the Marchioness of Normanby (ambassadress from 1846–52), acquired from the dealer, Mellon, in the rue St-Denis in 1846. She got into trouble with the Foreign Office when it was discovered that these charming, but sentimental bronzes had been acquired in part exchange for valuable Empire firedogs belonging to the Embassy. To the left of the chimneypiece hangs a portrait of the sculptor Antonio Canova by Sir George Hayter (1792–1871). Canova worked extensively for Napoleon and the imperial family, carving the celebrated statue of Pauline Borghese now in the Villa Borghese (a reduced replica of which is displayed in the Residence's Entrance Hall). After the fall of Napoleon in 1815 Canova was sent by Pope Pius VII to negotiate the return of looted works of art

Facing page: The Salon Jaune. Yellow silk was hung here in the Edwardian era (the original silk was replaced in 1986), but much of the furniture dates from Pauline Borghese's time. The splendid chandelier, of two tiers and eighteen lights, is described in old inventories as hanging in this room. To the right of the chimney hangs the portrait, *Queen Alexandra*, by Jacques Émile Blanche, c. 1905. To its right is the portrait, *Queen Henrietta Maria*, after Sir Anthony van Dyck, c. 1632–35.

from the musée Napoléon in Paris. The Duke of Wellington, then ambassador to France, was sympathetic and Canova would almost certainly have visited him at the Embassy. The portrait was probably painted in Rome in 1817 after Canova's return from his mission. It was commissioned by Canova's great patron, the 6th Duke of Bedford, for whom the sculptor carved a second version of *The Three Graces,* now jointly owned by the Victoria and Albert Museum and the National Galleries of Scotland. The portrait shows the sculptor working on the terracotta model for the statue, now in the musée de Beaux-Arts in Lyon. On the other side of the chimneypiece hangs a portrait of Queen Alexandra, wife of Edward VII, by Jacques Émile Blanche (1861–1942). Blanche, a society painter with strong links to Great Britain, wrote of this portrait in his autobiography *Portraits of a Lifetime…* (1937) 'I never finished the portrait — happily I kept the sketch — which I made of [the Queen Alexandra] in the majesty of her womanhood. I was not born an official portrait painter and the portrait horrified court circles.' This sitting took place in about 1905 and Blanche's impressionistic rendering of the queen, who was over sixty at the time, and deaf, betrays the influence of his mentor Edouard Manet. The picture, much more than a mere 'sketch', was given to the British Embassy by the family of the artist in 1951.

The picture on the east wall is the *Salon Carré and Grande Galerie of the Louvre* (1831), by John Scarlett Davis (1804–1845). James Jacques Tissot's (1806–1902) winsome study of a young woman entitled *On the River* (1877) hangs on the north wall. Below that picture, on the console, are glazed boxes containing interesting relics — the hair of the Duke of Wellington and his old adversary, the Emperor Napoleon.

Above: The clock in the Salon Jaune is called *Le Messager D'Amour* and depicts a lovelorn girl receiving a love letter from a dove. The ormolu furniture and pile of books on the clock base make this a particularly enchanting Empire-style tableau. *Facing page:* The Salon Jaune is used as a formal drawing room.

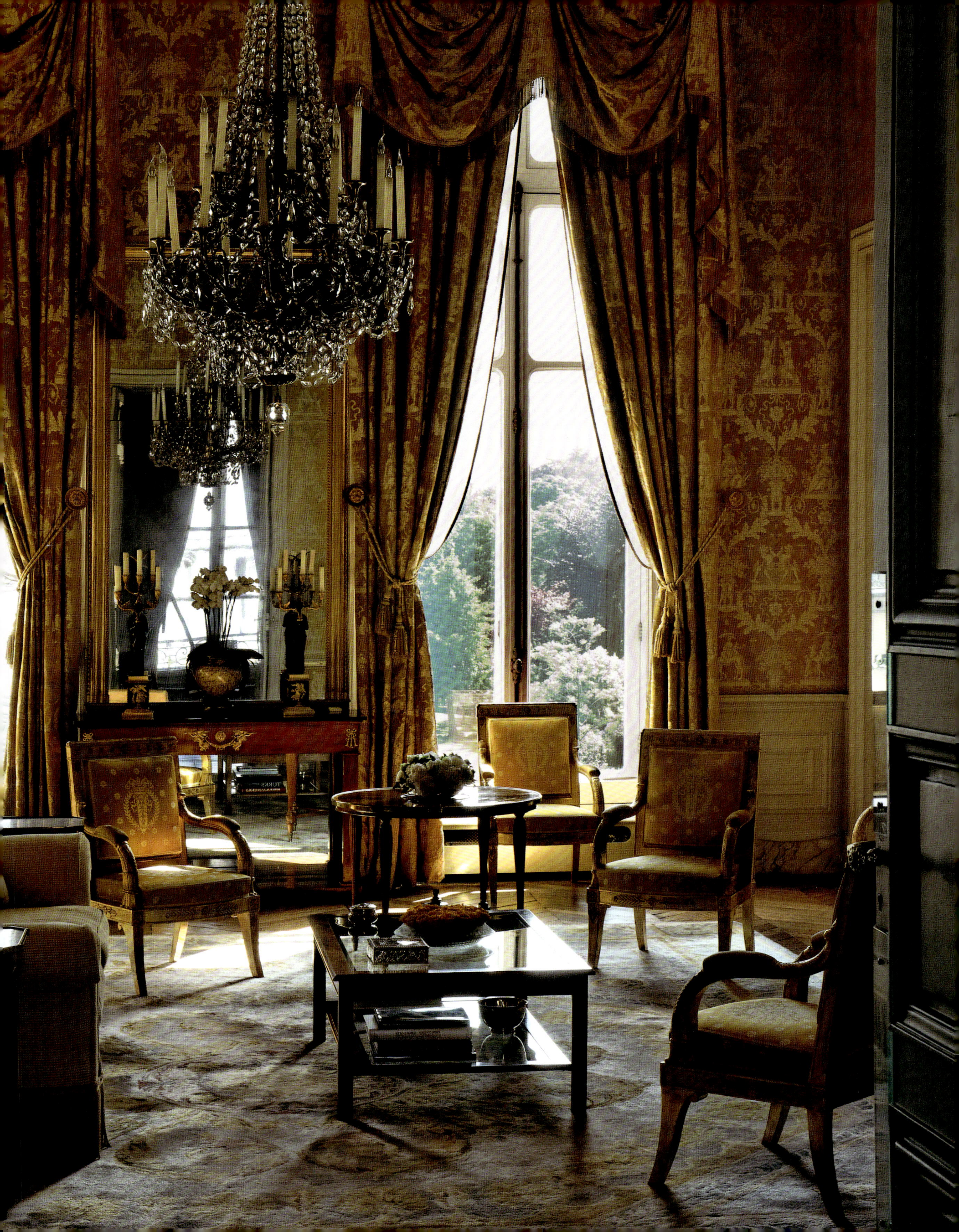

ANTONIO CANOVA
A PORTRAIT BY SIR GEORGE HAYTER

In the autumn of 1816, the young English painter George Hayter set off for Italy, intending to educate himself in Italian art and antiquities. He carried with him a letter of introduction to the celebrated sculptor Antonio Canova (1757–1822), in Rome, written by their mutual patron, the wealthy aristocrat and art lover John Russell, 6th Duke of Bedford (1766–1839). When Hayter arrived at the sculptor's studio, Canova was nearing completion of a version of *The Three Graces,* commissioned by Bedford. Canova spoke fluent English and was friendly and welcoming to the young painter. As President of the Accademia di San Luca in Rome, the sculptor supported Hayter in becoming the Accademia's youngest member in several generations. However, the kindness shown by Canova was not untypical. He was equally generous to many other young artists.

In May 1817, Bedford wrote to Canova announcing 'Hayter has engaged to paint your portrait for me'. He went on to request a bust of the sculptor, explaining: 'the regard and esteem I entertain for you makes me feel the likeness cannot be too often multiplied'. Later that year, Hayter sent his patron a rough sketch of his portrait of the sculptor, below which he explained: 'The general arrangement is like this but the likeness or character must not be looked for here...'. The resulting half-length portrait of Canova includes a terracotta model for *The Three Graces*. Canova looks more youthful than his sixty years, perhaps partly because, from 1810, he wore a black wig when sitting for portraits. As the more senior artist, it seems likely that Canova had a significant influence over the way he was presented. Before leaving Italy, Hayter showed his gratitude to Canova by dedicating an etching after Titian's *Assumption of the Virgin* to him. The original painting is located in the same Venetian church where Canova's heart would one day be buried. Hayter returned to England in January 1818. The portrait of Canova had reached Woburn Abbey, Bedford's country estate, by August that year, when the Duke mentioned in a letter to Canova how pleased he was with it. It was acquired for display at the Paris Residence by the Government Art Collection in 1957 for its connections with the history of the Residence. Between 1805 and 1808, Canova made a marble sculpture of former occupant Princess Pauline Borghese. A reduced version of the sculpture by Canova's pupil Adamo Tadolini is now on display in the Entrance Hall. Hayter also painted subsequent residents Charles Stuart, Lord Stuart de Rothesay (1779–1845) and his family (see pages 86-89).

Facing page: A perfect English tea served in the opulent Empire setting of the Salon Jaune. George Hayter's portrait, *Antonio Canova*, painted in 1817, hangs next to the chimney.

Text by Philippa Martin

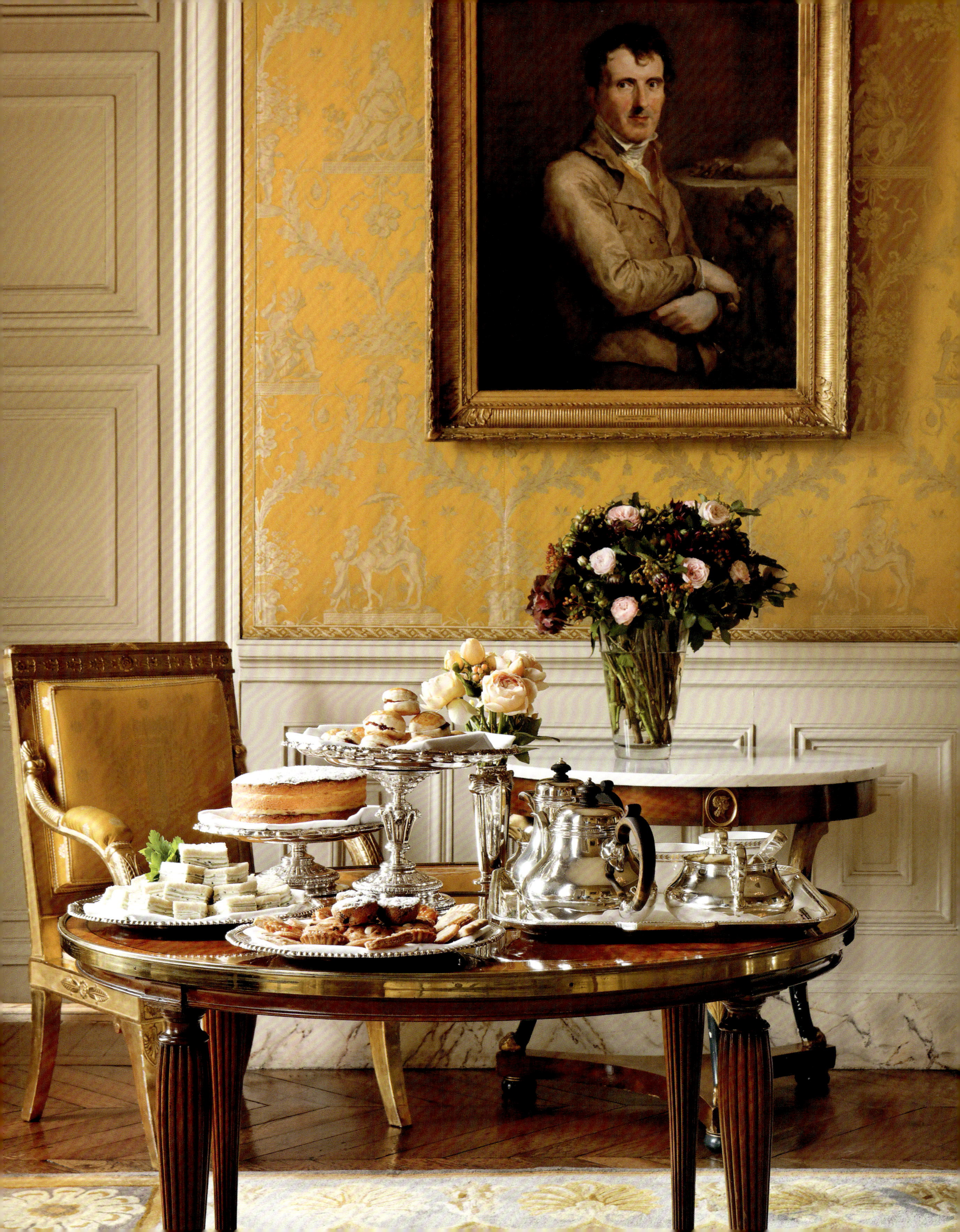

TAPESTRY DINING ROOM

Originally the chapel of the hôtel de Charost, by 1787 the room appears to have been virtually abandoned, as the inventory of that year lists only two firedogs and twenty cushions in different sizes and colours. In 1811, Pauline transformed it into a billiard room, with plans to build a conservatory on the terrace outside the window — a feature that was briefly, but tastelessly, realised under Earl Cowley in 1858–60. Nothing survives of Pauline's decoration and the current decor is Edwardian, supposedly inspired by a room in the château de Breteuil outside Paris that the designer, Georges Hoentschel, and his patron, Sir Francis Bertie, particularly admired. This was when it was hung with the set of late-seventeenth-century Brussels tapestries that had been discovered in store in the Foreign Office in London. They were produced in the factory of D. Leyniers and illustrate rustic pursuits — *Harbour Scene, Drawing Water from a Well, Fruit Sellers, Smokers* and *Milking the Cows* — after cartoons by David Teniers II and III. Many other such sets are known, but this is a very fine weaving, if somewhat faded. The room is now used as a breakfast and dining room. The chimneypiece garniture, notably the clock known as a *'pendule formant arcade'*, belonged to Pauline Borghese, but the admittedly charming firedogs with a poodle and a Persian cat are a souvenir of the Marchioness of Normanby's disastrous shopping spree in 1846.

Above left and right: Firedogs. *Facing page:* The Tapestry Dining Room is essentially a creation of 1905, incorporating a set of late-seventeenth-century Brussels tapestries with a chimneypiece and overmantel mirrors in the Louis XV taste.

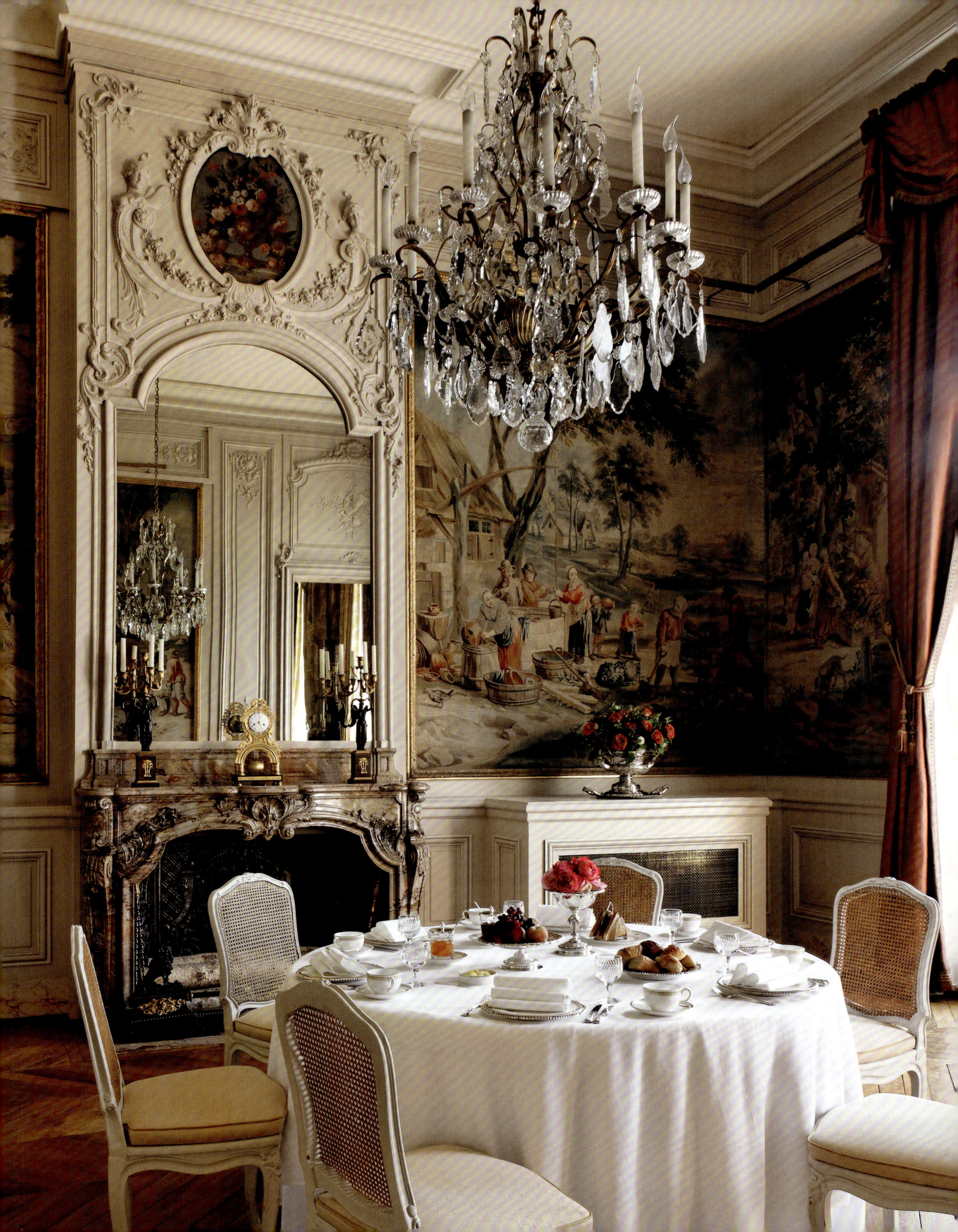

Above: The Brussels tapestries in the Tapestry Dining Room depict rustic pursuits, after cartoons by David Teniers II and III. They abound in charming details. *Facing page:* The curious clock in the Tapestry Dining Room, surmounted by a pair of ormolu billing doves, is described in Pauline Borghese's inventory as a *'pendule formant arcade'*.

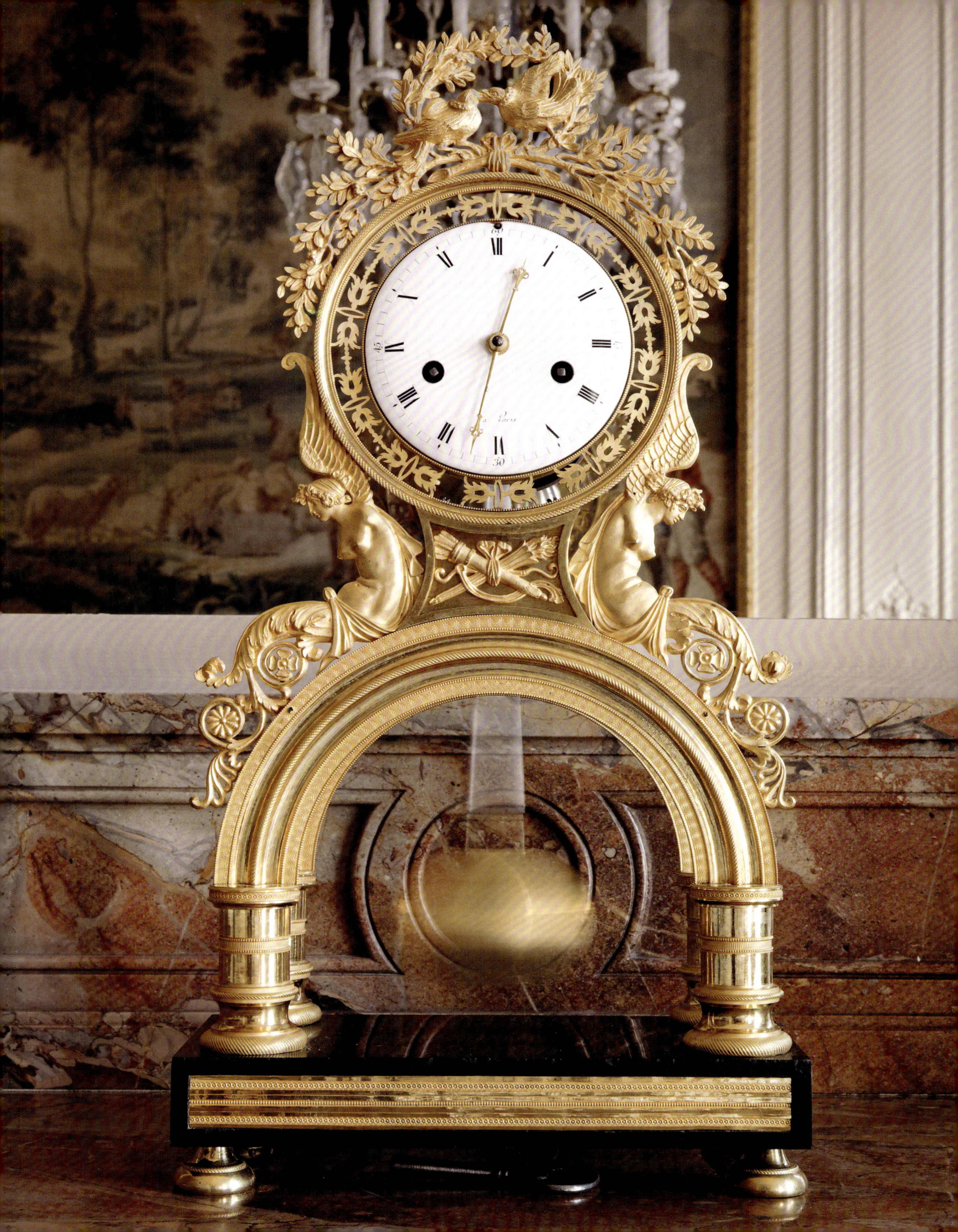

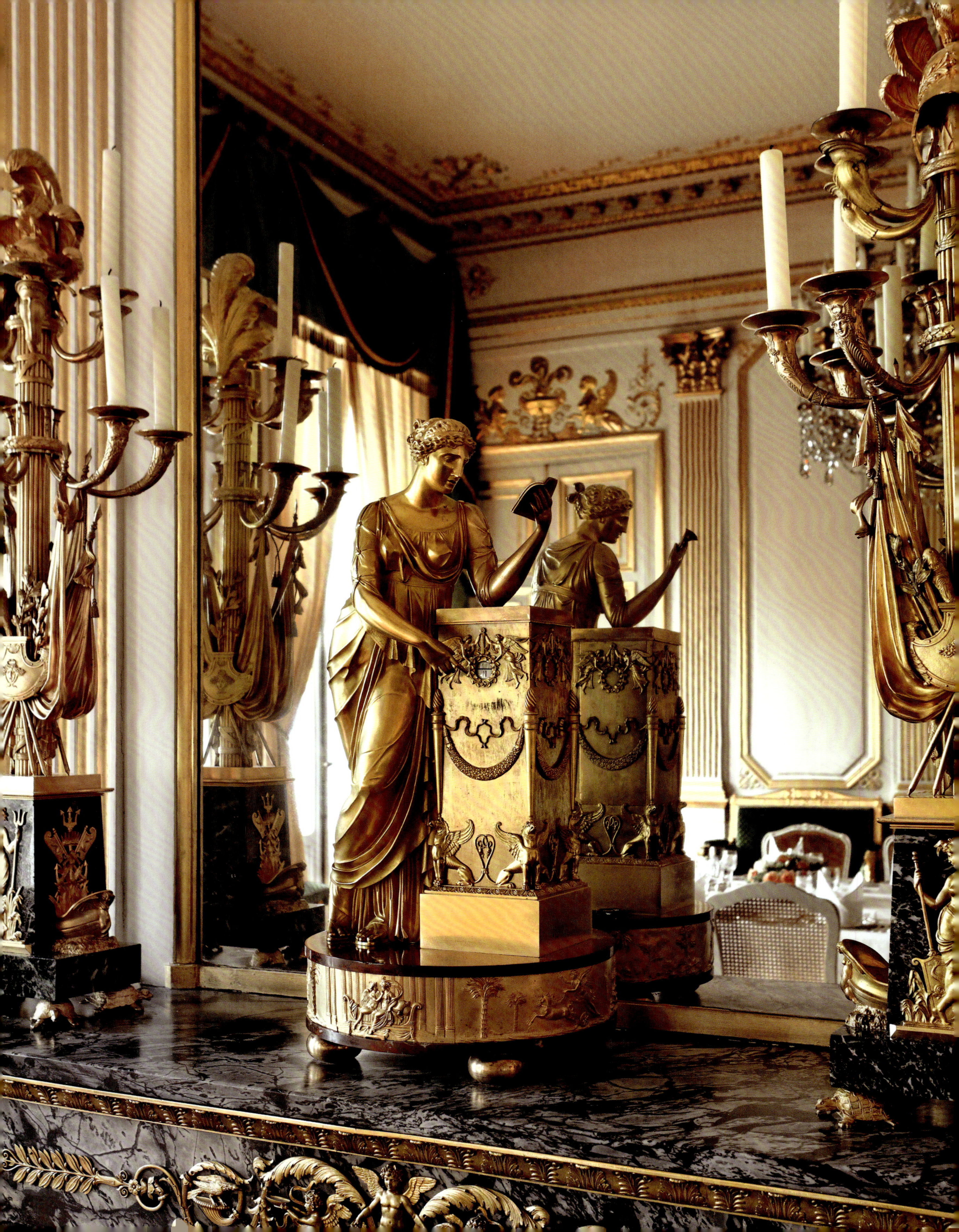

SALON VERT ET OR

The duc de Charost used this room as his salon, the principal room of his upstairs suite. By the mid-eighteenth century it was hung with part of a large set of tapestries depicting the Guise Hunt. Pauline Borghese transformed the room into her Grand Salon Vert, by hanging panels of green velvet, richly embroidered with gold thread, between the pilasters, and installing the magnificent chimneypiece of grey *bardiglio* marble with its ormolu mounts incorporating eagles and swans. But in the 1860s, additional ornaments were added to the frieze of the room and in 1904–05 Georges Hoentschel and Vye Parminter introduced the arched mirrors and white-and-gold panelling in place of wall-hangings. At this time the pilasters were given fluting and all the ornaments were picked out with oil gilding.

Despite these alterations to Pauline's principal state room, most of her original furnishings survive in place. These include the side table and the gilded seat furniture, with uprights in the form of winged caryatids. Recently restored and reupholstered, as originally, with green stamped velvet, they evoke Pauline's lost hangings. The clock on the chimneypiece, *L'Étude,* was here in 1814. Also here at that time were the flanking candelabra with plumed helmets and trophies of arms, and bases of green marble adorned with ormolu mounts representing Neptune and his attributes, including ships' prows and turtles. The chandelier, the largest and most splendid in the house, was returned to the room in 1991 from the Salon Pauline. Other Pauline items come from elsewhere in the house. The gilt-bronze firedogs with griffons came from the bedroom on the ground floor, while the candelabra on the console table in the form of vestals came from her Boudoir Violet (now the Throne Room).

The flat-weave carpet bearing the royal arms of Great Britain and Hanover is English and was probably made in Axminster by Thomas Whitty. It is an interesting and possibly unique survival of a royal armorial carpet of the early nineteenth century. This carpet is said to come from the old British Embassy in St Petersburg, but has been in Paris since at least 1894.

Facing page: Amongst the great glories of the British Ambassador's Residence are the gilt-bronze garnitures of candelabra, clocks and other ornaments for the chimneypieces. The clock in the Salon Vert et Or is entitled *L'Étude*, while the flanking candelabra are particularly magnificent. *Following pages:* The wall panelling of the Salon Vert et Or was redesigned in 1904–05. The chimneypiece and overdoors are from Pauline's day. To the left hangs the portrait, *Henrietta Anne, Duchesse d'Orléans*, by Pierre Mignard (d. 1695), c. 1665–70; to the right, *Prince James Francis Edward Stuart ('The Old Pretender')*, by Alexis Simon Belle (1674–1734), c. 1712–14.

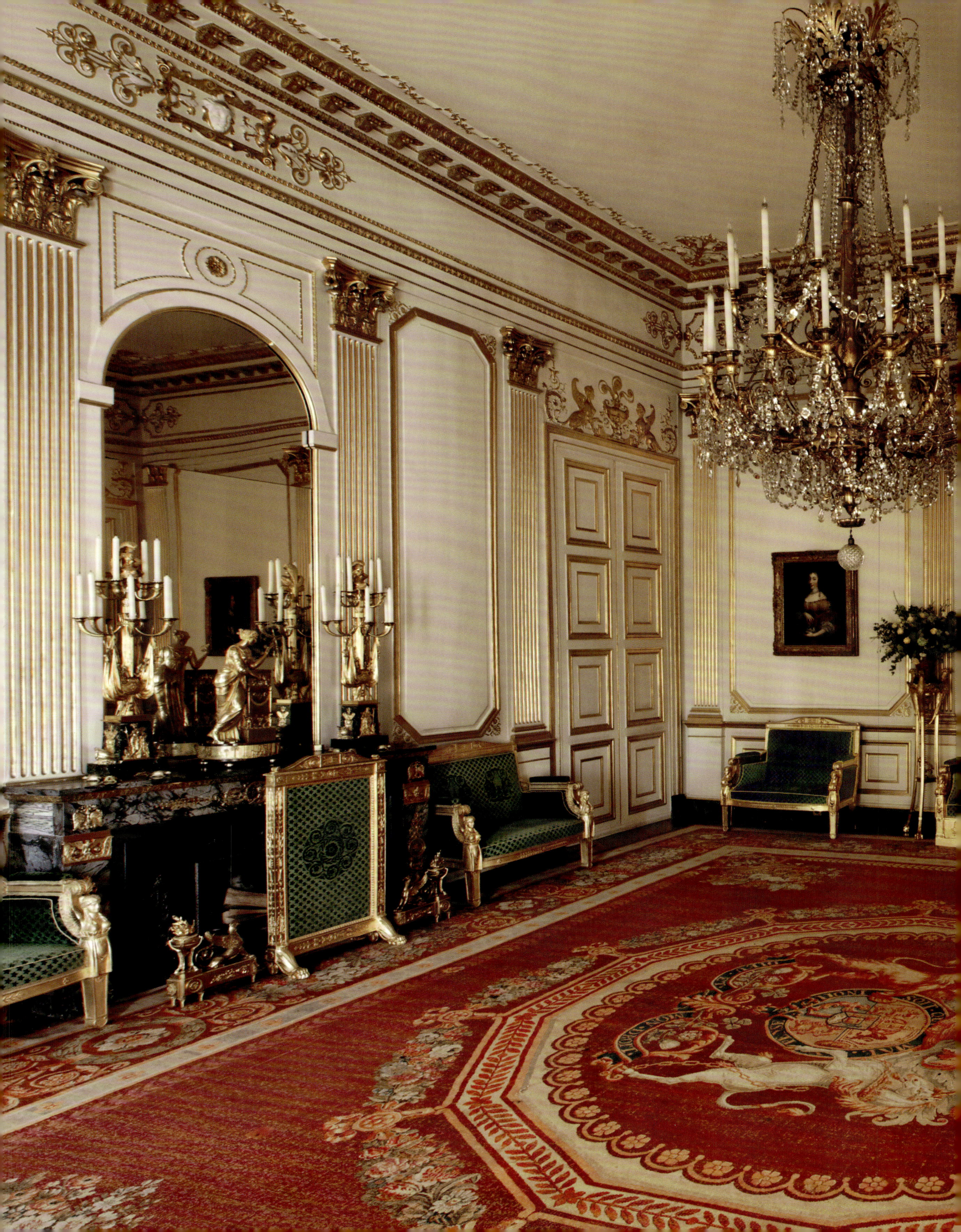

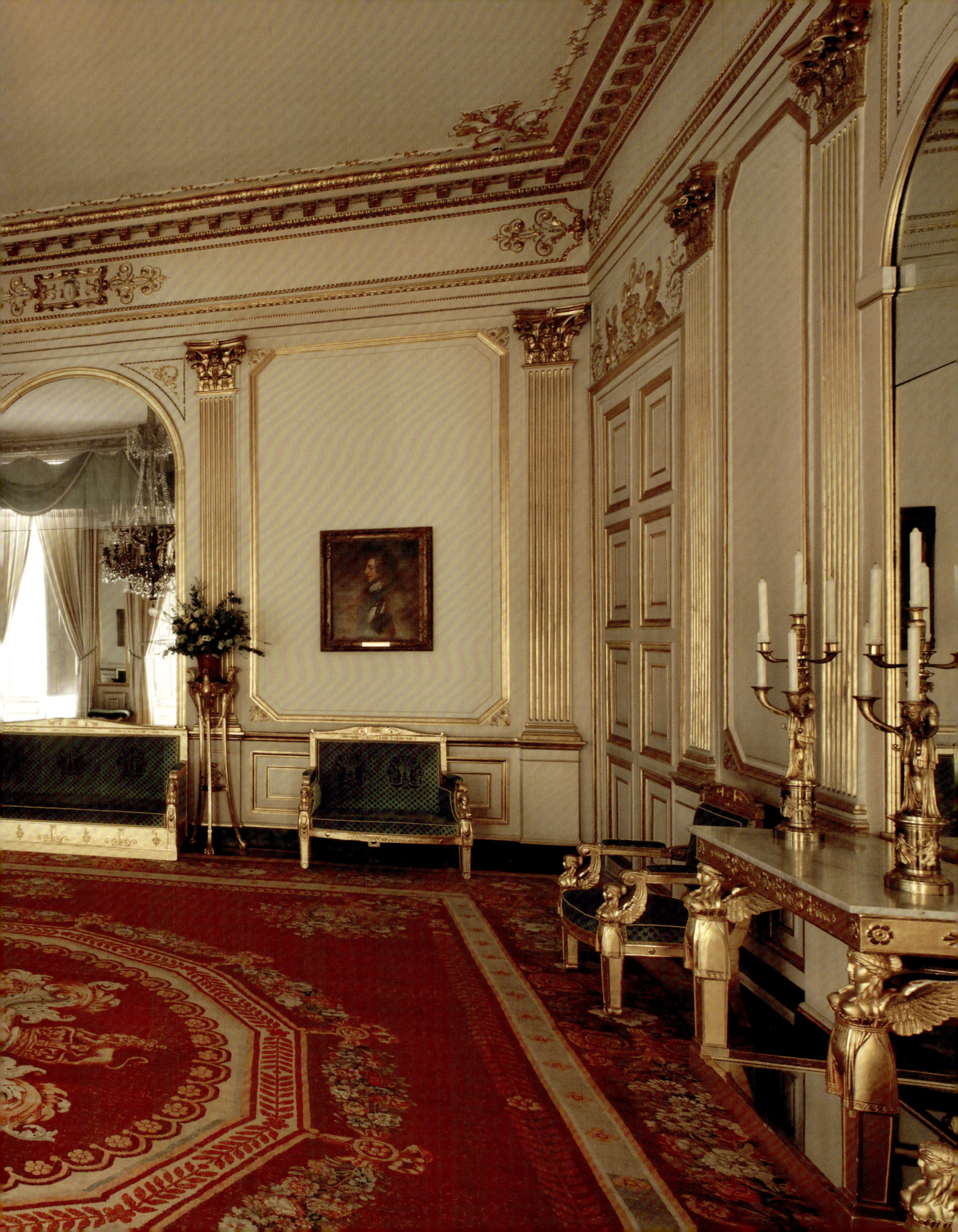

Above: The Salon Vert et Or is the only one which retains its original 1814 furniture and decorative objects *(clockwise from top left):* A martial trophy from the candelabra on the chimneypiece; the complete chimneypiece ensemble in the Salon Vert et Or, with clock, candelabra and griffon firedogs, the firescreen and flanking armchairs upholstered in stamped green velvet; detail of the firescreen; the portrait of Henrietta Anne, duchesse d'Orléans, daughter of Queen Henrietta Maria of England, whose portrait is in the Salon Jaune, hangs above a gilded tripod with eagle finials. *Facing page:* The thirty-light crystal chandelier hung here in Pauline Borghese's time and is the largest and most splendid chandelier in the house. The elaborate ceiling rose is probably a mid-nineteenth-century addition to the Empire decor.

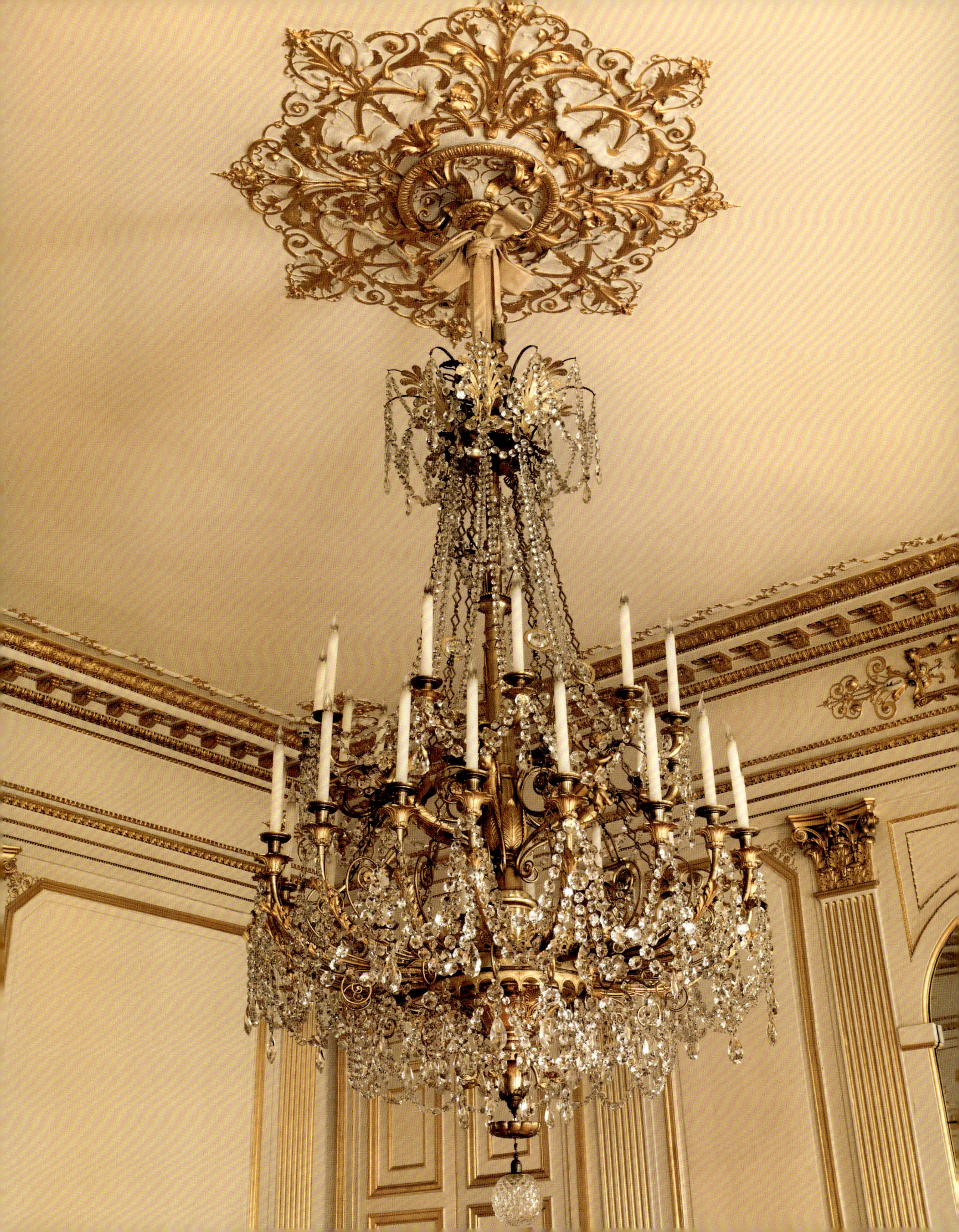

SALON VERT

For much of the early history of the house, this room was the principal bedchamber on the first floor. Here the 3rd duc de Charost — trusted friend of Louis XIV and adviser and mentor of his great grandson, Louis XV — died, aged 84, on the morning of 23 October 1747. All trace of his decor — three richly carved pier glasses and a matching gilded console table — have vanished. Decades later, Pauline's towering *lit de parade* (now in the Salon Pauline downstairs) stood here. In Pauline's time the Salon Vert was hung with white silk with gold rosettes, and was known as the Salon Bleu on account of the jasper-blue bed hangings. The white marble chimneypiece with gilt-bronze mounts and the mouldings on the ceiling were an addition of Pauline's, although the mouldings have been embellished by later work. Later, this room became a drawing room to successive British ambassadors; in 1825, Lady Granville hung it with straw-coloured chintz and laid out French and English newspapers and books of prints for her guests, while by 1842 the walls had panels of white satin paper. The colour that gives the room its name did not appear until 1852, under Earl and Lady Cowley, who described how they had it 'lined with green flake paper'. It has been green ever since.

Lord Lytton used the room during his last illness, dying here on 24 November 1891, but during the difficult times that followed the Second World War, Lady Diana Cooper hosted nightly salons of her intimate friends — artists, musicians and writers — as well as anyone else who happened to be passing through Paris. These brilliant candlelit assemblies buoyed up spirits in the war-torn capital, making the British Embassy one of the few places in Paris with a warm fire and an abundant supply of gin and gossip.

Today the room is an informal drawing room used by the ambassador, often containing the personal possessions of the resident family. Among its more notable contents are the chandelier originally from Pauline Borghese's large dining room, a fine mahogany *secrétaire,* attributed to Georges Jacob (1739–1814) and from the apartments used by Prince Borghese, and the delightful clock known as *La Négresse*. While some pictures in this room are liable to change, Eugène Louis Gillot's *George V and Queen Mary Descending the Staircase of the Paris Opera on their State Visit to France in April 1914,* and the charming anonymous painting *The British Embassy in Paris from the Gardens*, possibly commissioned by Lord and Lady Granville in 1841, usually hang here. The delightful *Paris-Plage, Picardy*, painted around 1905 by William Frederick Mayor, hung in Tony Blair's office in 10 Downing Street for three years until he resigned as prime minister in 2007.

Facing page: The Salon Vert is used as an informal sitting room by the resident ambassador, and with its inviting sofas and mix of mainly twentieth-century British pictures, is one of the most comfortable rooms in the house. To the left of the chimneypiece hangs *George V and Queen Mary Descending the Staircase of the Paris Opera on Their State Visit to France in April 1914,* by Eugène Louis Gillot (1868–1925), 1914; to the right *Paris-Plage, Picardy*, by William Frederick Mayor (1865–1916), c. 1905.

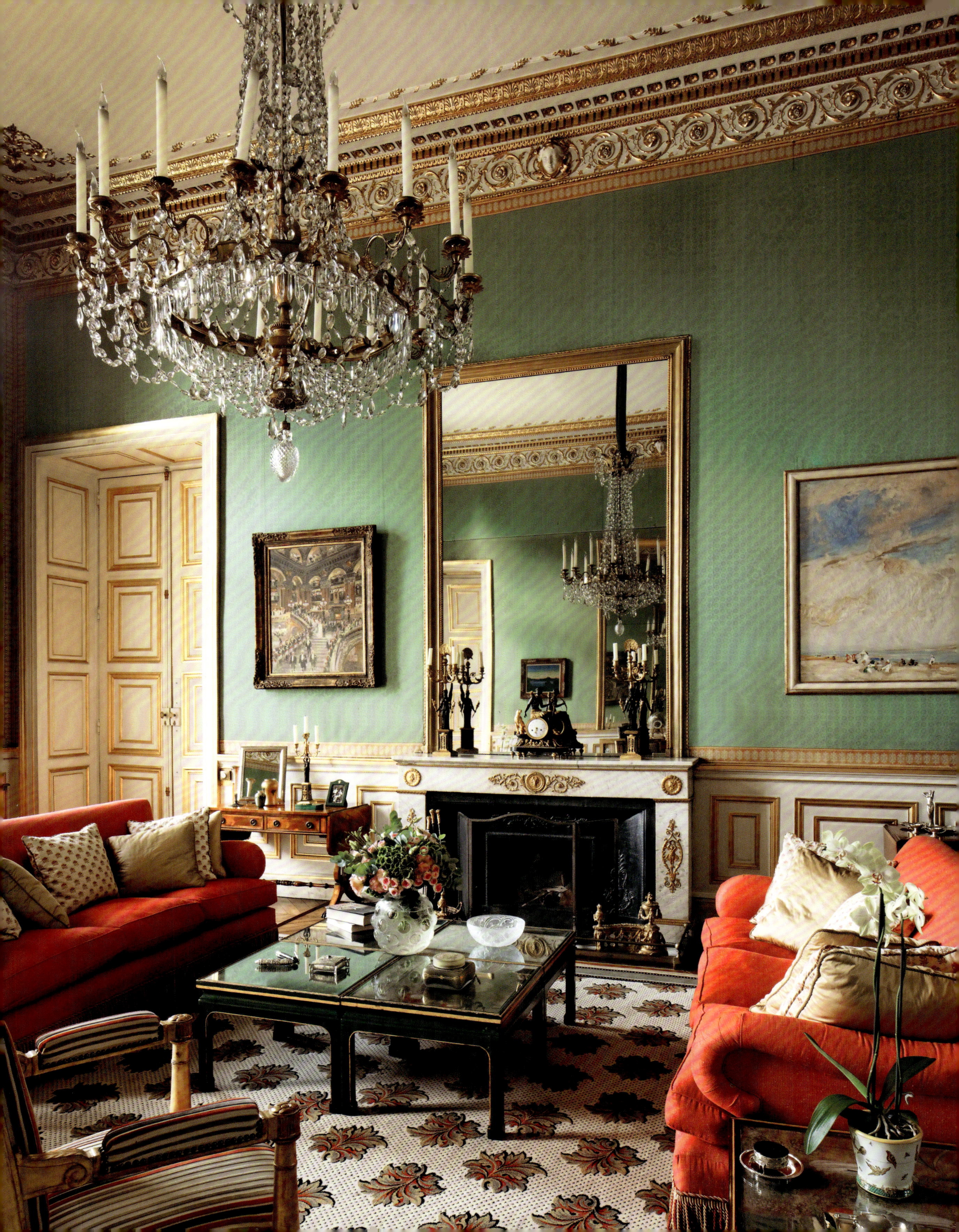

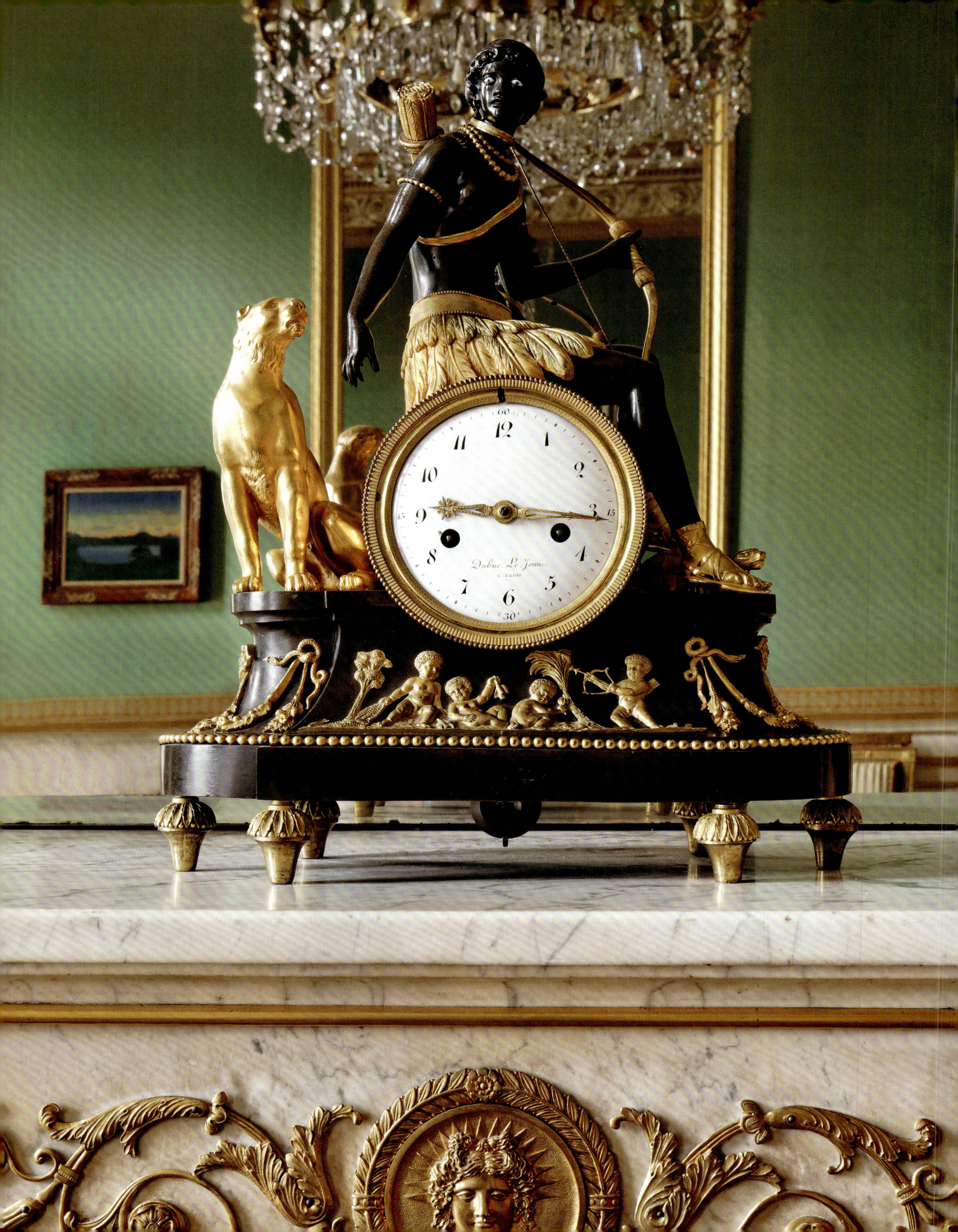
Dubuc. Le. Jeune
A. PARIS

Facing page: Perched on the Salon Vert chimneypiece is possibly the most exotic of all clocks in the Residence, *La Négresse*. The figure is probably a personification of the continent of Africa. *Above:* The mahogany *secrétaire* in the Salon Vert is recorded in old inventories in the apartments used by Prince Borghese. In this photograph it displays porcelain belonging to the ambassador and his family.

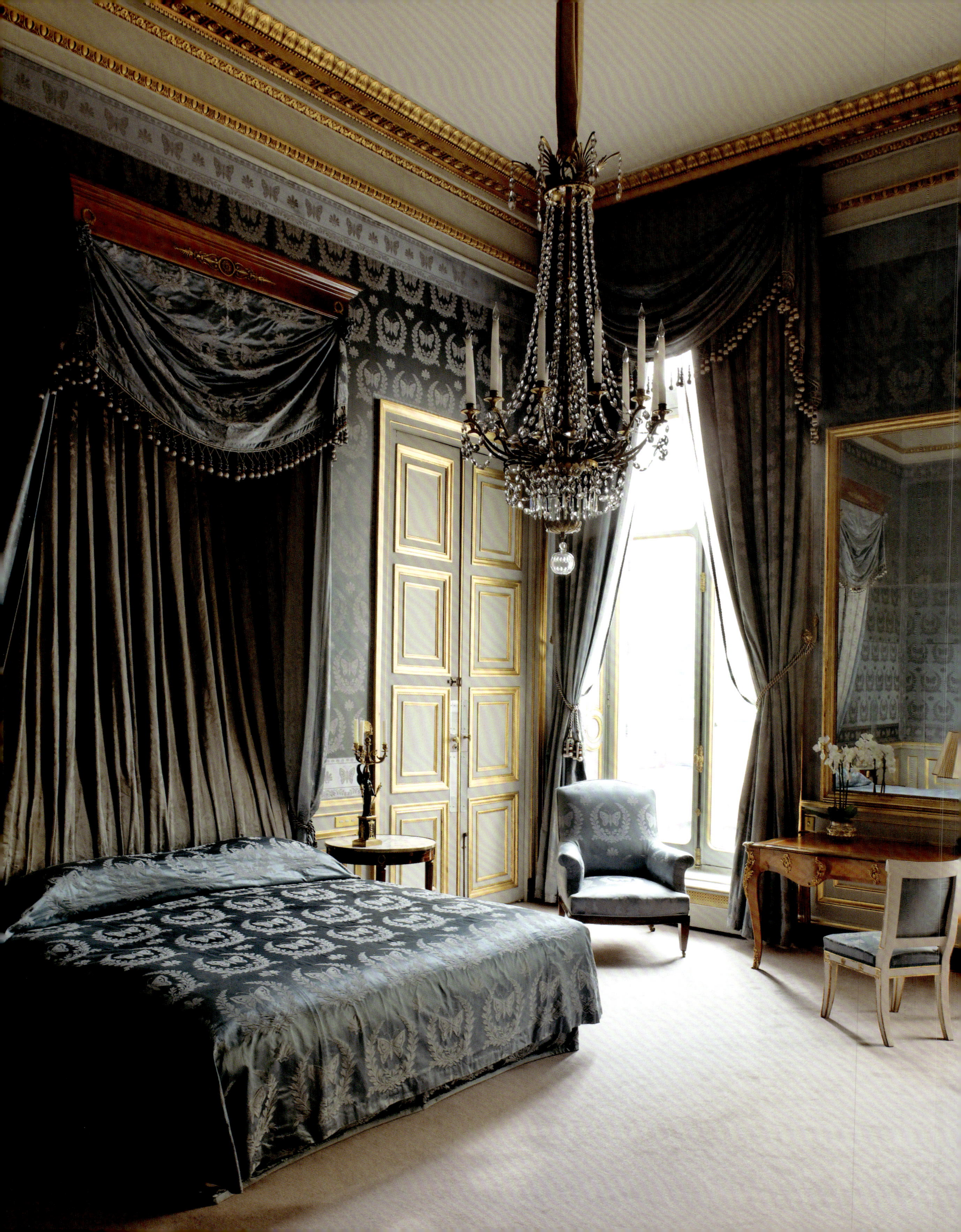

COOPER BEDROOM
AND BATHROOM

What is now the Cooper Bedroom began life as the 3rd duc de Charost's richly fitted-up Grand Cabinet, adjoining his bedchamber. Pauline Borghese used it as her library — despite it having only a single bookcase — and hung it with white and orange lampas, with orange silk curtains and matching seat furniture. After the British took over it was hung at first with a striped chintz and later with crimson flock wallpaper, and was known as the *'chambre à coucher de Milady'*. The famous Pauline bed was moved in here, its canopy shorn of the imperial eagle, which was relegated to the attic. The fine Empire chimneypiece of *verde di Prato* and Siena marbles was brought here from elsewhere in the house in 1853.

The room underwent something of a revival in 1903, when Edward VII slept here during his state visit. Old photographs show it filled with monumental Empire furniture, much of it borrowed from the Mobilier National, with the bed reunited with its canopy and eagle. After the Second World War, Lady Diana Cooper slept in Pauline's bed and hung the room with ox-blood red silk woven with wreaths and butterflies. The present hangings are a blue-grey version installed in 1983.

Although Pauline's grand bed was moved downstairs in 1985, the room retains a few notable pieces of furniture, particularly a mahogany dressing table with gilt-bronze ornaments, mounted with an octagonal mirror, which is signed by François Joseph Loven, cabinetmaker, and which came from Pauline's bathroom. The present bed incorporates an Empire bed canopy that appears on the second floor in the inventory of 1814. This room is now used as one of the principal guest bedrooms.

The bathroom adjoining the Cooper Bedroom has always served this purpose. In Pauline's day it had an iron bathtub painted in imitation of granite and a 'greensward velvet pile carpet'. Later, in 1946, Lady Diana Cooper persuaded Christian Bérard to conjure up a miniature Napoleonic marshal's tent in her bathroom, economically achieved in red-and-white striped butcher's cloth. Replaced three times since its creation, the cloth is now blue and white to match the scheme of the adjoining bedroom. Some of the bathroom fittings have been altered, but the room, with its mirrored bath alcove, is a rare survival of a stylish Empire Revival interior.

Facing page: The Cooper Bedroom is dominated by a large half-tester bed hung, like the walls of the room, with a blue-grey silk woven with wreaths and butterflies. *Page 148:* Another view of the Cooper Bedroom, which is named after Sir Duff Cooper. Lady Diana Cooper slept here during her husband's embassy between 1944 and 1947. Then it was hung with ox-blood red silk and Pauline Borghese's bed — now downstairs — stood on the east wall. *Page 149:* The dressing table is a work by the rare but interesting cabinetmaker, François Joseph Loven, and came from Pauline Borghese's bathroom.

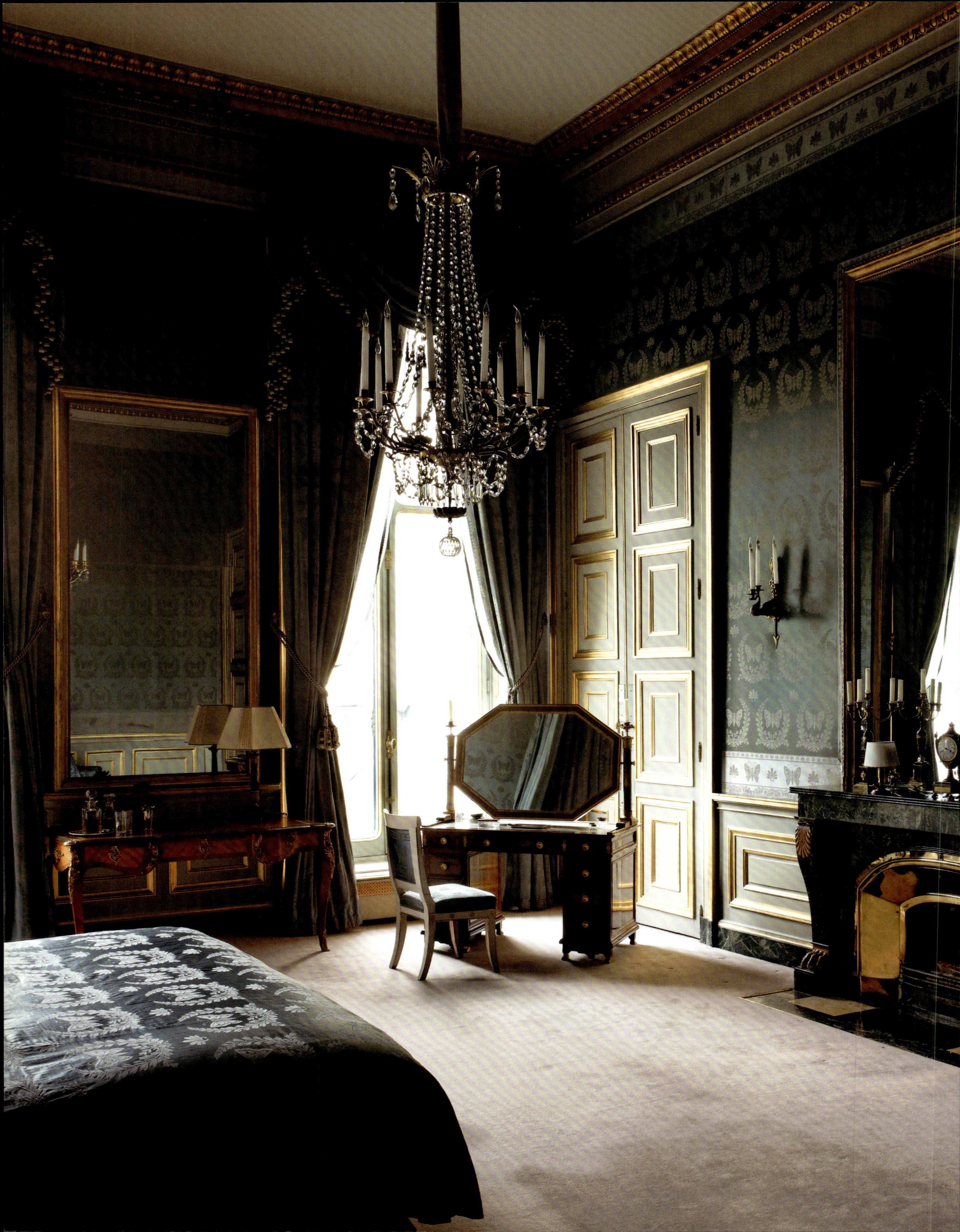

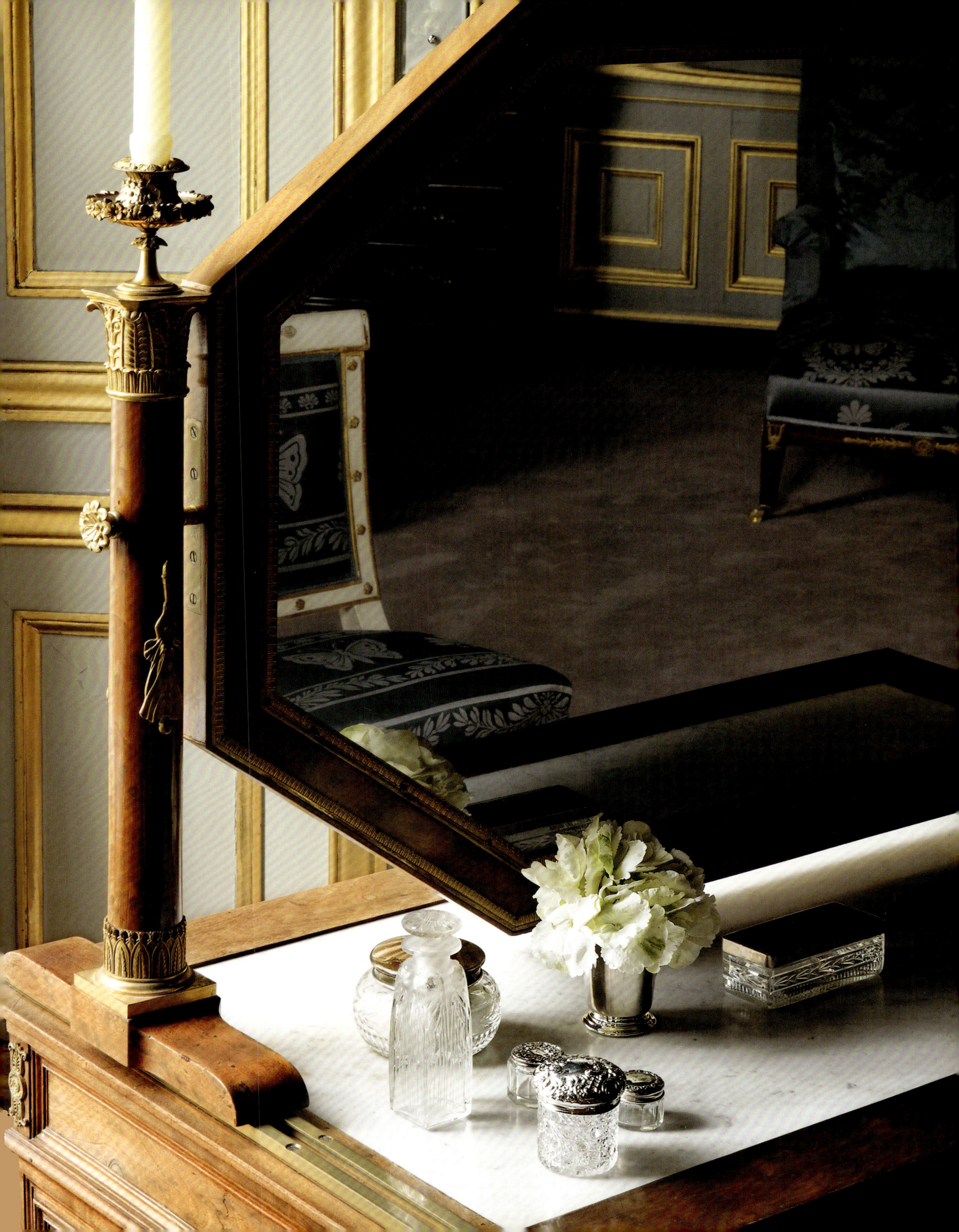

Above: The ensuite bathroom to the Cooper Bedroom is hung with striped butcher's cloth and imitates a Napoleonic tent. First devised by Christian Bérard for Lady Diana Cooper in 1946, this is its third reincarnation.
Facing page: Reflected in the overmantel mirror, the sombre splendour of the Cooper Bedroom.

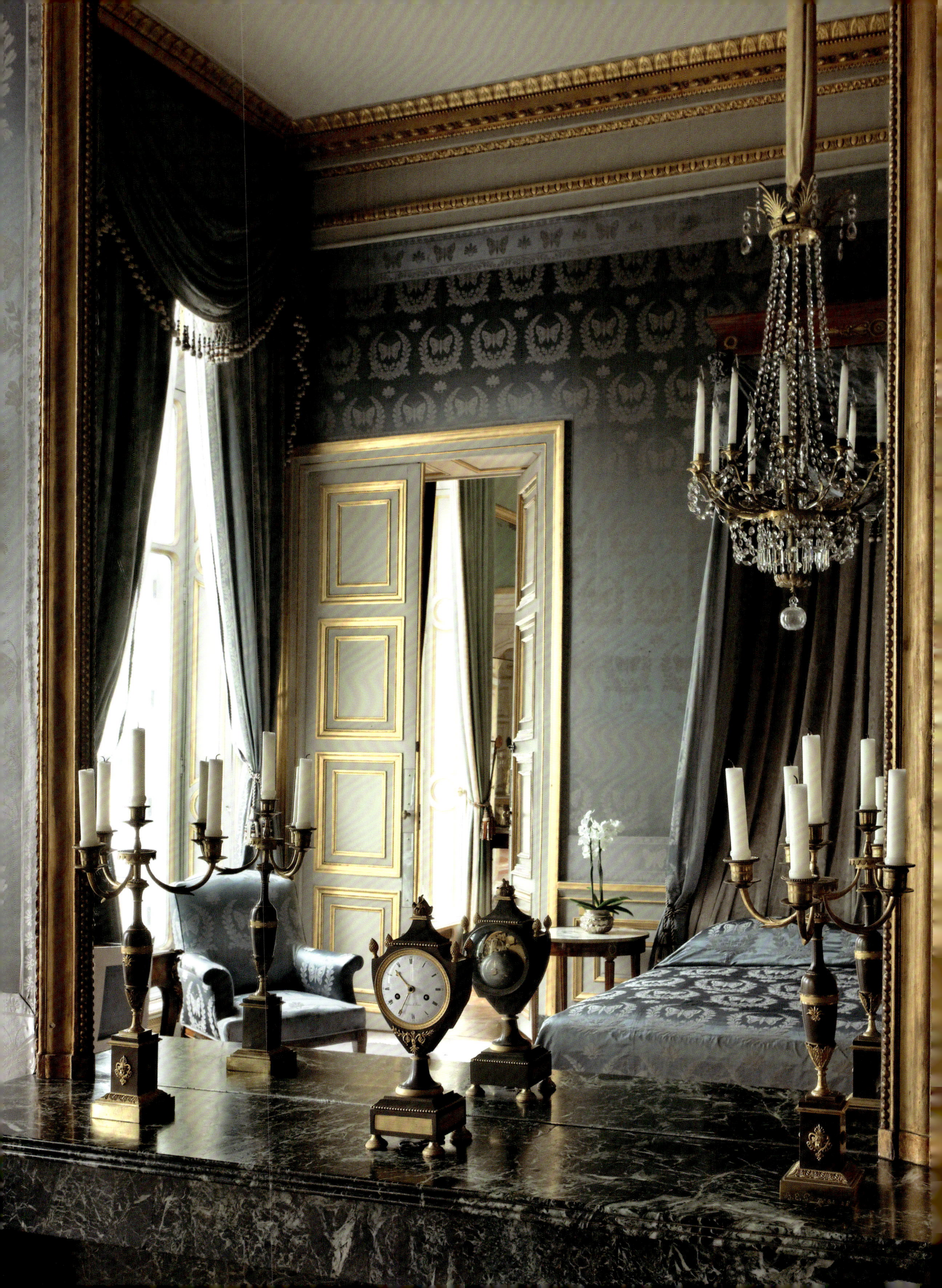

DUFF COOPER LIBRARY

Originally the bedchamber of the duc de Béthune, in Pauline's day her estranged husband Prince Borghese used this room, while she sulked in her apartments downstairs or removed herself altogether. Pauline decorated it with 'American green' taffeta combined with poppy red draperies of the same material, whence the name 'Cabinet Vert'. It contained the lemonwood suite of furniture that is now in the Wellington Room, and the *La Négresse* clock now in the Salon Vert. Later ambassadors used this room as a study, but it was always considered rather gloomy, so its transformation into a library by Duff Cooper was a masterstroke. In the third volume of her memoirs, *Trumpets from the Steep* (1960), Lady Diana described how the design came about: 'There was no library at the Embassy and Duff had the generous idea of establishing one by giving his collection when his mission as ambassador ended. The Office of Works agreed in exchange to install elegant shelves on which to range it. The lofty room in which he [Duff Cooper] worked was ideal in size and position, and the decoration must naturally be worthy of the rest of the house. Charles de Beistegui, whom I had known for twenty-odd years, volunteered, with the help of Georges Geoffroy, to design a library which all agreed became, with its deep cornice, its slender pilasters, its busts and vases and green-fringed shelves, perhaps the most perfected room in the Embassy.... Bébé Bérard chose the colour of the carpet and curtains and arranged the placing of the furniture.'

The Ministry of Works actually needed quite a lot of persuading to allow this theatrical room to be constructed in an era of post-war austerity, but the Coopers could charm and knew all the right people. The resulting room is a testament to the ingenuity of its designers, particularly Bérard's impeccable sense of colour and knack of conjuring up luxurious effects out of cheap materials. The colonnettes supporting the frieze are hollow tubes, and the busts and urns are plaster casts, as are the medallions of Wellington and Pauline Borghese. Paint effects suggest a luxurious tortoiseshell-like wood, but only the gilding is real. The Latin inscription around the frieze was added later, by Sir Gladwyn Jebb, and translates as 'Duff Cooper, fortunate Ambassador to France, dedicated this place to the silent friendship of books so that readers might be numbered among his friends. Hail, friend and read.' The books in the Library comprise a good general collection of classics and works of the Coopers' era, with a special emphasis on Franco-British relations. Books are still added to the Library, keeping it up to date, and it remains the ambassador's study. The chandelier was Pauline's, and came from her Boudoir Violet, while the candelabra came from her Library, now the Cooper Bedroom. Between the windows is a humorous sketch of Lady Diana Cooper by her friend Cecil Beaton.

Facing page: Said to be inspired by 'a palace in Saint Petersburg', the Duff Cooper Library was created in 1946–47 by Charles de Beistegui, with the help of Georges Geoffroy and Christian Bérard. It houses the books donated by Sir Duff Cooper to the Residence. *Following pages:* With its gilding and graining suggesting a luxurious tortoiseshell-like wood, the Duff Cooper Library is a rich and atmospheric setting for the books in the Residence. The gilded inscription on the frieze was added by one of Cooper's successors, Sir Gladwyn Jebb.

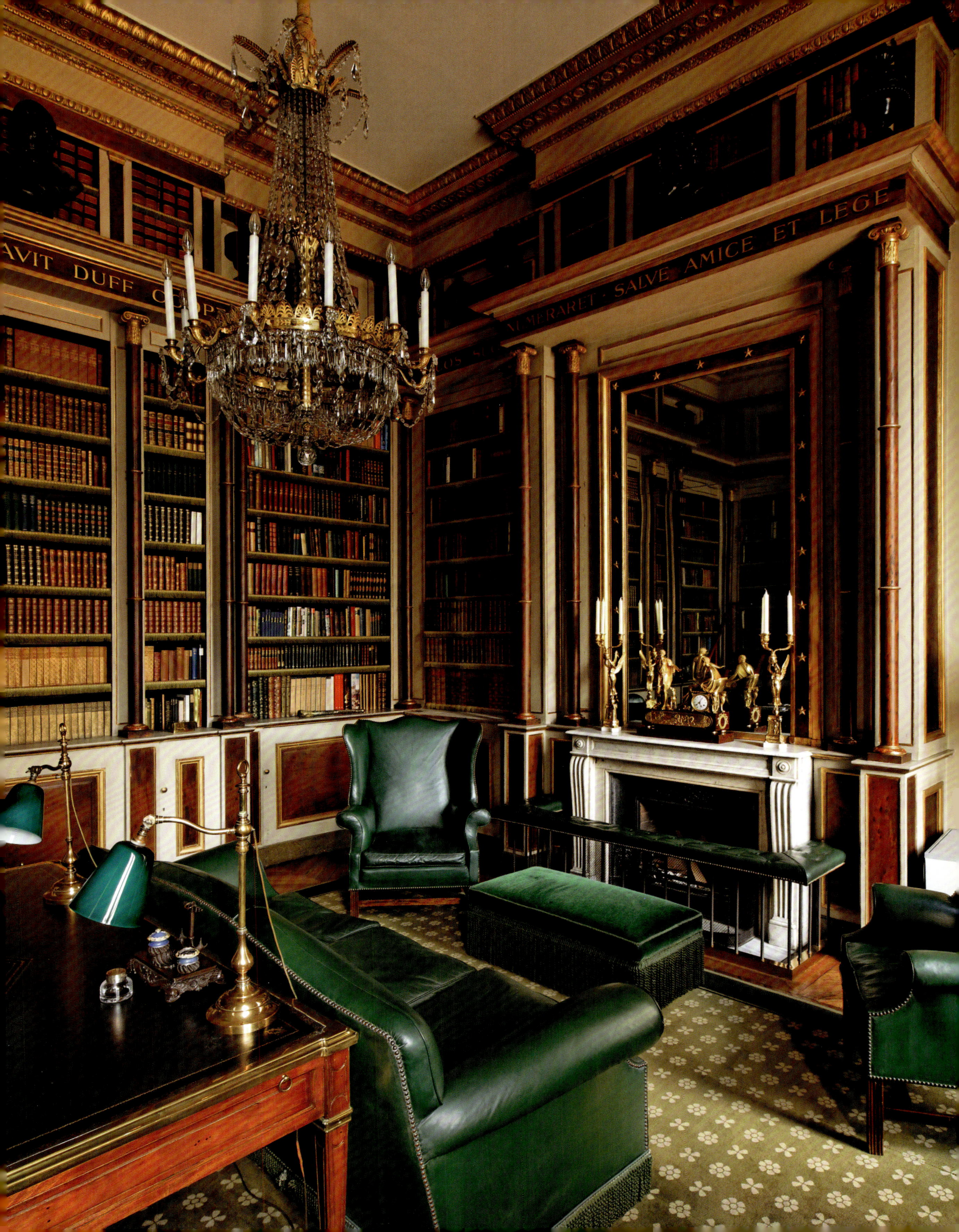
AVIT DUFF
SALVE AMICE ET LEGE

DEDICAVIT DUFF COOPER

UT LECTORES INTER AMICOS

WELLINGTON ROOM

This room was originally used by the duc de Béthune to store his saddlecloths, of which there were several very lavish examples, such as one in blue velvet with pistol holders and a fringe of fine silver thread; another, in apricot-coloured velvet, embroidered with silver thread; and a third in daffodil-coloured velvet, trimmed with fine gold thread. Under Pauline, this became Prince Borghese's salon, resplendent in blue silk with blue and yellow trimmings, with mahogany furniture upholstered to match. The first British ambassadors used it as a conference room and then a waiting room and library before it became the Ambassadress's Study in the late twentieth century. Since being redecorated in 2003 on the advice of John Cornforth it is used for meetings and conferences. Now called the Wellington Room, the walls are hung with prints depicting the Iron Duke. A handsome suite of lemonwood seat furniture, inlaid with ebony, has been arranged around the walls. This furniture may have been commissioned by Pauline before 1803 and thus may have belonged to her first husband, General Leclerc. The chairs have arms supported by Egyptian-style heads, and the *demi-lune* console table is supported by four animal legs terminating in hoofs.

Above: Detail from a lemonwood armchair in the Wellington Room. The armrests are supported by Egyptian busts.
Facing page: The Wellington Room is used for meetings and conferences. The walls display prints depicting the Duke of Wellington (1769–1852).

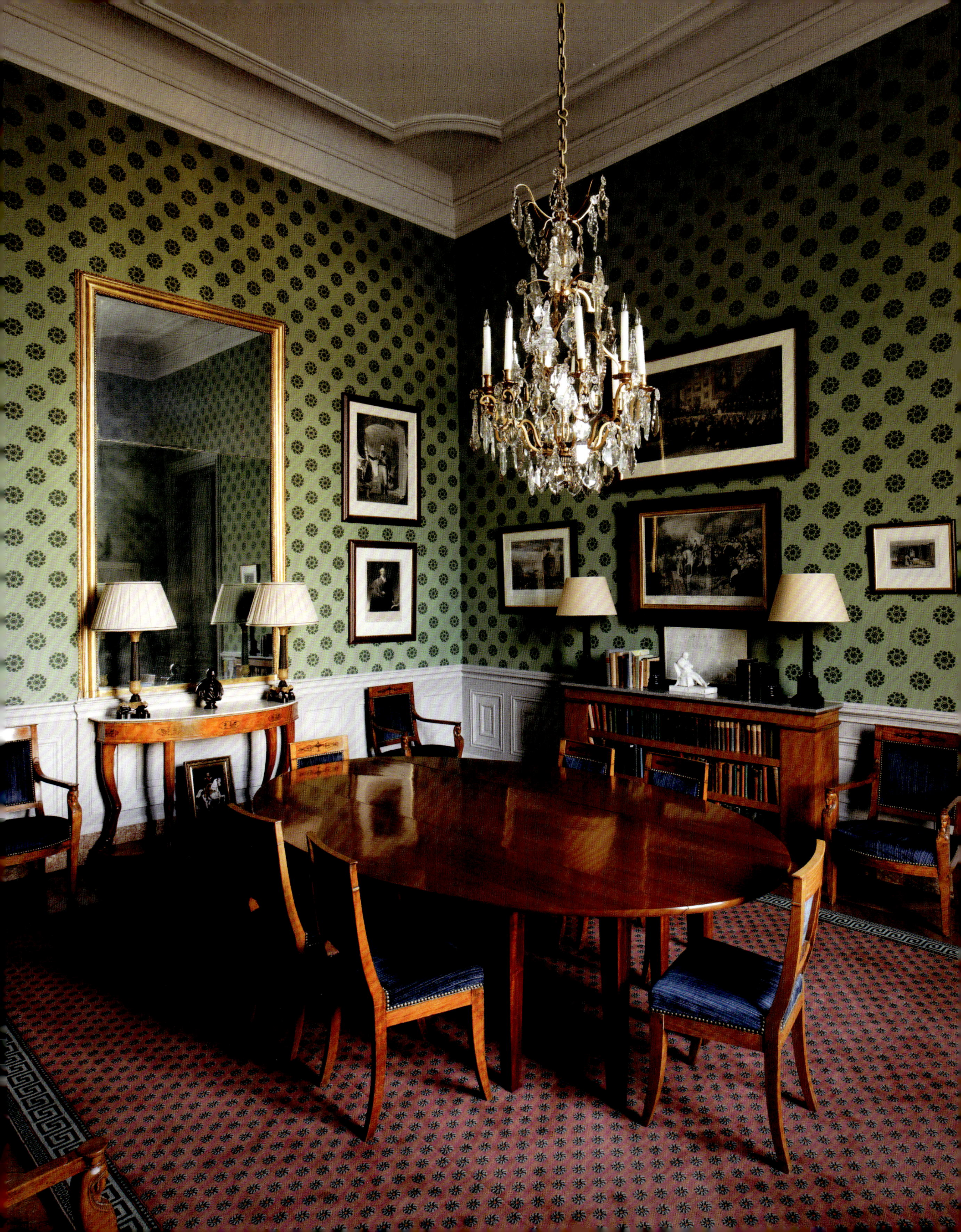

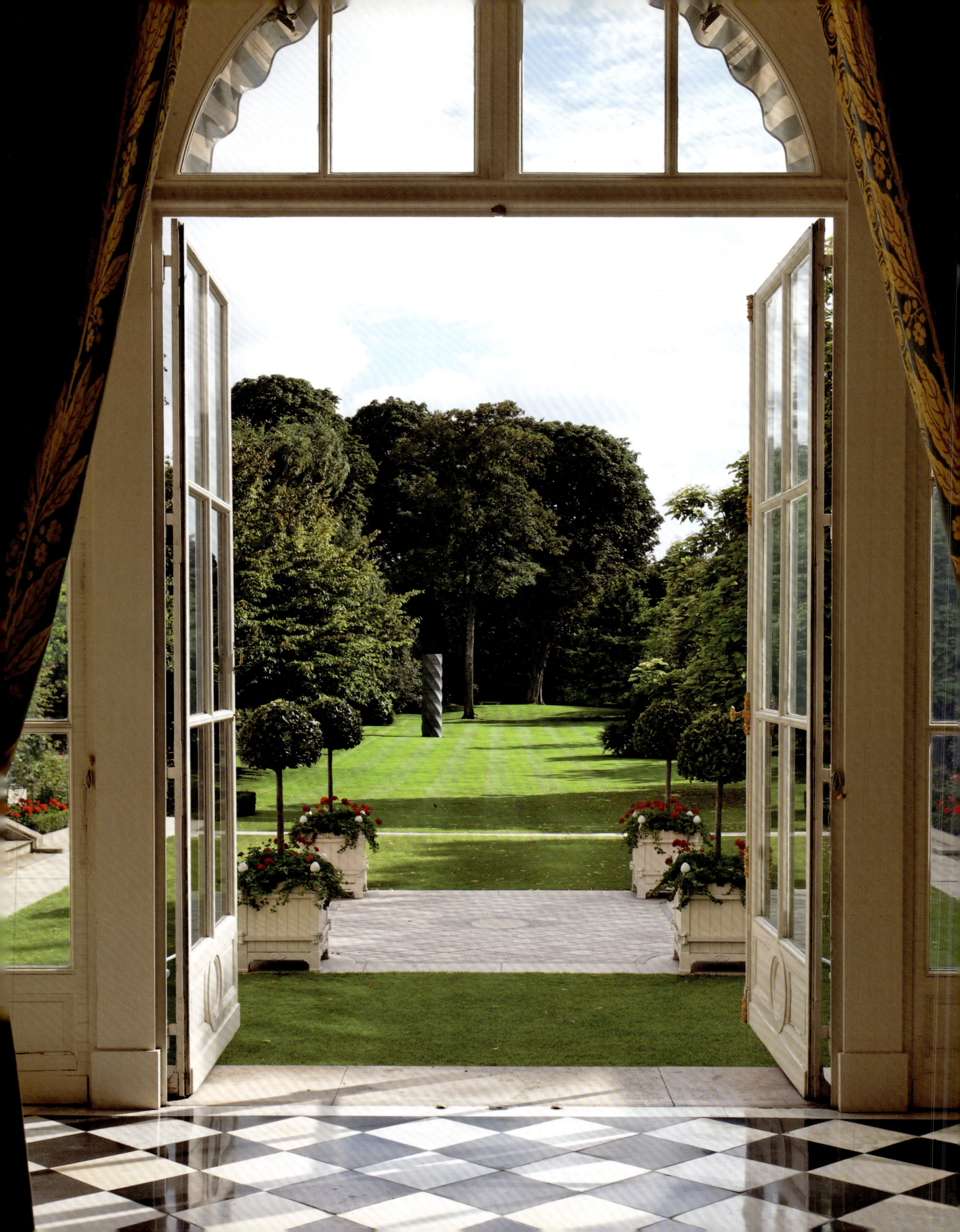

GARDEN FRONT AND GARDEN

Backing directly onto the avenue Gabriel, the large garden of the Residence has always been one of its greatest assets. Turgot's 1739 map of Paris suggests that the south front of the hôtel de Charost looked onto an elaborate parterre and beyond that a quincunx of lime trees. The leasehold agreement signed between the 5th duc de Charost and the comte de La Marck in April 1785 stipulated that, among other improvements to the property, Charost must lay out the garden in the fashionable informal 'English' style. This took the form of a large central lawn with a grove at its southern end, crossed by paths and bounded by trees and shrubbery. In the winter of 1808–09, the Emperor Napoleon himself made use of this private gate (which still opens onto the avenue Gabriel) for nocturnal visits to his mistress, Madame de Mathis, one of his sister's ladies-in-waiting. Between 1811 and 1814, Pauline Borghese spent considerable sums on maintenance and improvements.

The British, inevitably, made the garden their own, particularly after Visconti's addition of the Gallery to the south front in 1825 — which regrettably necessitated the removal of much of the Louis XV carved stonework and iron balconies from the façade. But Lady Granville was delighted, writing in June 1826 to her sister, 'How enjoyable it is at the moment. It is perfect retirement, and as fresh and as fragrant as if it was fifty miles from a town. Roses and orange trees are all in bloom, and the grass, having had no heat great enough to blight its new-born greenness, is to French eyes what Herbault's caps are to English ones.' The garden walls were raised in 1838, and replaced by high railings in 1844, neither of which prevented the storming of the garden by French government troops in May 1871.

Edward VII planted a chestnut tree in the garden on his state visit of May 1903, and the following year Visconti's fountain was removed from between the wings of the Gallery and banished to the far end of the garden. It now languishes in the garden of the Embassy next door. One of the more eccentric denizens of the garden between the wars was Lady Tyrrell, wife of Lord Tyrrell (1866–1947), ambassador between 1928 and 1934. Interminably engaged in researching a vast book on the history of the world, she would retire to the upper recesses of a large tree to work undisturbed. When visitors came to call, a footman would station himself under the tree and whistle, whereupon Lady Tyrrell would drop down from the branches in her voluminous skirts and go into the house to receive them.

Trees are regularly planted in the garden by important visitors, including two by HM The Queen during her state visits to France in 1957 and 1972, and three by the late Queen Elizabeth The Queen Mother — just as well since many of the older trees were lost in the storms of 1999. In 1998, a focal point was added to the famous lawn, in the form of *The Extended Shadow* (1994), a sculpture by the British-Iranian artist Shirazeh Houshiary (b. 1955), a spiral of forty-nine partly gilded lead heptagons. Amongst the shrubs is a battered marble drum decorated with garlands and *bucrania*, or ox skulls. Much eroded from exposure to the weather, it is an ancient Roman sacrificial altar, and may have been left behind by one of the more adventurous nineteenth-century ambassadors.

Facing page: The garden seen from the Gallery. On the famously manicured lawn stands *The Extended Shadow*, a lead sculpture by Shirazeh Houshiary, 1994.

Above: The magnificent Residence garden, stretching down to avenue Gabriel, is a place of many moods and surprises. Most of the roses planted in 2007 and 2008 are David Austen perfumed roses.
Facing page: The Gallery was first erected in 1825 for Lady Granville and still provides a link between house and garden. *Following pages:* The Residence seen from the garden — a green oasis less than five hundred metres from the place de la Concorde.

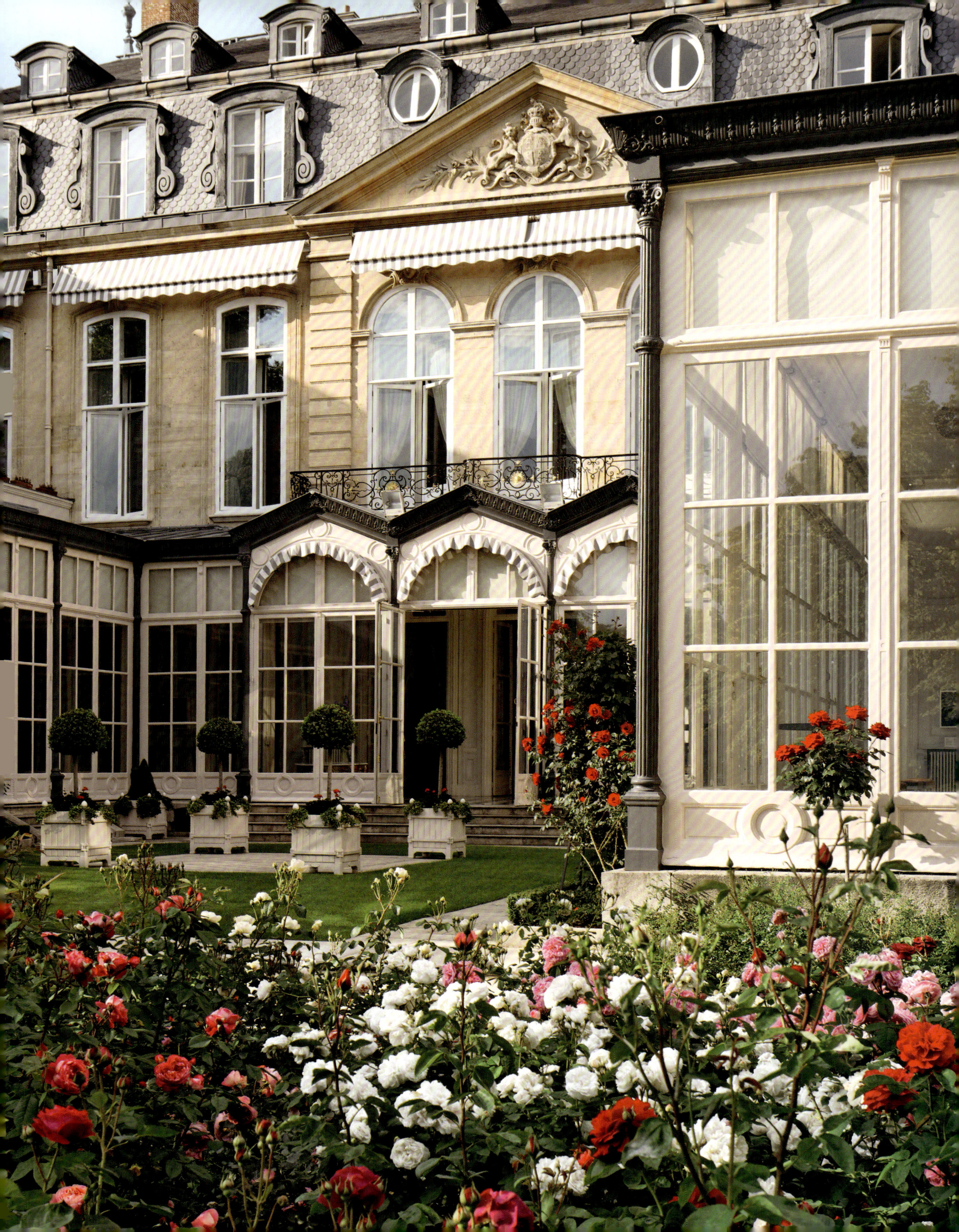

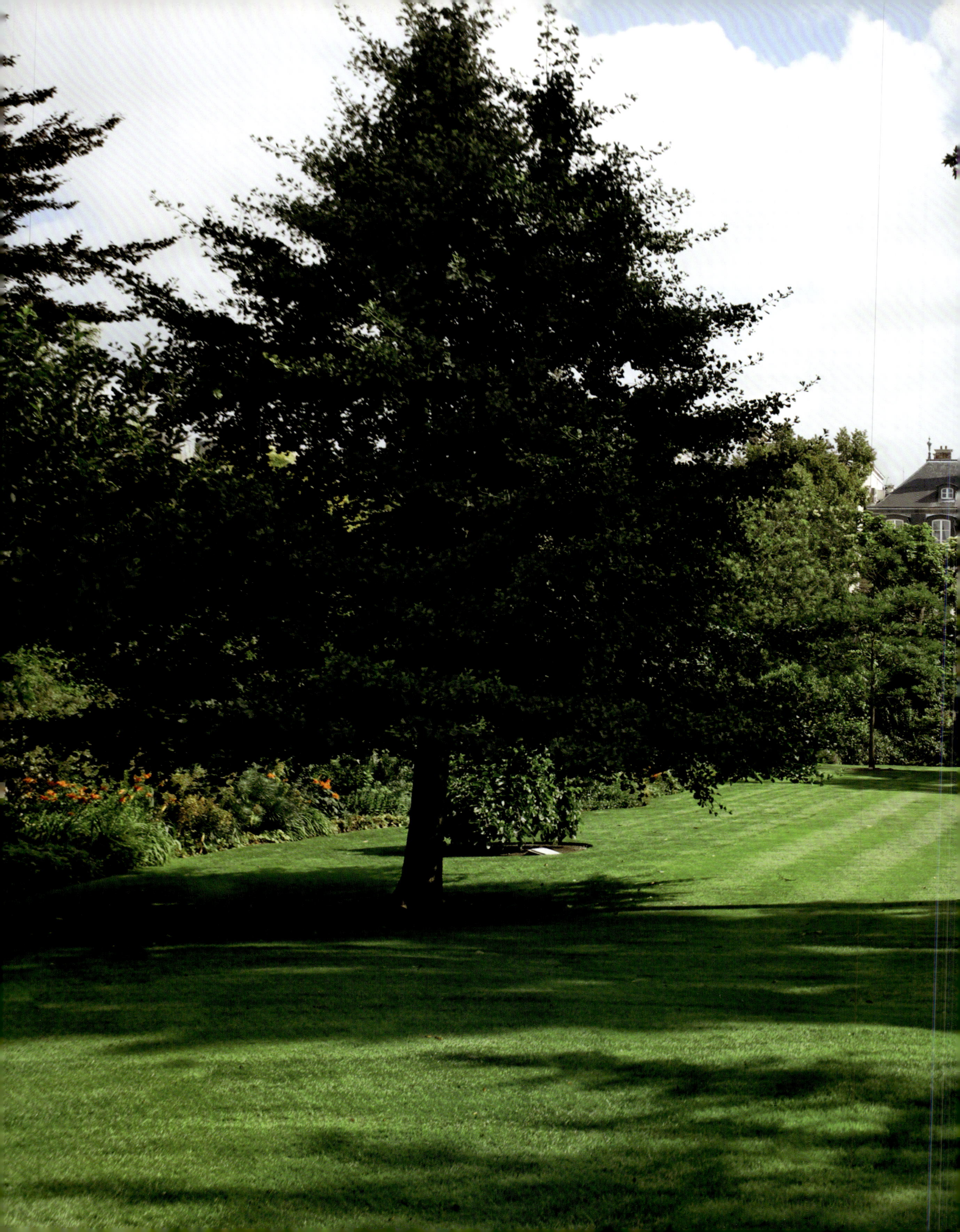

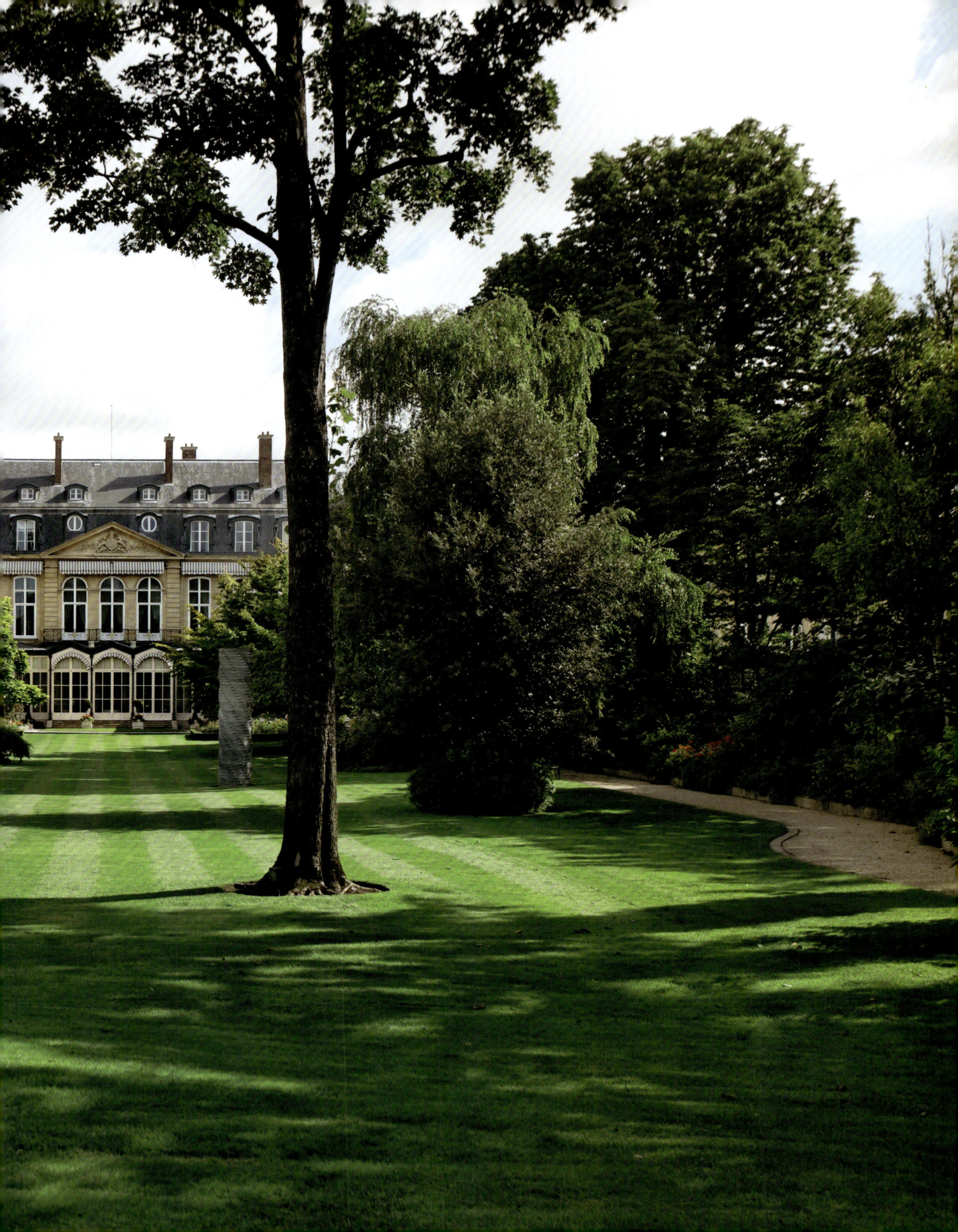

RESIDENTS OF THE HOUSE 1725 TO PRESENT

1725–1747	Armand de Béthune-Charost, 3rd duc de Charost (1663–1747)
1725–1759	Paul François de Béthune-Charost, marquis d'Ancenis, duc de Béthune (1724), 4th duc de Charost (1724) (1682–1759)
1725–1737	Julie, duchesse de Béthune (d. 1737)
1725–1735	Armand Louis, marquis de Charost (1711–1735)
1725–1739	Francois Joseph de Béthune-Charost, marquis d'Ancenis, duc d'Ancenis (1737) (1719–1739)
1737–1784	Élisabeth de La Rochefoucauld de Roye, duchesse d'Ancenis (1720–1784)
1738–1762	Armand Joseph de Béthune-Charost, marquis d'Ancenis, duc d'Ancenis (1739), 5th duc de Charost (1747) (1738–1800)
1785–1791	Auguste Marie Raymond d'Arenberg, comte de La Marck (1753–1833)
1792–1792	Dom Vicente de Sousa Coutinho, Portuguese Ambassador to the French Republic (1726–1792)
1799–1799	Régie Nationale des Hôpitaux Militaires
1802–1803	Earl Whitworth, British Ambassador (1752–1825)
1803–1814	Pauline Bonaparte, Princess Borghese (1780–1825)
1814–1814	Emperor of Austria (1768–1835)
1814–1815	Arthur Wellesley, 1st Duke of Wellington (1769–1852)
1815–1824	Sir Charles Stuart (later Lord Stuart de Rothesay) (1779–1845)
1824–1828	Viscount Granville (later the Earl Granville) (1773–1846)
1828–1831	Lord Stuart de Rothesay (1779–1845)
1831–1835	The Earl Granville (1773–1846)
1835–1835	Lord Cowley of Wellesley (1773–1847)
1835–1841	The Earl Granville (1773–1846)
1841–1846	Lord Cowley of Wellesley (1773–1847)
1846–1852	The Marquess of Normanby (1797–1863)
1852–1867	The Earl Cowley (1804–1884)
1867–1887	Lord (later Viscount) Lyons of Christchurch (1817–1887)
1887–1891	The Earl of Lytton (1831–1891)
1891–1896	The Marquess of Dufferin and Ava (1826–1902)
1896–1905	Sir Edward Monson (1834–1909)
1905–1918	Sir Francis Bertie (later Lord Bertie of Thame) (1844–1919)
1918–1920	The Earl of Derby (1865–1948)
1920–1922	Lord Hardinge of Penshurst (1858–1944)
1922–1928	The Marquess of Crewe (1858–1945)
1928–1934	Sir William Tyrrell (later Lord Tyrrell of Avon) (1866–1947)
1934–1937	Sir George Clerk (1874–1951)
1937–1939	Sir Eric Phipps (1875–1945)
1939–1940	Sir Ronald Campbell (1883–1953)
1940–1944	Under protection of American then Swiss Embassy
1944–1947	Sir Duff Cooper (1890–1954)
1948–1954	Sir Oliver Harvey (1893–1968)
1954–1960	Sir Gladwyn Jebb (1900–1996)
1960–1965	Sir Pierson Dixon (1904–1965)
1965–1968	Sir Patrick Reilly (1909–1999)
1968–1972	Mr (later Sir) Christopher Soames (1920–1987)
1972–1975	Sir Edward Tomkins (1915–2007)
1975–1979	Sir Nicholas Henderson (1919–2009)
1979–1982	Sir Reginald Hibbert (1922–2002)
1982–1987	Sir John Fretwell (b. 1930)
1987–1992	Sir Ewen Fergusson (b. 1932)
1993–1996	Sir Christopher Mallaby (b. 1936)
1996–2001	Mr (later Sir) Michael Jay (b. 1946)
2001–2007	Sir John Holmes (b. 1951)
2007–2011	Sir Peter Westmacott (b. 1950)

Detail from an armchair in the Salon Vert et Or. This suite of seat furniture was supplied to Pauline Borghese for use in this room.

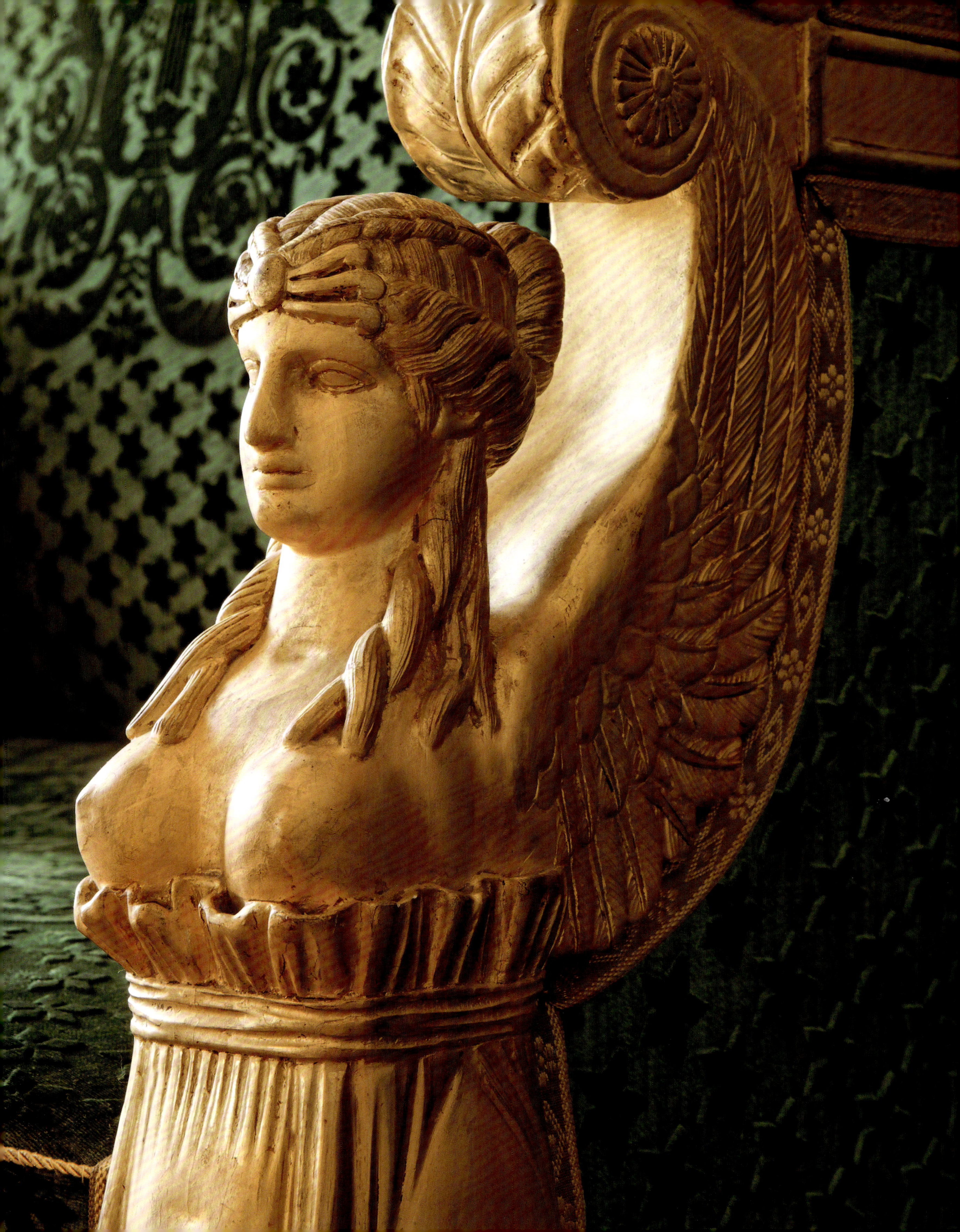

Top: Armand Joseph, 5th duc de Charost. Engraving by Ephraïm Conquy, date unknown. *Above left:* The coat of arms of Louis de Béthune, comte de Charost, ancestor of the marquis d'Ancenis, who built the hôtel de Charost in 1722. A carved stone trophy of similar arms and supporters — semi-naked warriors bearing clubs — adorned the gatehouse of the house before the Revolution. *Above right:* Paul François, 4th duc de Charost. Engraving by Nicolas Dauphin de Beauvais, date unknown.

GENEALOGICAL CHART

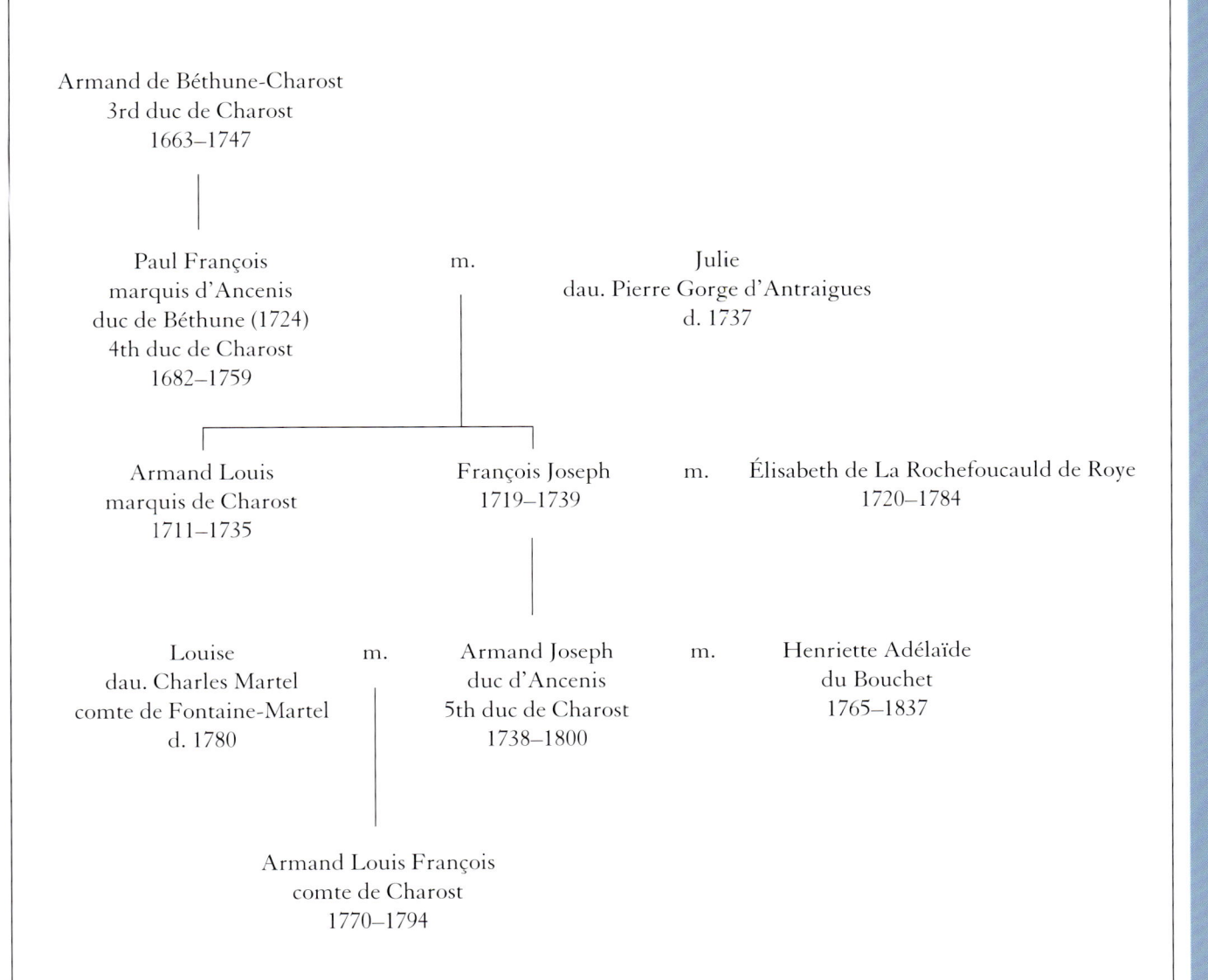

Armand de Béthune-Charost
3rd duc de Charost
1663–1747
|
Paul François   m.   Julie
marquis d'Ancenis   dau. Pierre Gorge d'Antraigues
duc de Béthune (1724)   d. 1737
4th duc de Charost
1682–1759

Armand Louis   François Joseph   m.   Élisabeth de La Rochefoucauld de Roye
marquis de Charost   1719–1739   1720–1784
1711–1735

Louise   m.   Armand Joseph   m.   Henriette Adélaïde
dau. Charles Martel   duc d'Ancenis   du Bouchet
comte de Fontaine-Martel   5th duc de Charost   1765–1837
d. 1780   1738–1800

Armand Louis François
comte de Charost
1770–1794

SELECTED BIBLIOGRAPHY

Beal, Mary, and John Cornforth, *British Embassy, Paris: The House and its Works of Art* (London: Government Art Collection, 1992).

Cooper, Lady Diana, *Trumpets from the Steep* (London: Rupert Hart-Davis 1960).

Friedman, Joseph, *British Embassy, Paris: History of a House* 1725–1985 (unpublished typescript in four volumes, 1985).

Friedman, Joseph, *A Catalogue of the Bonaparte-Borghese Collection of Furniture and Bronzes, British Embassy, Paris* (unpublished typescript in two volumes, 1985).

Foreign and Commonwealth Office, *Short History of the British Embassy, Paris* (limited edition, HMSO London, 1990).

Gladwyn, Cynthia, *The Paris Embassy* (London: Constable and Company, Ltd, 1976).

Ronfort, Jean Nérée, and Jean-Dominique Augarde, *À l'Ombre de Pauline: La résidence de l'Ambassadeur de Grand-Bretagne à Paris* (Paris: Editions du Centre de Recherches Historiques, 2001).

Willson, Beckles, *The Paris Embassy 1814–1920: A Narrative of Franco-British Diplomatic Relations* (London: T. Fisher Unwin Ltd/Ernest Benn Ltd, 1927).

Facing page: A secret door in the Duff Cooper Library — cunningly disguised with dummy book spines — gives access to a hallway leading to the Salon Vert.

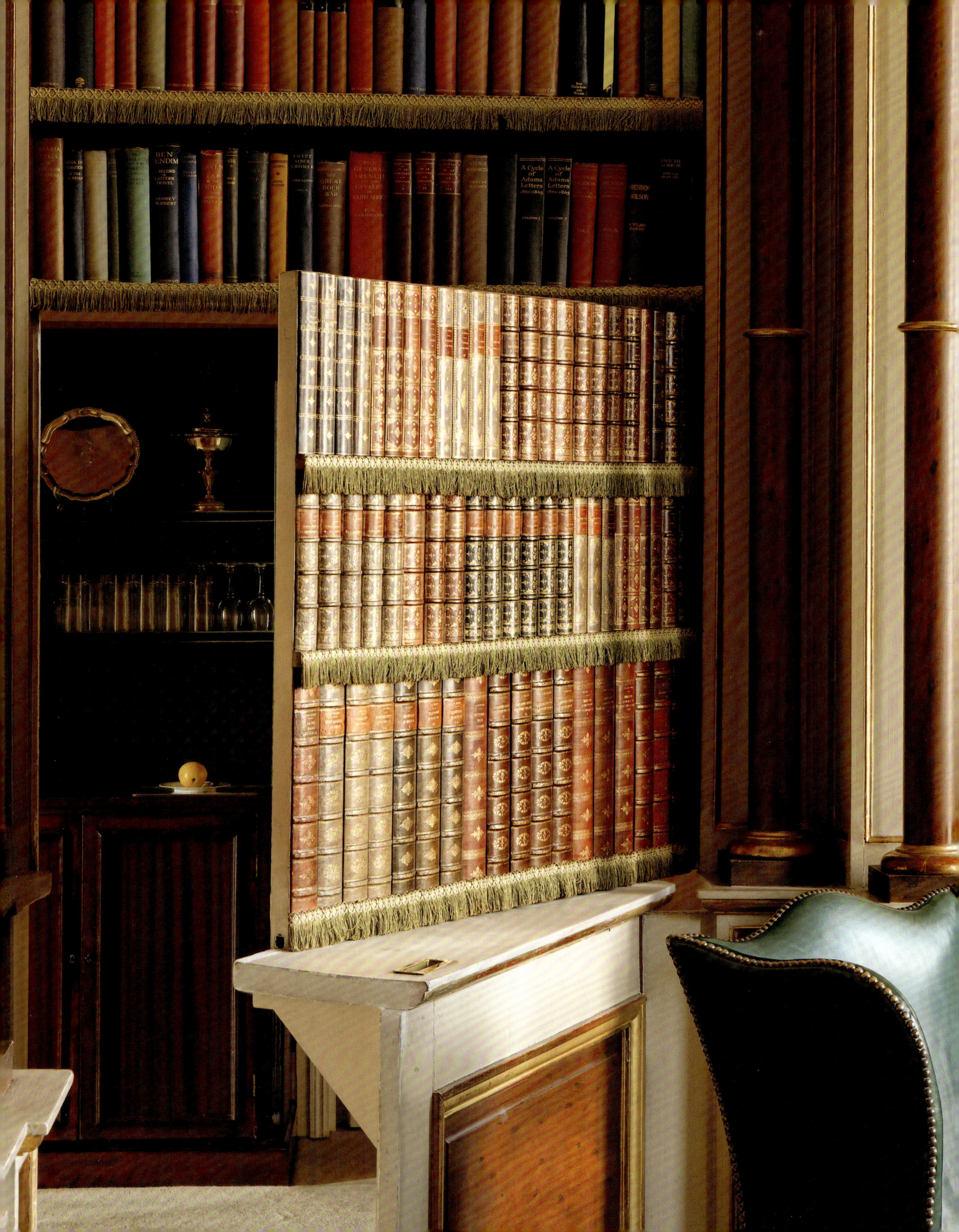

INDEX

Page numbers in italics refer to captions.

A

Albano, Benedict 51, 117
Alexandra, Queen consort (of Edward VII, King) 78, *127*, 128
Angell, Joseph 100
Antoine, Jacques Denis 90
Aubusson 90, *90*, 95, 100
Austria, Francis I, Emperor of 23, 46

B

Barnard, Lady Anne *49*
Beaton, Cecil 66, *66*, 152
Beauharnais, Eugène de 40
Beauvais, Nicolas Dauphin, *166*
Bedford, John Russel, 6th Duke of 86, 128, 130
Beistegui, Charles de 66, 81, 152, *152*
Belle, Alexis Simon *137*
Bénard, Pierre Nicholas 40, 45, 105, 117
Bérard, Christian 66, 147, *150*, 152, *152*
Berlin, Sir Isaiah 66
Berlioz, Hector 58
Bernhardt, Sarah 60
Berry, Agnes 86
Berry, Mary 86
Bertie, Sir Francis, later Lord Bertie of Thame 24, *56*, *57*, 60, *61*, 65, *65*, 78, 132
Béthune, Julie, duchesse de 24, 34, 81, 90, 95
Béthune, Louis de, comte de Charost *166*
Béthune-Charost, Paul François de, marquis d'Ancenis, duc de Béthune, 4th duc de Charost 24, 30, 33, 152, 156, *166*
Blair, Tony, prime minister (1997–2007) 14, 142
Blanche, Jacques Émile *127*, 128
Blount, Edward 55
Blücher, Field Marshal, Prince Von 123
Bonaparte, Joseph 37, 40
Bonaparte, Pauline, Princess Pauline Borghese 23, 24, *26*, *33,* 37, *37,* 40, *42*, 45, *45*, 46, 49, 51, 55, 60, 65, *66*, 75, 76, 78, *78*, 81, 90, *90*, *93*, 95, *95*, *98*, 100, 105, 117, 120, 123, *123*, 125, *125*, 127, *127*, 130, 132, *134*, 137, *137*, 140, 142, 147, *147*, 152, 156, 159, *164*, *175*
Borghese, Prince Camillo 37, 40, 45, 142, *145*, 152, 156
Boucher, François 100
Boullée, Etienne Louis 40
Brice, Germain 33
Brion, Pierre Gaston 81, 123
Brown, Gordon, prime minister (2007–2010) 14
Bute, John Stuart, 3rd Earl of, prime minister (1762–1763) 86

C

Cameron, David, prime minister (2010) 14
Campbell, Sir Ronald 65
Campbell, Lady 65
Canning, Charles *88*
Canning, George *88*
Canova, Antonio 78, *78*, 127, 128, 130, *130*
Carrington, Lord 68
Castlereagh, Lord 23
Charles X, King 49, 75
Charost, Armand de Béthune, 3rd duc de 24, 33, 127, 137, 142, 147
Charost, Armand Joseph, de Béthune-Charost, marquis d'Ancenis, duc d'Ancenis, 5th duc de *24,* 34, 37, 123, 159, *166*
Charost, Armand Louis François, comte de 37
Charost, Henriette Adélaïde du Bouchet, later duchesse de 37, 40
Chateaubriand, (François René de Chateaubriand, known as) *40*
Chaudet, Antoine Denis *71*, 76
Chirac, Jacques 14
Chrystie, William R. 65

Churchill, Lord Randolph 58
Churchill, Sir Winston, prime minister
    (1940–1945 and 1951–1955) 13, 14, 23, 58, 76
Cocteau, Jean 66
Colette, (Sidonie-Gabrielle Colette, known as) 66
Connolly, Cyril 66
Conquy, Ephraïm *166*
Contet, Frédéric 55
Cooper, Sir Alfred Duff *13,* 14, 24, 65, 66, *147,*
    152
Cooper, Lady Diana 14, 65, 66, *66*, 142, 147, *147,*
    150, 152
Corden, William 76
Cornforth, John 68, 156
Coward, Noel 66
Cowley, Henry Wellesley, 1st Lord 49
Cowley, William Henry Wellesley, 2nd Lord,
    later 1st Earl 51, 75, 100, *102*, 105, *105*, 117,
    132, 142
Cowley, Lady 142
Craddock and Reid *120*
Craufurd, Quentin 23, 46
Crewe, Robert Crewe-Milnes, 1st Marquess of 65
Curzon, George Nathaniel, Marquess Curzon of
    Kedleston,
    Viceroy of India 65

D
David, Jacques Louis 123
Davis, John Scarlett 128
Denon, Dominique Vivant, baron 98
Derby, 17th Earl of 65
Dickens, Charles 108
Dorset, Arabella Diana, dowager Duchess of,
    later Lady Withworth 37
Dufferin and Ava, Frederick Hamilton-Temple-
    Blackwood, Marquess of 60
Dumas, Alexandre 60
Dyck, Sir Anthony van *127*

E
Edward VII, King 10, *55*, 60, *60*, *61*, *63*, 78, 95,
    120, 123, 127, 128, 147,159
Eliot, T. S. 66
Elizabeth, The Queen Mother 95, 159
Elizabeth II, Queen 14, *18*, 23, 159
Eluard, Paul 66

Epinay, Prosper d' 78
Epstein, Sir Jacob 76
Eugenie, Empress 51

F
Fontaine, Pierre François Léonard 37, *37*, 40
Friedman, Joseph 68, 90

G
Gamelin, General 76
Garnier, Charles 51
Garrard and Co. 120
Gaulle, Charles de, president 14
Geoffroy, Georges 66, 152, *152*
George IV, King 49
George V, King 65, 142, *142*
Gérard, François Pascal Simon, Baron *23*, 123,
    125, *125*
Gilbert, P. R. 120
Gillot, Eugène Louis 142, *142*
Gladwyn, Lady Cynthia 68
Gladwyn Jebb, Hubert Miles, 1st Baron
    Gladwyn 68, 152, *152*
Goering, Hermann 14, 65
Goscombe John, William 10, 123
Grahame, George 65
Granville, Leveson-Gower, 1st Earl 24, 46, 49,
    59, 100, 105, *105*, 112, 120, 142
Granville, Lady 24, 49, *59*, 90, 105, 112, 127, 142,
    159, 160
Gronow, Rees Howell, Captain 46
Guise, duc de 137

H
Hallé, Antoine *2*, 33, 76
Hardinge, Charles, 1st Baron of Penshurst,
    Viceroy of India 65
Harvey, Sir Oliver 108
Harvey, Lady 108
Haydon, Benjamin Robert 85
Hayter, Sir George *51*, *81*, 85, 86, 100, 127, 130,
    130
Hennell, Robert *20*, *52*, 120
Henrietta Maria, Queen consort (of Charles I,
    King) 127. *140*
Héricourt, Jean-Baptiste 90

Hesp, Charles 68
Hirst, Damien 112
Hitorff, Jacques Ignace 105
Hoentschel, Georges 60, *63*, 76, 132, 137
Houshiary, Shirazeh 112, 159, *159*
Huxley and Co., Messrs 75

J

Jacob-Desmalter, François Honoré 46
Jacob, Georges 142
Jerome, Jennie 58

K

Kent, William 76

L

Labouchère, Henry 55
La Marck, Auguste Marie Raymond d'Arenberg, comte de 24, *24*, 34, 37, 90, *90*, 123, 159
La Marck, comtesse de 90, *90*
Lardin, Jean-Baptiste 33
Leclerc, Dermide 37, 40
Leclerc, Marie-Paulette *see* Bonaparte, Pauline 37
Leclerc, Victor Emmanuel, General 37, 156
Leczinska, Maria, Queen consort (of Louis XV, King) 127
Lefèvre, Robert 37, 123
Leigh, Vivien 66
Leyniers, D. 132
Leys 117
Loraine, Percy 65
Louis XIII, King 33
Louis XIV, King 2, 30, 33, 76, 142
Louis XV, King 30, 33, 127, 142, 159
Louis XVI, King 34
Louis XVIII, King 23, 33, 46, 125
Louis-Philippe, King 51, 90
Loven, François Joseph 147
Lwoff, Princess Elisabeth, Vilma von Parlaghy-Brachfeld 60
Lyons, Richard Bickerton Pemell, Lord Lyons of Christchurch 55, 58
Lytton, Edward Robert Bulwer-Lytton, 1st Earl of 58, 60, 76, 108, 142

M

Malet, Edward 55
Malraux, André 66
Manet, Edouard 128
Manière, Charles Guillaume 90
Manny, Henri 65
Marie-Antoinette, Queen 34, 127
Mary, Queen consort (of George V, King) 142, *142*
Mathis, Madame de 159
Maugham, William Somerset 58
Mayor, William Frederick 142, *142*
Mazin, Antoine 33, 40, 75
Mellon 127
Mercy-Argenteau, Florimond, comte de 34
Michelot, Jean Paul Louis 23, 40, 46
Mignard, Pierre *137*
Mirabeau, (Honoré Gabriel Riquetti, known as) comte de 34
Mitford, Nancy 24, *66*
Mlinaric, David 68, 123
Moinet, Aîné *40*
Monson, Sir Edward 24, 60
Moore, John *52*, 120
Morgan, Lady (Sydney Owenson, known as) 49

N

Napoleon I, Bonaparte, Emperor 13, 23, 37, 40, *42*, 46, *71*, 76, 125, 127, 128, 159
Napoleon III, Louis-Napoleon Bonaparte, Emperor 51, 55
Nicolson, Harold 66
Normanby, Constantine Henry Phipps, Marquess of 51, 75, 105
Normanby, Marchioness of 51, 127, 132
Norris, William 55

O

Olivier, Herbert Arnould 125, *125*, *176*
Olivier, Sir Laurence 66, *66*, *176*
Onslow-Ford, Edward 100
Opie, Julian 112
Orléans, duc d' 30
Orléans, Henrietta Anne, duchesse d' *137*, *140*
Orsay, (Alfred Guillaume Gabriel de Grimaud, known as) comte d' *13*, *46*, 85
Osler and Company, F. and C. 105, *108*

P

Paignault, Louis 33
Palairet, C. Michael 65
Parker, Cornelia 68
Pernon, Camille 81
Perregaux, bankers 46
Pirou, Eugène 56, 65
Pius VII, Pope 127
Powell, T. 65
Praz, Mario 95
Proust, Marcel 23, 60

R

Ramsay, Patrick 65
Raveau, Etienne 51, 100, 105, *105*, *108*, 117
Reilly, Lady 68
Reilly, Sir Patrick 68
Reynaud, Paul 76
Richelieu, (Armand Jean du Plessis known as) Cardinal and duc de 33
Ruskin, John 88

S

Shaw, Isabella 58
Scipio Africanus, (Publius Cornelius Scipio Africanus known as) 81
Simpson, William 58
Smirke, Sir Robert 49
Smithson, Harriet 58
Soames, Sir Christopher 14
Sousa Coutinho, Dom Vincente de 34
South, Simeon 127
Spender, Stephen 66
Spurgeon, Ernest Edward 65
Stuart, James Francis Edward, Prince *137*
Stuart, Charlotte, later Countess Canning 86, *88*
Stuart, Louisa, later Marchioness of Waterford 86, *88*
Stuart, Sir Charles, later 1st Baron Stuart de Rothesay 23, 24, 46, 49, *81*, 85, 86, *86*, 120, 130
Stuart, Lady Elizabeth, later Lady Stuart de Rothesay 46, *49*, 85, 86, *88*

T

Tadolini, Adamo 78, *78*, 130
Teniers II, David 132, *134*
Teniers III, David 132, *134*
Thackeray, William Makepeace 23, 58
Thatcher, Margaret, prime minister (1979-1990) 14, 23, 78
Thomire, Pierre Philippe *40*, *85*, 120, *120*
Tissot, James Jacques 128
Titian, (Tiziano Vecellio, known as) 130
Turgot, (Anne Robert Jacques Turgot, baron de l'Aulne known as) 159
Tyrrell, Lady 159
Tyrrell of Avon, Sir William 159

V

Vaillant 123
Victoria, Queen 23, 24, 51, *51*, 60, 76, *88*, 100, 105, *108*, 117
Vilmorin, Louise de 66, *66*
Visconti, Louis Tullius Joachim 49, 51, 105, *105*, 112, 117, 159
Vitry, Robert 33
Vye Parminter, Arthur 60, *63*, *76*, 137

W

Wallner, Jean André 95
Waterford, Henry de la Poer Beresford, 3rd Marquess of 88
Watson, Musgrave L. *71*, 76
Watts, George Frederic 88
Weisweiller, Adam 127
Wellington, Arthur Wellesley, 1st Duke of 13, *13*, 23, *23*, 24, 46, *46*, 49, *71*, 76, *81*, 85, 123, 125, *125*, 128, 152, *156*
Wellington, Duchess of 46
Whiteread, Rachel 112, *112*
Whitty, Thomas 137
Whitworth, Earl 37
Wilde, Oscar 60
Winterhalter, Franz Xaver 76

Y

Yarde-Buller, Henry, Colonel 65
Yass, Catherine 112, 114
Yorke, Lady Elizabeth *see* Stuart, Lady Elizabeth 46

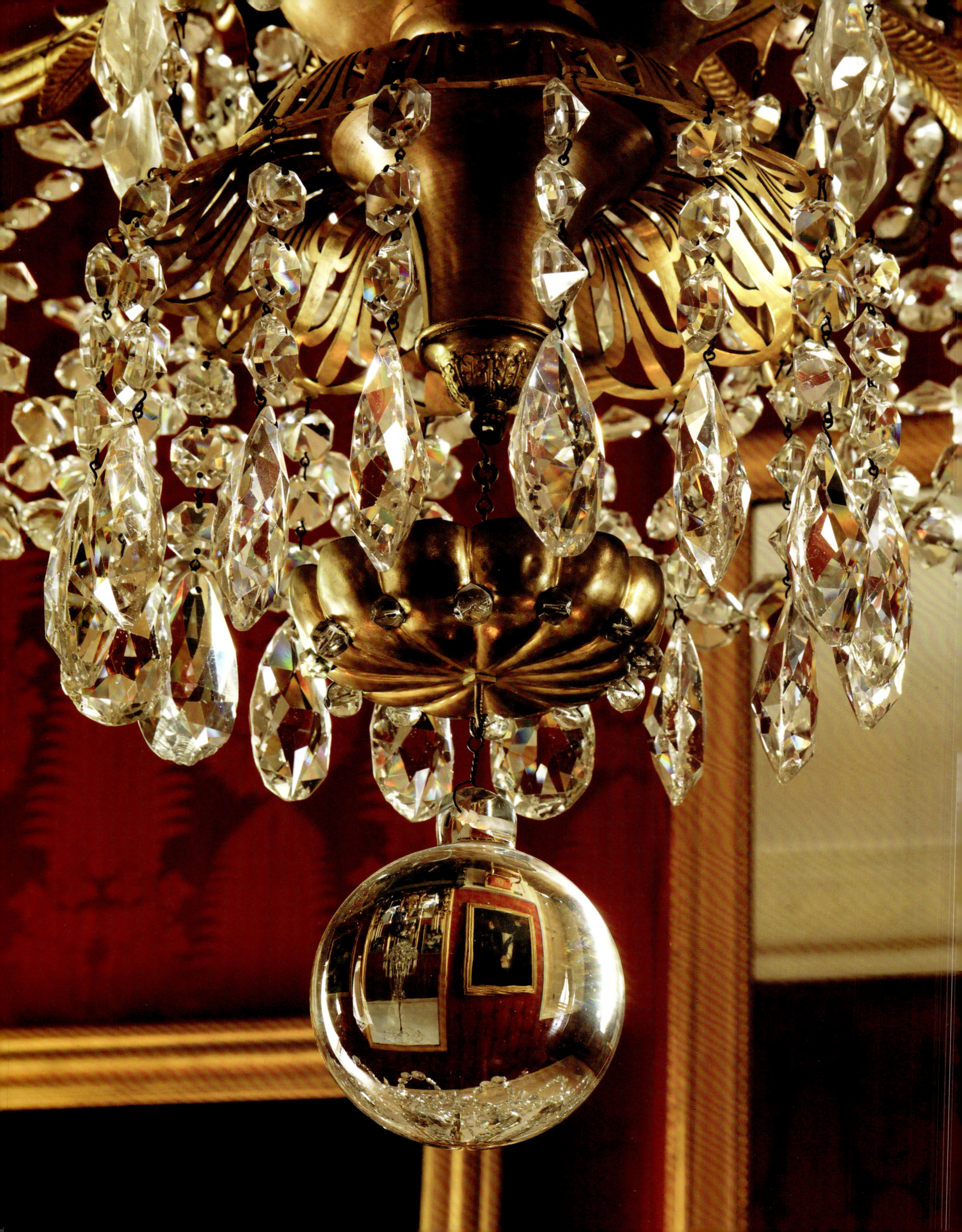

PHOTOGRAPHIC CREDITS

All photographs in this book were taken by Francis Hammond except:

18–19 (left to right, top to bottom): © British Embassy; © British Embassy; © Francis Hammond; © W.A. Dudley; © British Embassy; © Francis Hammond; © British Embassy; © British Embassy; © British Embassy; © W.A. Dudley; © W.A. Dudley; © W.A. Dudley; © British Embassy; © Francis Hammond; © British Embassy; © W.A. Dudley; © British Embassy; © British Embassy; © Francis Hammond, © Hulton Archives (photo Peter Macdiarmid); © W.A. Dudley; © Francis Hammond; © W.A. Dudley; © W.A. Dudley; © British Embassy; © W.A. Dudley / 30: © British Embassy / 38–39: Courtesy of Talabardon and Gautier / 47: © Crown copyright: UK Government Art Collection / 48: © Lord Balniel / 51: © Crown copyright: UK Government Art Collection / 54–55 (above left): © Private collection (photographer unknown) / 55 (above right)–57: © Private Collection of Tim Knox and Todd Longstaffe-Gowan, London / 58–60: © Crown Copyright: UK Government Art Collection / 61 (top): © Private Collection of Tim Knox and Todd Longstaffe-Gowan, London / 61 (above): © British Embassy / 64: © Crown copyright: UK Government Art Collection / 66 (above left): © Cecil Beaton Studio Archives – Sotheby's Picture Library / 66 (above right): © Cecil Beaton Studio Archives – Sotheby's Picture Library, courtesy UK Government Art Collection / 67: © Cecil Beaton Studio Archives – Sotheby's Picture Library / 69: © Cornelia Parker, courtesy of UK Government Art Collection (photo Francis Hammond) / 87–89: © Crown copyright: UK Government Art Collection / 114–115: © Catherine Yass, courtesy of UK Government Art Collection / 130: © Crown copyright: UK Government Art Collection / 166: © British Embassy.

The painting of Pauline Borghese on page 36 is reproduced courtesy of The Rayne Foundation.

The Rayne Foundation

Facing page: A detail of the chandelier in the Salon Rouge, with twenty-four lights, originally in Pauline's bedchamber.

Above: The narrow panels of the Ante-Room are hung with 'drops' of forty small oil sketches by Herbert Arnould Olivier (1861–1952), *Representatives, Delegates and Supporting Staff at the Supreme War Council Meetings, Versailles 1918–19*. The sketches represent the officials who participated in the discussions leading up to the Treaty of Versailles in 1919, and were preparatory sketches for two huge finished paintings; *The Council in Session on 3 July 1918*, and *The Council Meeting on 3 and 4 November 1918*. Olivier, a British painter who had studied at the Royal Academy Schools and the uncle of the actor Sir Laurence Olivier, was given access to Versailles during the deliberations and made these rapidly painted sketches from life. No preliminary drawing was used, although the artist did take photographs to work from and some of the sitters granted him sittings in private. These lively records, which include portraits of all the major figures attending the Council, are on loan to the British Embassy in Paris from the artist's family.